IMAGES
of America

LYN-LAKE

ON THE COVER: In August 1927, the Buzza Card Company's women's softball team, the Buzza Bees, took on the men's team, the Slo-Pokes. "A wild and rugged game to the bitter death took place between the Slo-Pokes and the Buzza Bees," reported the company's newsletter, the *Bee Hive*. Ultimately the "gals" won in the end, with the final score "about" 20 to 9. (Hennepin County Library.)

IMAGES
of America

LYN-LAKE

Thatcher Imboden and
Cedar Imboden Phillips

ARCADIA
PUBLISHING

ISBN 978-0-7385-8331-0

Published by Arcadia Publishing
Charleston, South Carolina

Printed in the United States of America

Library of Congress Control Number: 2010937899

For all general information, please contact Arcadia Publishing:
Telephone 843-853-2070
Fax 843-853-0044
E-mail sales@arcadiapublishing.com
For customer service and orders:
Toll-Free 1-888-313-2665

Visit us on the Internet at www.arcadiapublishing.com

For the people of Lyn-Lake: past, present, and future

Contents

Acknowledgments

The stories and images shared in this book were the result of the assistance of many dedicated community members. In finding the photographs and stories, we had the opportunity to meet and learn from both current and former residents, business owners, employees, and many others who have been involved with Lyn-Lake, both past and present. It was an incredible process, and the result is just a fraction of the stories and photographs that are out there. Consider this a snapshot view of its rich and robust history and an invitation to delve deeper.

We want to specifically thank the following individuals and organizations, in no particular order, for their contributions to the book: Peg Carlson, Heather Lawton, Ian Stade, Nick Steffel, Al Hagen, the Schatzlein family, Paul Newman, Aaron Hanuer, Diane Armstrong, Linda McHale, Rev. Jen Nagel, Jeremy Nichols, Elizabeth Archerd, Louise Pearson, Jim Flanders, Todd Ferrara, Furniture Industries, Inc., Leonard Schnack, Cheryl Walsh Bellville, Gil and Mary Ann Maple and the Redeemer Residence, Minneapolis Public Schools, Craig Steiner and Robert McCune of the records management division of the Office of the City Clerk in Minneapolis, the Lyn-Lake Business Association, Hennepin County Library Special Collection's Minneapolis Collection, the Minnesota Historical Society, Susan Larson-Fleming and the Hennepin History Museum (HHM), Rev. Jen Nagel and the Salem English Lutheran Church (SELC), Joyce Battcher-Malchow and the Lyndale United Church of Christ (LUCC), David Cargo and Judie Cilcain of St. Francis Liberal Catholic Church (SFLCC), Chris Hudok and the Minneapolis Police Department (MPD), Mohn Electric Company, Caroline Griepentrog and the Lowry Hill East Neighborhood Association (LHENA), Mark Hinds and the Lyndale Neighborhood Association (LNA), Scott Engel of the Calhoun Area Residents Action Group (CARAG), and the Whittier Alliance.

We would like to thank our parents, Durant and Cheryl, and Cedar's mother-in-law, Susan, for their advice, support, and babysitting; brother Anders for his humor and leads; Thatcher's wife, Melissa, for her support and patience; Cedar's husband, Andrew, and son, Jack, for their patience and willingness to listen to all things Lyn-Lake.

INTRODUCTION

The Lyn-Lake neighborhood of Minneapolis encompasses one of the city's oldest commercial districts and serves as home for thousands of residents of all ages and backgrounds. Although it defies formal definitions, for the purpose of this book we intend to cover the portions of Lake Street, Lyndale Avenue, and neighboring streets that we view as within the greater Lyn-Lake sphere of influence. Formal neighborhoods within the boundaries of Lyn-Lake include Lyndale, Lowry Hill East (the Wedge), CARAG, and Whittier; given that the city's formal neighborhoods are so often defined by major commercial corridors, in this case Lyn-Lake's namesake Lyndale Avenue and Lake Street, it is easy to see why Lyn-Lake as an informal district or neighborhood can truly be called a crossroads.

Lyn-Lake's strategic location between several streetcar lines connecting downtown Minneapolis and St. Paul with Minneapolis's chain of lakes helped it to develop as one of the oldest commercial districts in Minneapolis outside of downtown. Even today its commercial core is filled with buildings dating to the 1880s and 1890s. The Lyn-Lake district experienced another boom decade following 1905, when a new and improved streetcar was laid the length of Lake Street. The residential streets in the neighborhood soon filled in, with thousands of people living in a blend of apartments, duplexes, and single-family homes. Everything they needed was within an easy walk from home—stores, work, churches, schools, and entertainment.

Just one block north of Lake Street, the Twenty-ninth Street rail corridor was to play an essential role in Lyn-Lake's history, past and present. A rail corridor made it possible for the Lyn-Lake district to develop a bustling industrial economy. Businesses of all sorts lined the corridor, and in the first decade of the 20th century an ambitious project lowered the railway into a deep trench (now the Midtown Greenway). Grain elevators, lumberyards, dairies, stables, and manufacturers of all types—everything and anything that needed a location with rail access—found a home along the Twenty-ninth Street Corridor. The Chicago, Milwaukee, and St. Paul Railroad Grade Separation is now listed on the National Register of Historic Places. After trains stopped using the tracks in the late 1990s, it was reconfigured for use as an urban biking and walking "highway," and while some industry remains, now much of its Lyn-Lake frontage is lined with new and adapted condos and retail businesses.

By the 1960s, Lyn-Lake had also started to take on a distinctive artistic flavor. Lured by cheap rent and the variety of housing, artists and musicians began to flock to the area. Acts such as Peter, Paul, and Mary performed in so-called "3.2 joints" lining Lake Street, and record shops proliferated. In the 1980s, Lyn-Lake was the background for the vibrant Minneapolis music scene; The Replacements was just one of many groups to have Lyn-Lake roots. Visual and performing arts have also long been a presence; the Jungle Theater has been at Lyndale Avenue and Lake Street for nearly 20 years, and the area is now one of the most artist-intensive neighborhoods in the country.

Today Lyn-Lake is a mixture of the old and the new. Many of its oldest buildings remain, and its historic nature (including its industrial background) contributes to its reputation as a regional destination for those looking for something unique and distinctive. It has built upon its artistic past to establish itself firmly as an artistic center of the Twin Cities. Its diversity has also continued to evolve and shift; the greater Lyn-Lake district was home to one of the metropolitan area's first pizza places (considered "ethnic" in its day), the state's first and oldest Ethiopian restaurant, and in more recent years the country's first Somali "mall."

One

INDUSTRY

After a rail line was built through the area along Twenty-ninth Street between 1879 and 1881, Lyn-Lake became home to many manufacturers, wholesalers, and other industry.

Upon construction of the Twenty-ninth Street railroad depression in the first decade of the 20th century, most buildings adjacent to the tracks were retrofitted. The result was a period of massive investment along the tracks, with many buildings adding new storehouses, mills, or docks. The area boasted a central location, industrial land and buildings, a strong workforce, and a railroad corridor.

In the early 1900s, the need to provide coal to buildings and building materials to nearby construction sites made the land adjacent to the railroad tracks attractive as a distribution point. In the years following World War II, some businesses moved to the suburbs because of a need for additional space that was cheaper, newer, and more accessible.

Industrial businesses along the main commercial corridors, Lyndale Avenue and Lake Street, were slowly replaced by retailers and restaurateurs who wanted foot traffic and higher visibility and were willing to pay more for it. The conversion of the railroad track to a bike trail and the city's interest in revitalizing the industrial land, increasing the tax base, and expanding housing options led to direct action by the city and subsequent market forces to convert the industrial land into new housing. Today very few industrial businesses are left in Lyn-Lake.

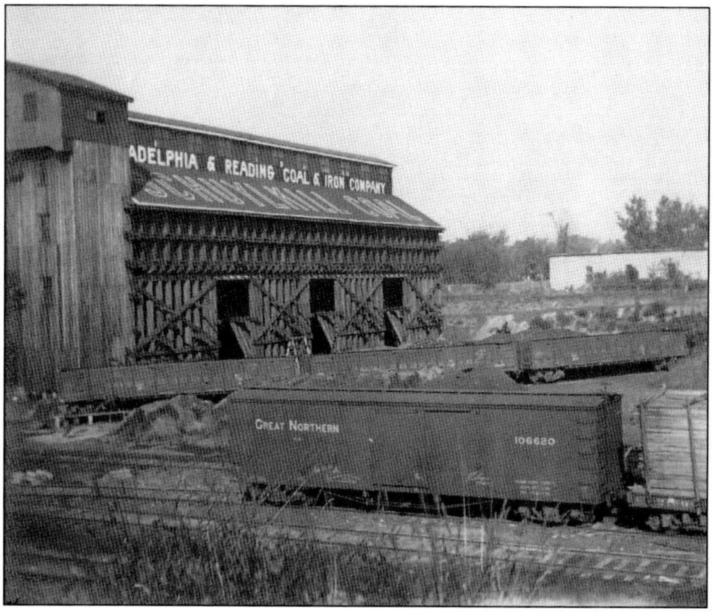

In 1913, the Philadelphia and Reading Coal Company excavated the property located on the northwest corner of the Milwaukee Road railroad tracks and Dupont Avenue so that the company could directly serve its coal elevator via a siding on its property. The coal elevator was converted into a warehouse in 1951, and the *Minneapolis Star and Tribune* built a small newspaper distribution building there in 1965. (Hennepin County Library.)

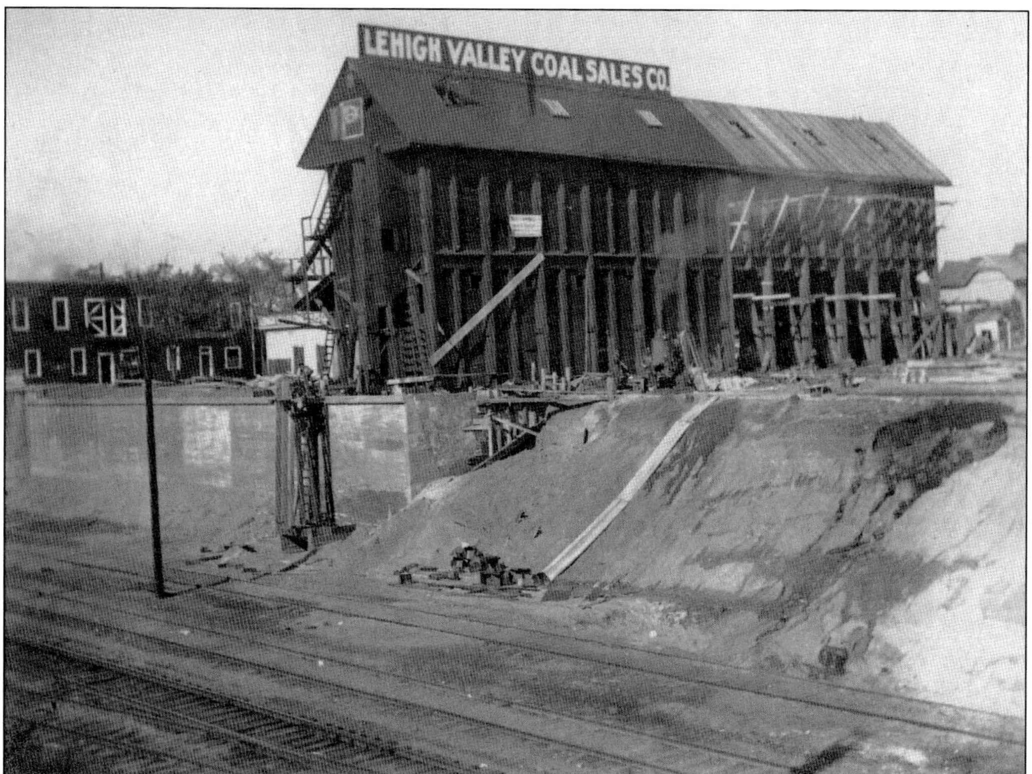

This photograph, taken around 1915, shows the Leigh Valley Coal site at 2835–2847 Colfax Avenue. The first coal elevator was built there in 1905; a new one was constructed in 1914 with the construction of the Milwaukee Road railroad depression. In 1931, Rex Oil Company built oil storage tanks on the property and occupied it for several decades until it was purchased by the Sowles Crane Company. (Hennepin County Library.)

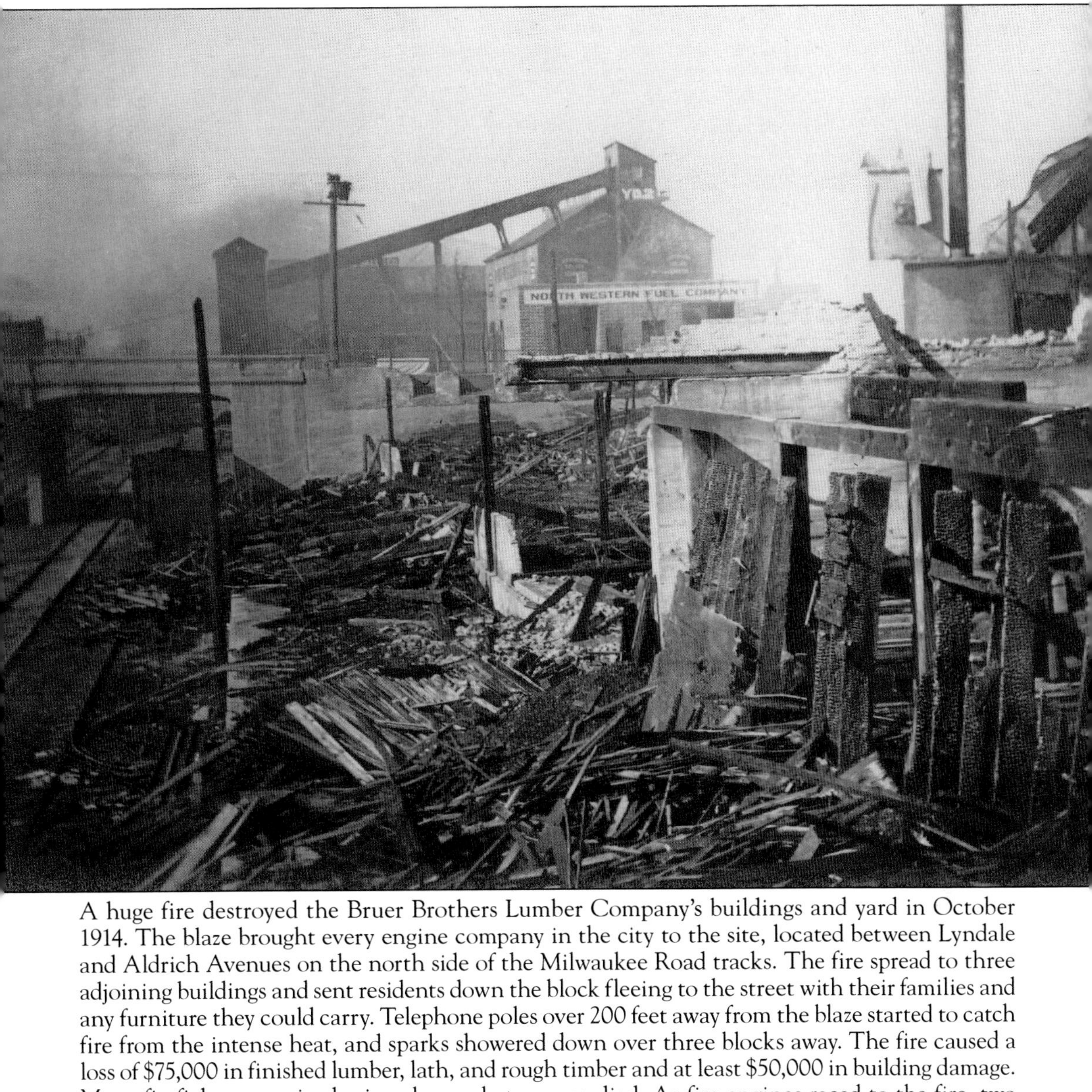

A huge fire destroyed the Bruer Brothers Lumber Company's buildings and yard in October 1914. The blaze brought every engine company in the city to the site, located between Lyndale and Aldrich Avenues on the north side of the Milwaukee Road tracks. The fire spread to three adjoining buildings and sent residents down the block fleeing to the street with their families and any furniture they could carry. Telephone poles over 200 feet away from the blaze started to catch fire from the intense heat, and sparks showered down over three blocks away. The fire caused a loss of $75,000 in finished lumber, lath, and rough timber and at least $50,000 in building damage. Many firefighters received minor burns, but no one died. As fire engines raced to the fire, two pedestrians were struck along Twenty-eighth Street nearby. Bruer Brothers Lumber Company rebuilt on the site. (Hennepin County Library.)

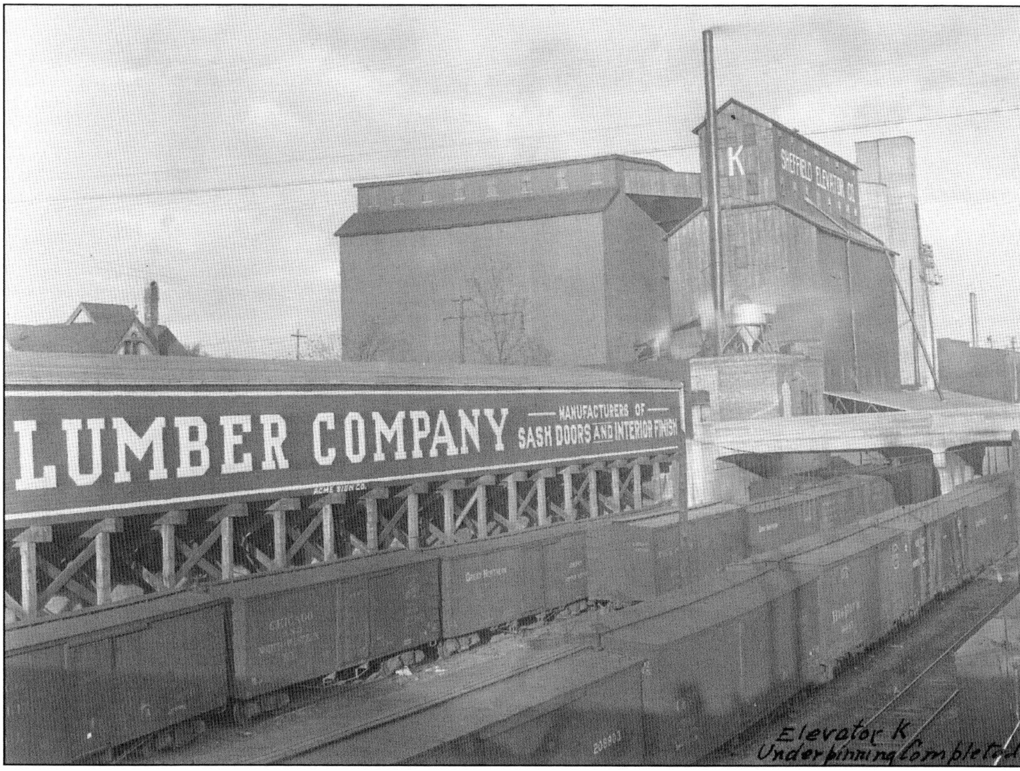

Bruer Brothers Lumber Company also owned a lumberyard on Lyndale Avenue across from its main building. This photograph, from about 1915, shows the company's storage yard, the Garfield Avenue Bridge, and the Sheffield Elevator Company. Bruer Brothers sold the yard in 1915 for $18,000 to Berwind Fuel Company for coal storage. The site became home to George Cook Construction in 1950; it remained there until the first decade in the 21st century. (Hennepin County Library.)

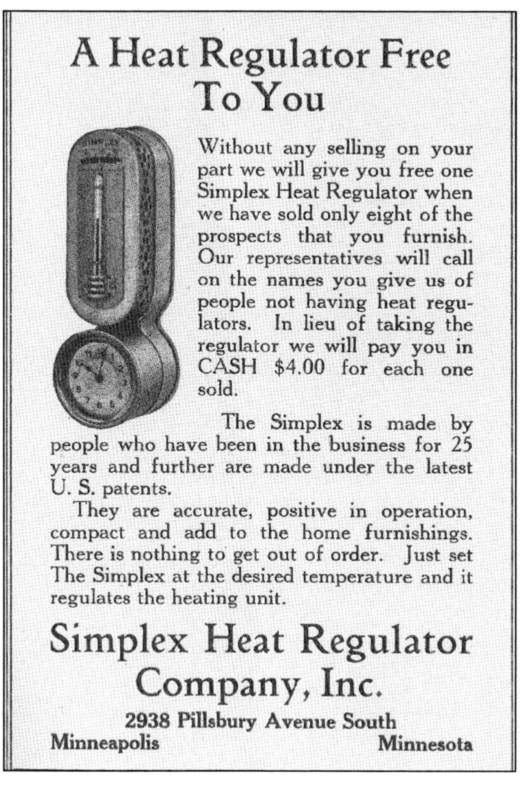

Lyn-Lake has a rich manufacturing history, representing items of all shapes and sizes and purposes. This temperature gauge was produced and sold by the Simplex Heat Regulator Company on Pillsbury Avenue, and this image is of a 1926 advertisement placed in a Lake Street guide, published by Lyndale Avenue's Ballentine VFW post. (Hennepin History Museum.)

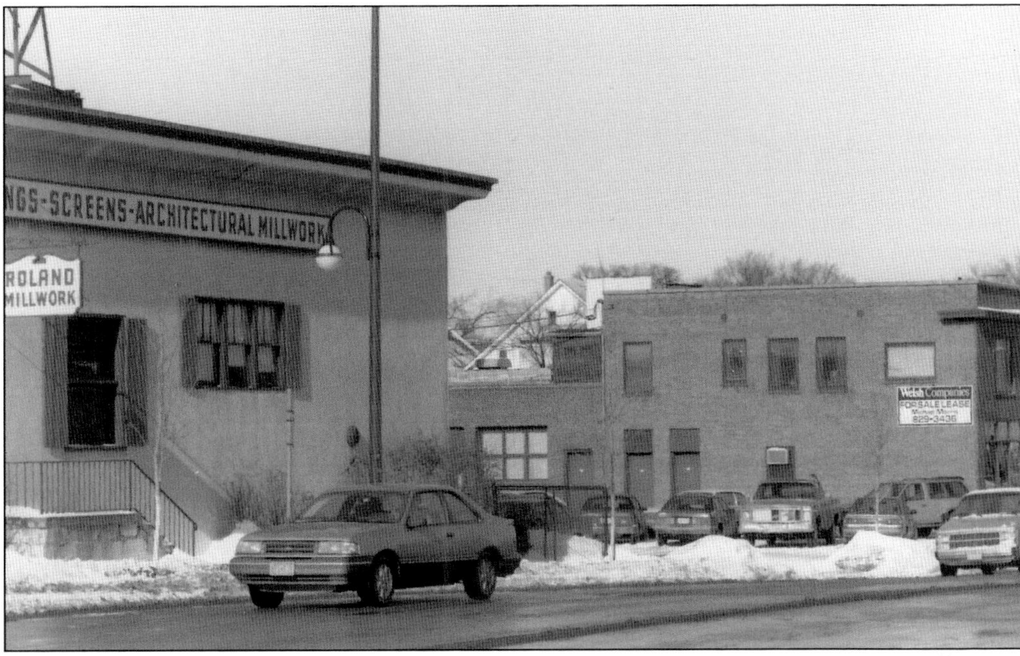

Roland Millwork occupied the one-time Bruer Brothers Building at 2836–2846 Lyndale Avenue. The building was constructed in 1901 as a mill for Bruer Brothers and rebuilt starting in 1914 after a devastating fire. Bruer Brothers was replaced by Lawson & Nelson Sash & Door in approximately 1960 and Roland Millwork shortly after that. The building had a planing mill in its basement. (Paul Newman.)

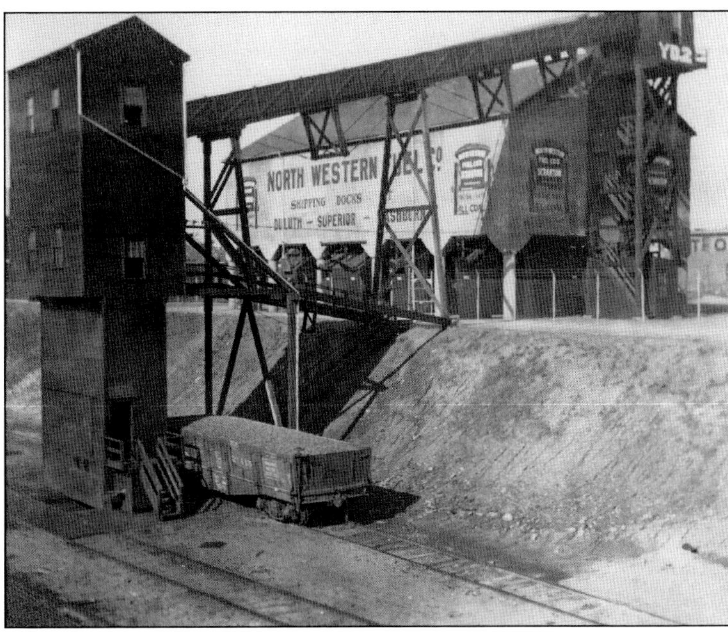

North Western Fuel Company first constructed a coal shed and office at 2840 Aldrich Avenue in 1899 before expanding in 1907. In 1914, it constructed new buildings, shown here, to work with the newly depressed railway. Just months later, the offices were destroyed by the Bruer Brothers fire. In 1939, the buildings were demolished, and the Twin City Read Mix Concrete Company soon opened on the site. (Hennepin County Library.)

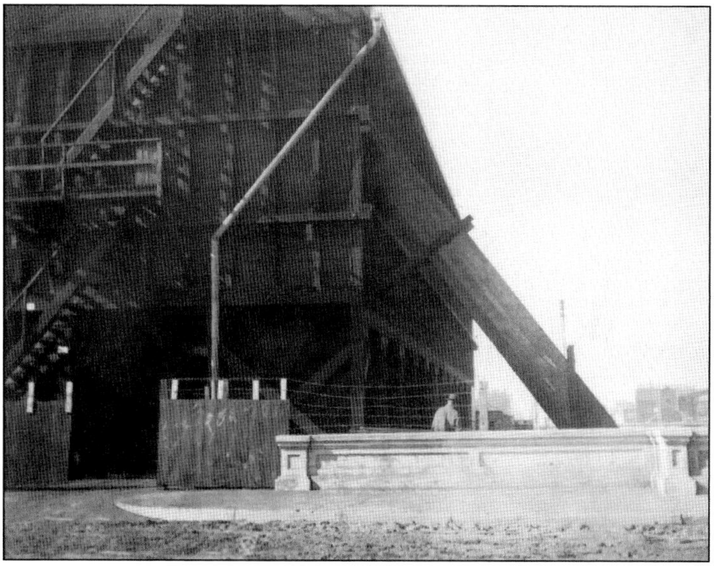

Sullivan Coal Company built a coal elevator in 1914 on the south side of the Milwaukee Road tracks between Garfield Avenue and Lyndale Avenue. The company used hoists for lifting coal from the railcars from the depressed tracks below. Coal piles were kept on the south side of the elevator. This photograph was taken between 1914 and 1916. (Hennepin County Library.)

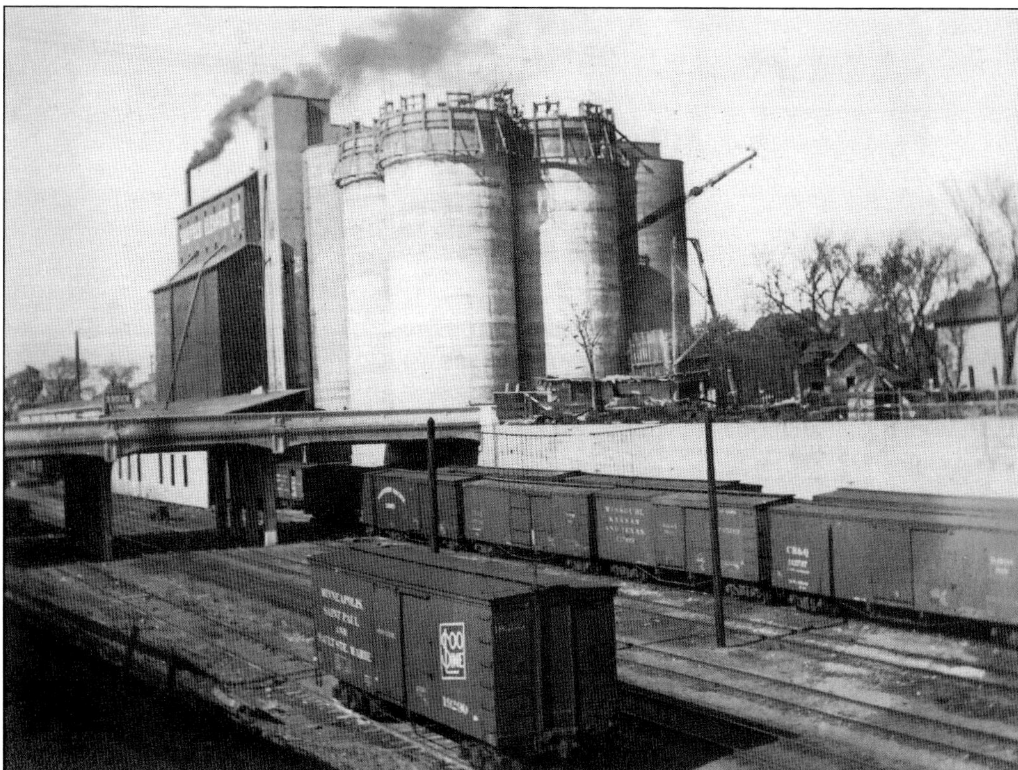

The Sheffield Elevator Company started out as a wood elevator in 1886 at 2843–2847 Garfield Avenue. The company expanded numerous times from 1905 through 1919, adding a new weighing house, powerhouse, sheds, and numerous new grain tanks. In 1925, the company added additions to the silos and new sheds. This photograph was taken in 1914 or 1915. (Hennepin County Library.)

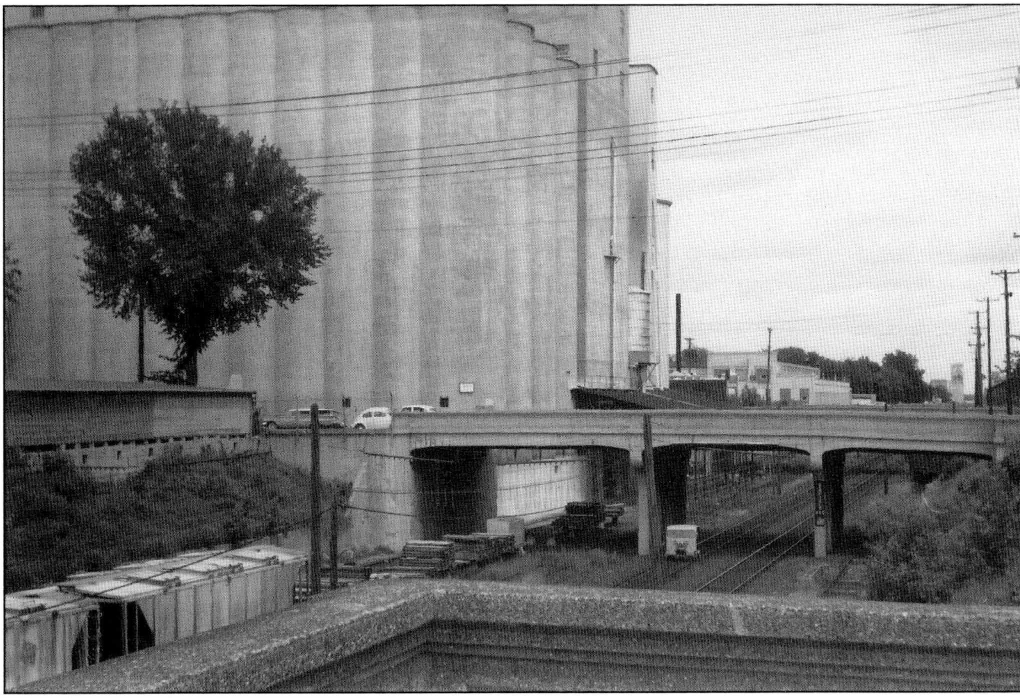

The Sheffield Elevator Company was incorporated in 1901 with the goal of "constructing, buying, owning, leasing, maintaining, and operating grain elevators and warehouses," as well as the buying and selling of grain and other goods. Sheffield's Elevator K was located on Garfield Avenue. The elevator had a 1.6 million-bushel capacity. (Minnesota Historical Society; photograph by Charles P. Gibson.)

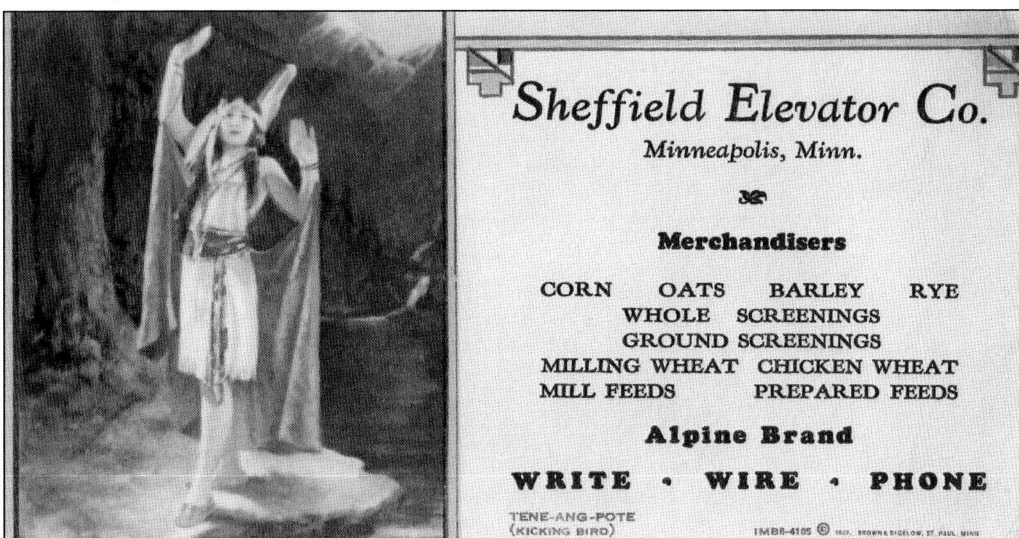

This ink blotter was part of a 1927 series created for the Sheffield Elevator Company by the St. Paul company Brown and Bigelow. Advertising materials like this were intended to keep the Sheffield name fresh in customers' mind. Those living and working in the greater Lyn-Lake area scarcely needed a reminder of Sheffield's presence; the large elevators, located at Twenty-ninth Street and Garfield Avenue, dominated the Lyn-Lake skyline. (Cedar Phillips.)

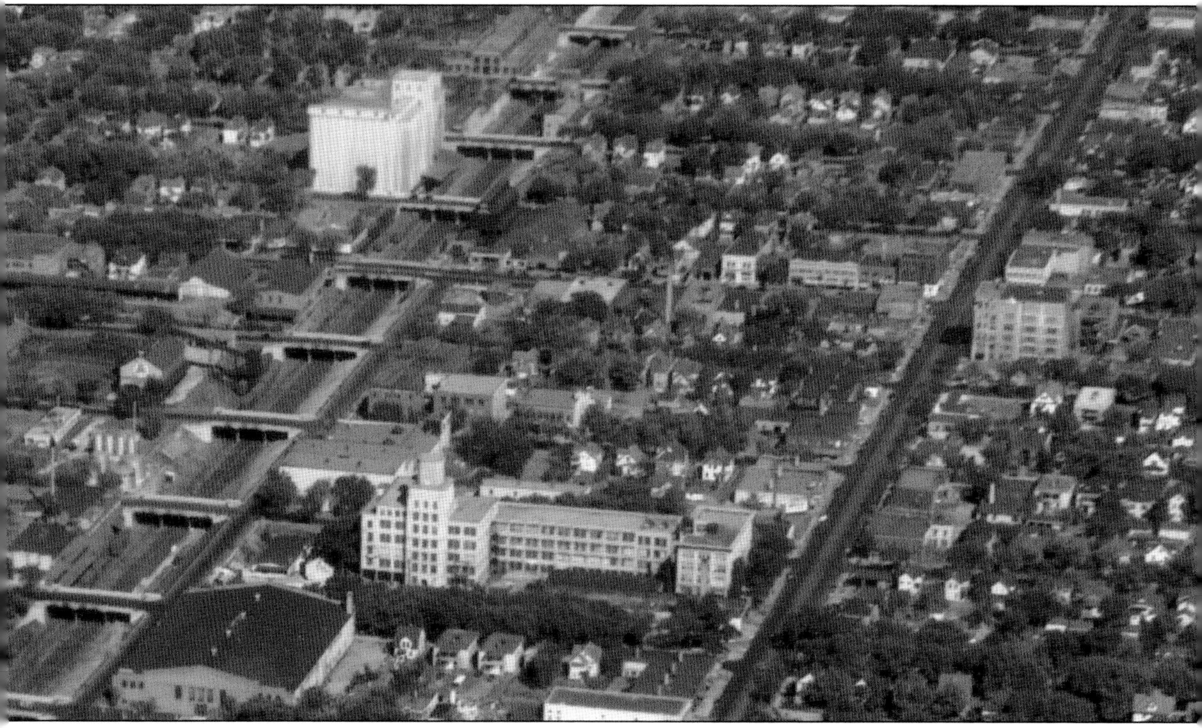

This aerial view of the industrial core of Lyn-Lake gives a good visual overview of the layout of the neighborhood. On the left side of the photograph, running below the series of bridges, is the depressed railroad trench; industrial buildings lined this corridor. The Sheffield Company's K elevator fills the sky in the upper left portion of the image, while the sprawling Buzza Card Company complex fills nearly an entire block in the lower part. Lyn-Lake was historically an important manufacturing neighborhood and has a rich industrial heritage, but that background has often been overlooked due to the physical geography of the industrial landscape. Industry was always there in the background, but it did not define the area. Its greatest physical influence was the shaping of smaller neighborhoods within the district. While both residents to the north and to the south of the railroad trench shared a common sense of community that was forged through the central business core as well as neighborhood parks, schools, and institutions, the tracks did create distinct micro-environments within the greater Lyn-Lake area. (MPS.)

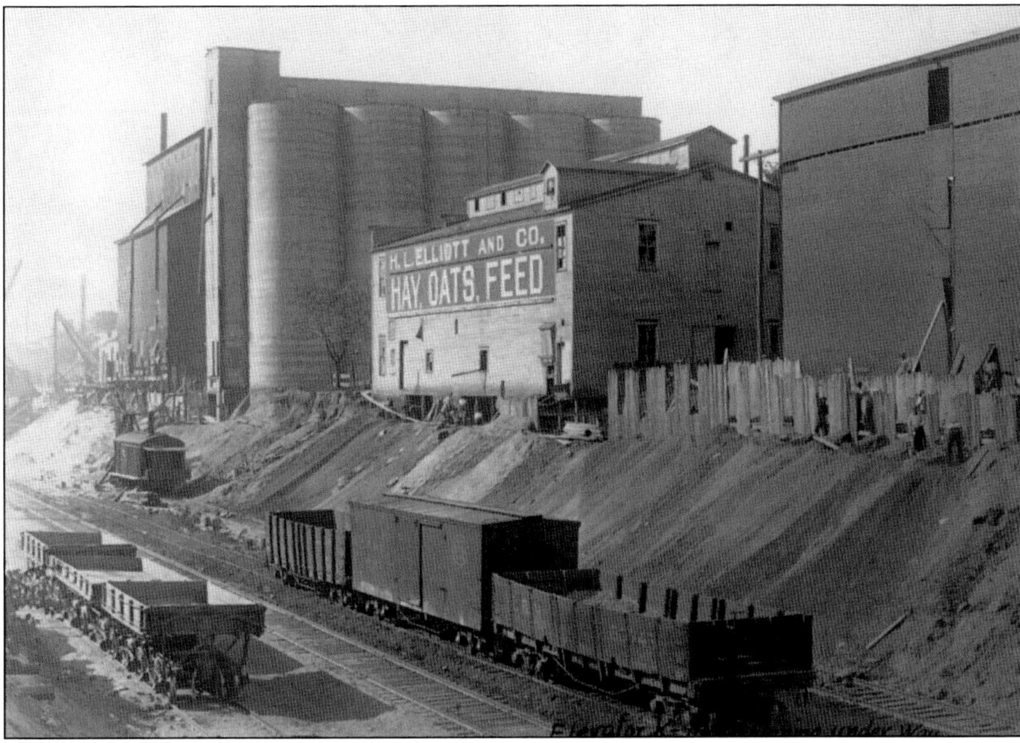

The H. L. Elliot and Company, at 2849 Harriet Avenue, is shown here approximately in 1912 when it operated as a feed barn. In 1914, the building, by then housing the Crassweller & Nelson Sash & Door plant, burned to the ground. The fire damaged the neighboring Cedar Lake Ice Company and two homes. Thousands of people were reported to have watched the fire, though many scattered when electrical wires snapped. (Minnesota Historical Society.)

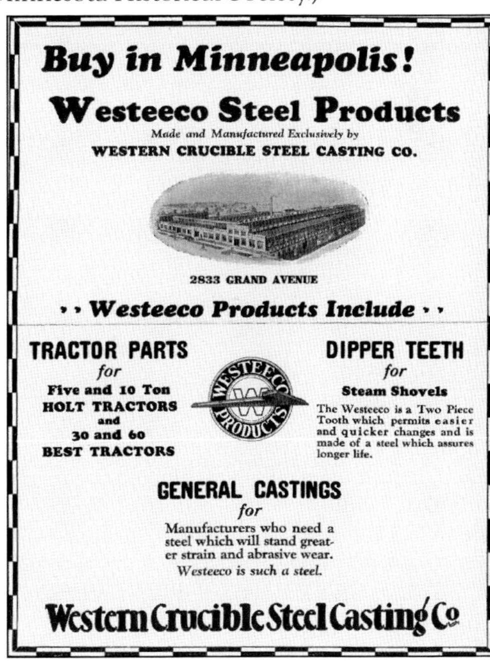

The Western Crucible Steel Casting Company, at 2833 Grand Avenue, was another longtime Lyn-Lake manufacturer. The company was founded in 1896 by George Honstain, J. H. Hopper, and Ray Merritt. This advertisement was published in 1928, several decades and several expansions later. The business enjoyed significant commercial success and shipped its steel castings nationwide. (Hennepin History Museum.)

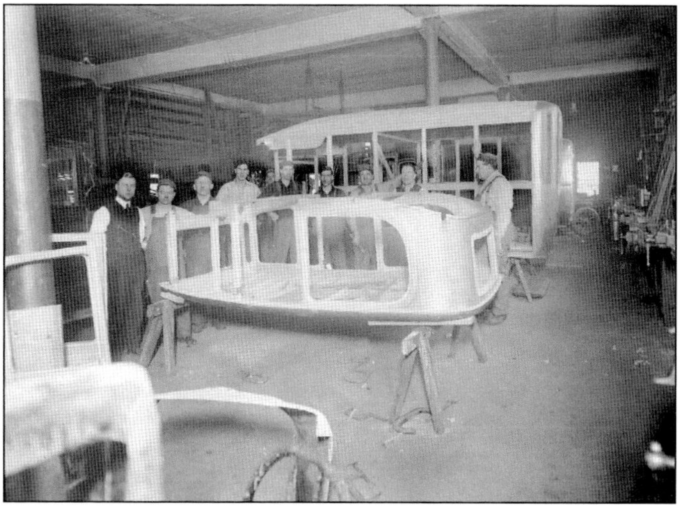

The Eckland Brothers Company moved into its new space at 2800 Lyndale Avenue in 1915. The business developed a national reputation as an expert in bus construction, and together with chassis builder C. H. Will built the first buses used by Greyhound Lines, which was based in Hibbing, Minnesota. This photograph dates to around 1912, which was shortly after the company had moved into its new space at 2800 Lyndale Avenue. (Al Hagen.)

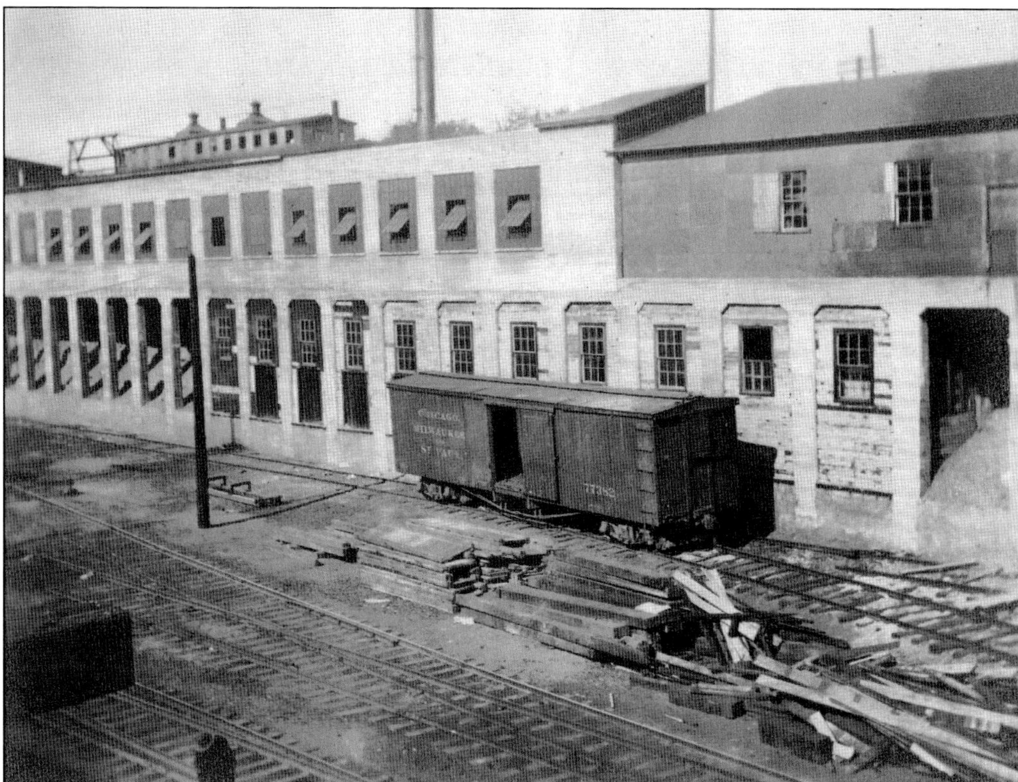

Western Crucible Steel Casting Company, at 2833 Grand Avenue, manufactured machinery materials. The plant featured a large street-level foundry with a large storeroom and a shipping room on the track level. In 1916, it was reported that the company was the largest steel casting company in the West. At the time, the company manufactured the castings for the boilers on two U.S. battleships. (Minnesota Historical Society.)

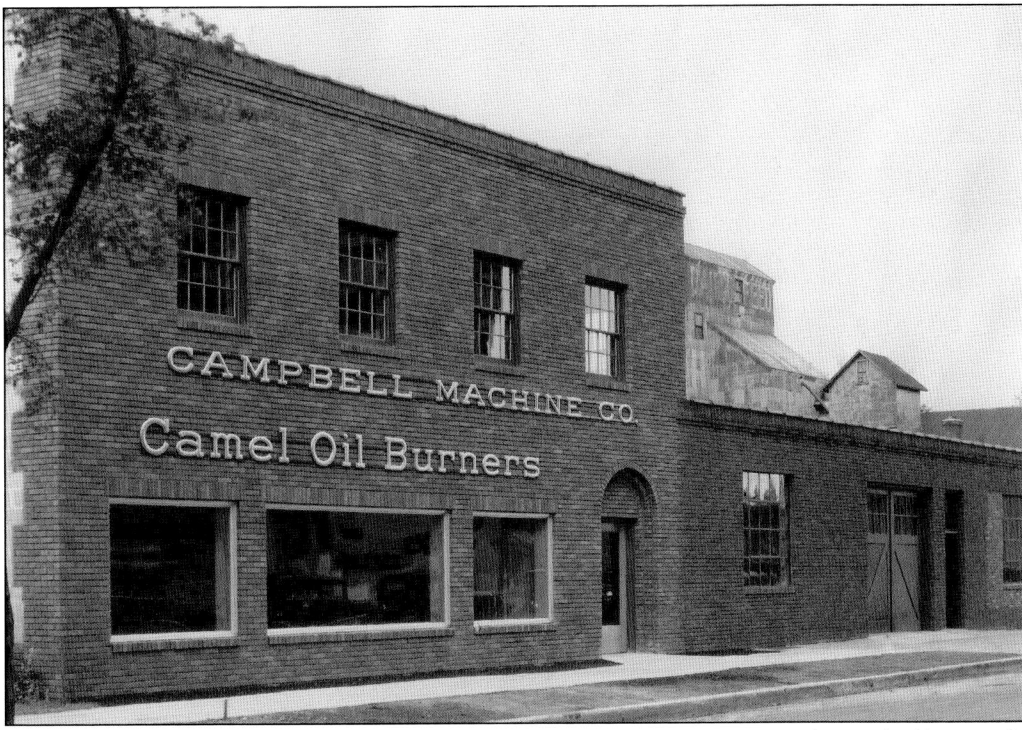

The Campbell Machine Company, located at 2845–2851 Harriet Avenue, manufactured oil burners for a national audience. The firm was founded in 1920. It grew rapidly, expanding three times in 14 years. This photograph, taken in 1934, shows the newest 40-foot-by-87-foot brick and concrete expansion, built at a cost of $10,000. (Hennepin County Library; photograph by Norton and Peel.)

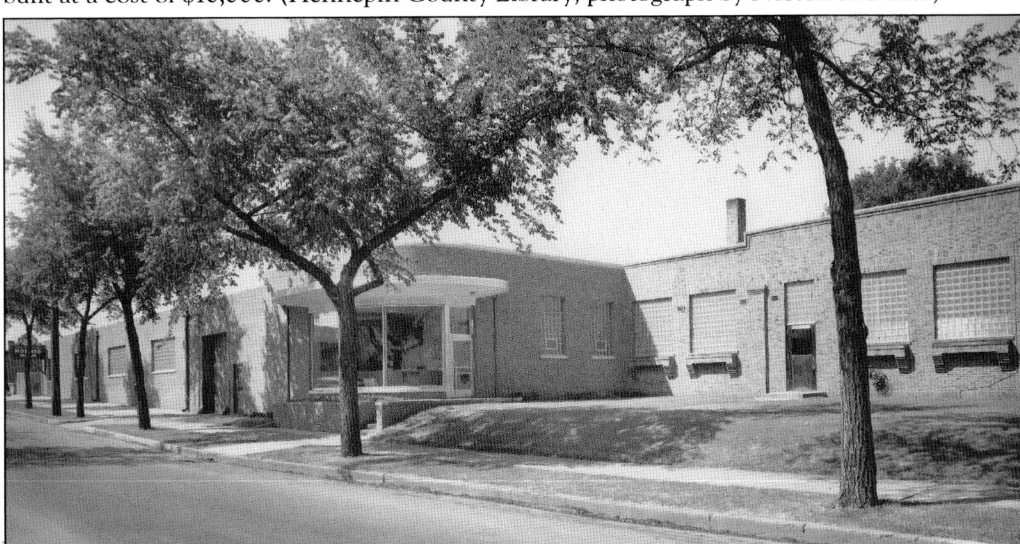

Norris Creamery, at 2924 Emerson Avenue, began in 1910 as Johnson Pure Milk Company. Renamed Norris Creamery in 1926, it began acquiring other dairies, including Isles Dairy at 2720 Lyndale Avenue and Young America Dairy at 2832 Bryant Avenue. The business delivered milk to over 50,000 people in the 1950s before discontinuing the service in 1973. The plant moved to Woodbury in 1980. This photograph was taken around 1947. (Hennepin County Library.)

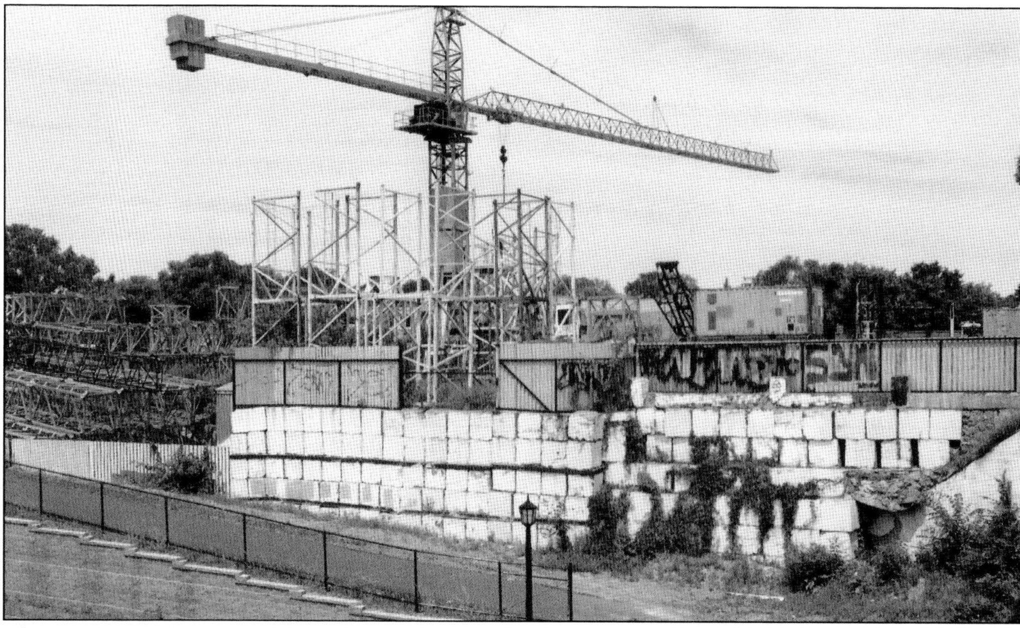

The L. H. Sowles Company was founded in 1961. The crane rental company, located at 2813 Bryant Avenue, had a role in the building of many Minneapolis skyscrapers, including the iconic 1967 IDS Tower. The City of Minneapolis bought the property in 2003 as a part of the Urban Village redevelopment, which was a series of housing projects replacing industrial property along the old rail corridor. This photograph was taken in 2001. (LHENA.)

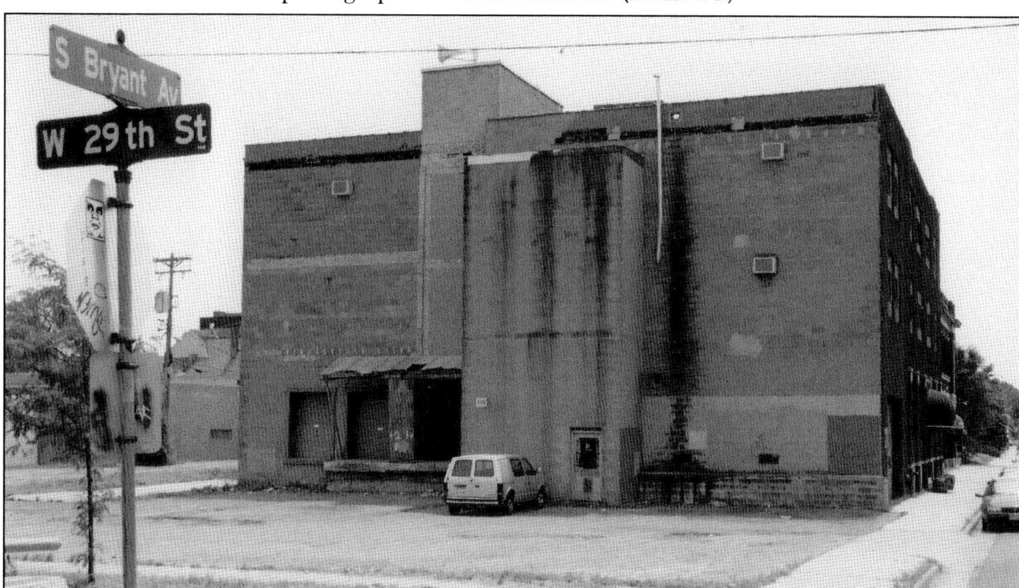

Furniture Industries, Inc. (FII), located at Twenty-ninth Street and Bryant Avenue, moved into this building in 1965 and has been there ever since. The family-owned business began as furniture manufacturers and upholsterers and gradually evolved into experts in hospitality industry design. Although near, but not on, the railroad tracks, the business has always been truck-based. Today the building serves as office and warehouse space for products now manufactured elsewhere. (LHENA.)

Two

COMMERCE

Ever since its earliest years in the 1880s, it seems that the Lyn-Lake neighborhood has always been either the current "it" neighborhood or the next "hot" and up-and-coming neighborhood. "The section of Lake Street known as the Lyndale-Lake Center has long been 'on the map' as one of the outstanding business centers of south Minneapolis," wrote local boosters in 1926, while the newspapers of later decades have always been filled with stories about the district's "renaissance."

In many ways, they are all right. Lyn-Lake has long been a commercial center, although the specific nature of its commerce has ebbed and flowed with time. In the 19th century, Lyn-Lake far eclipsed its sleepy neighbor at nearby Hennepin Avenue and Lake Street; by the first decade of the 20th century, new city regulations and streetcar routes had led to the rise of Uptown as a district, eclipsing Lyn-Lake in preeminence by the 1920s. In more recent decades, Lyn-Lake has been held up as the "anti-Uptown," the neighborhood where independent shops and a diverse blend of residents and customers give it a more bohemian flavor than the more gentrified Uptown.

One phrase that repeatedly comes up, decade after decade, is "crossroads." Lyn-Lake's businesses reflect the crossroads of south Minneapolis, the location where people representing all different ethnic backgrounds, socioeconomic levels, and with a dramatic range of tastes and interests, converge. It is where new immigrants mingle with native old-timers, where young hipsters belt out karaoke with aging veterans, where customers can shop for everything from feminist sex toys, English riding saddles, hand-crafted contemporary jewelry, to 1940s party dresses. Lyn-Lake's businesses have long had something for everyone, a tradition that continues today.

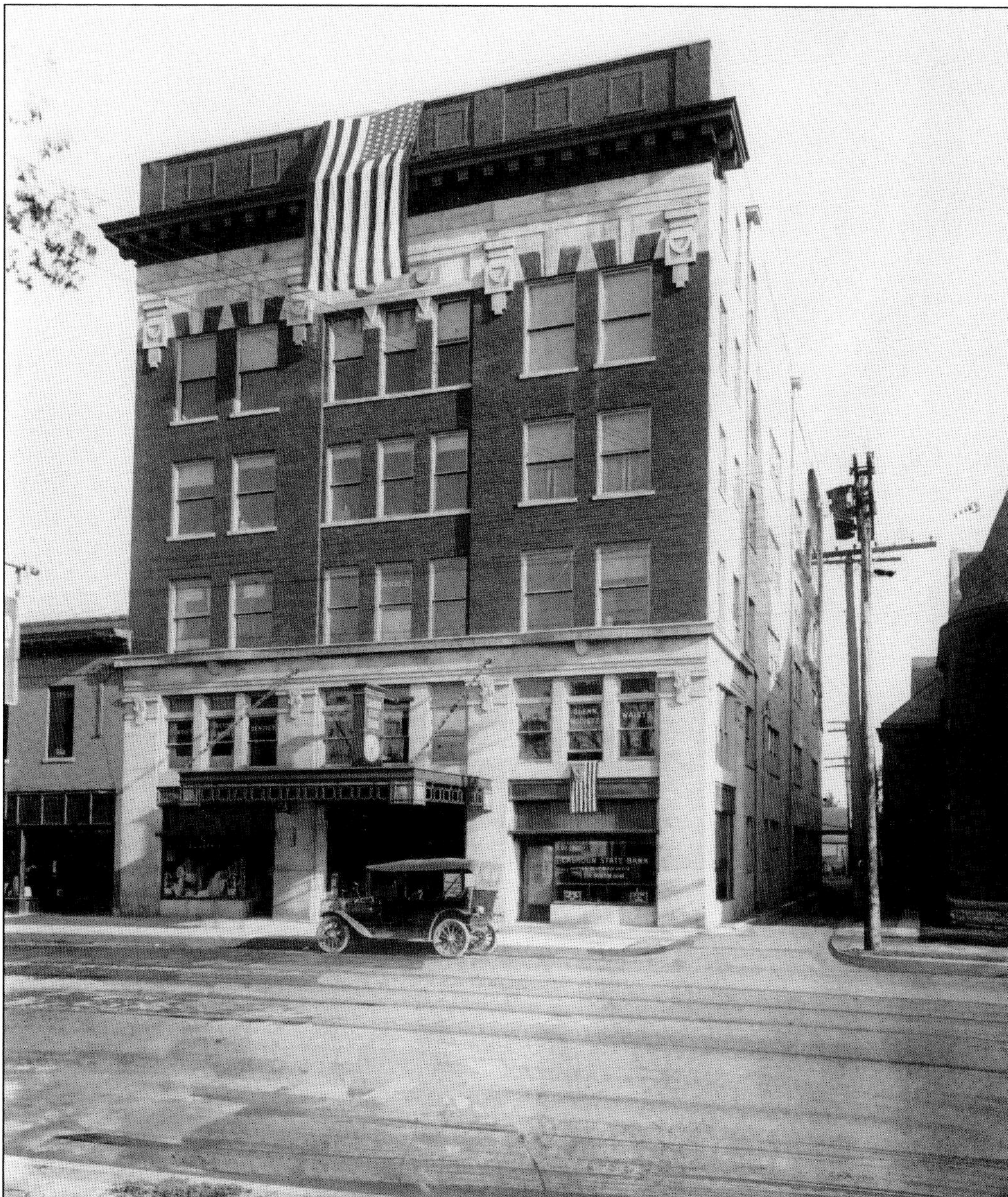

The Calhoun Commercial Club Building opened in 1914 to considerable fanfare. The six-story building featured three floors of stores and offices in addition to a reception hall, ballroom, and club rooms. It quickly became the regular gathering place for many of Lyn-Lake's most prominent businessmen. By July 1913, more than a year before the building or the club opened, more than 250 people had joined it; the number had swelled to more than 500 by the time it opened. The goals of the Calhoun Commercial Club and those of some of the district's businesses did not always neatly align. In 1915, for example, members voted to oppose additional movie theaters in the district after citing "artistic" concerns. In response, some retailers, anticipating increased customers and foot traffic, started a petition in support of the theaters. Generally, however, the goal of the Calhoun Commercial Club and the majority of Lyn-Lake businesses was the same—to encourage a safe, economically robust, vibrant commercial district. (Hennepin County Library.)

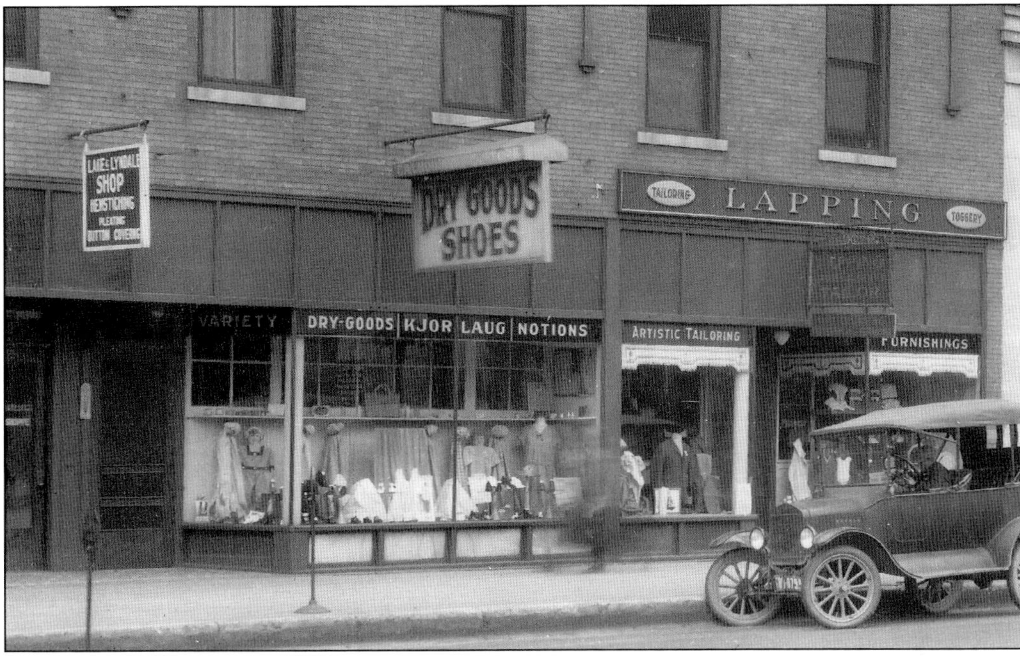

The businesses at 709 West Lake Street enjoyed a prime location near the southwest corner of the heavily traveled Lyndale Avenue and Lake Street intersection. Photographed around 1915, the businesses here included tailor Abraham Lapping and notions dealer Mons Kjorlaug. Both men lived near their work: Lapping lived at 3140 Harriet Avenue and Kjorlaug at 3120 Bryant Avenue. (Hennepin County Library; photograph by H. E. Vanderwater.)

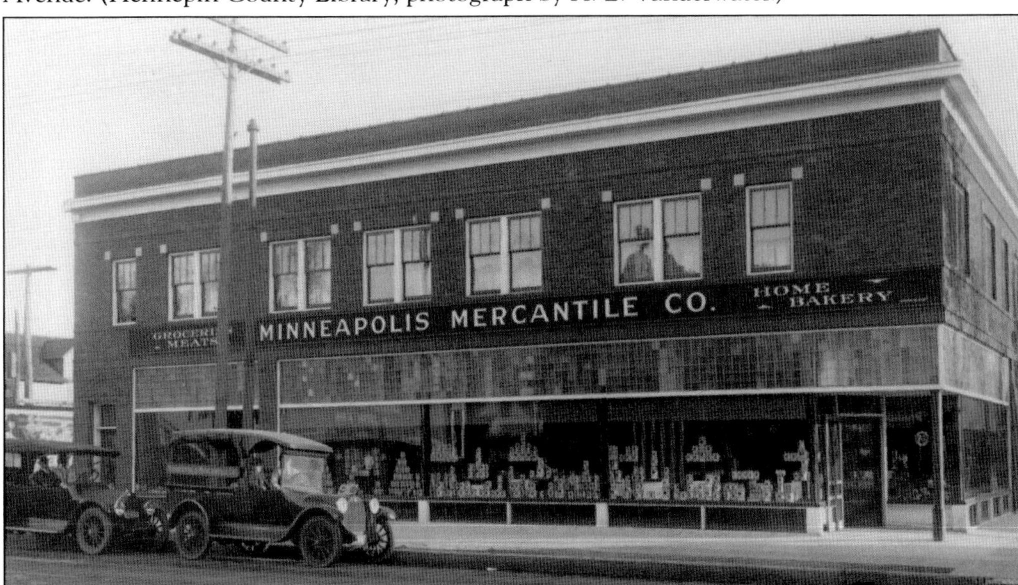

The Minneapolis Mercantile Company, located on the southeast corner of Lake Street and Colfax Avenue, offered groceries, meats, and a bakery. The building, constructed in 1916, housed both the family business as well as many of the family members themselves. Samuel, Richard, Arthur, and Victor Sandberg, family matriarch Lizzie, and Samuel's wife and two young daughters lived in the apartments above the store. (Mohn Electric Company.)

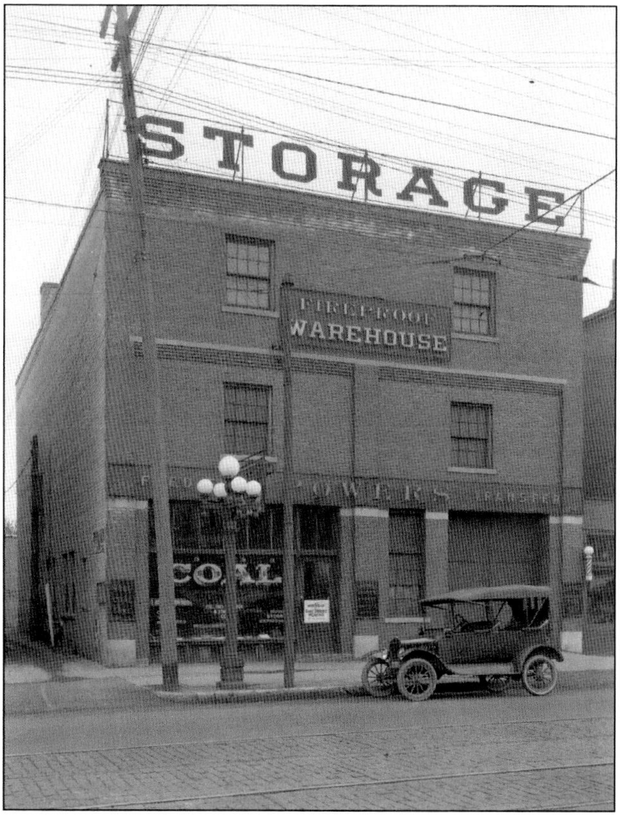

The Powers Transfer Building, located just west of Lyndale Avenue at 611 West Lake Street, sold fuel, moved goods, and had storage available for household items. In this 1920 photograph, its building sign advertises the fireproof storage warehouse. The company was well aware of the dangers of fire; in 1910, they had suffered a serious fire in the barn, stable, and storage building. (Minnesota Historical Society.)

The Grand Avenue and Lake Street intersection was a streetcar transfer point and as a result was home to many consumer-oriented businesses. The southeast and southwest intersections in this *c.* 1941 photograph were home to a taxidermist, Earl's Food Market, Chas Drug, a tavern, Grand Cash Market, and Scandia Furniture. (City of Minneapolis.)

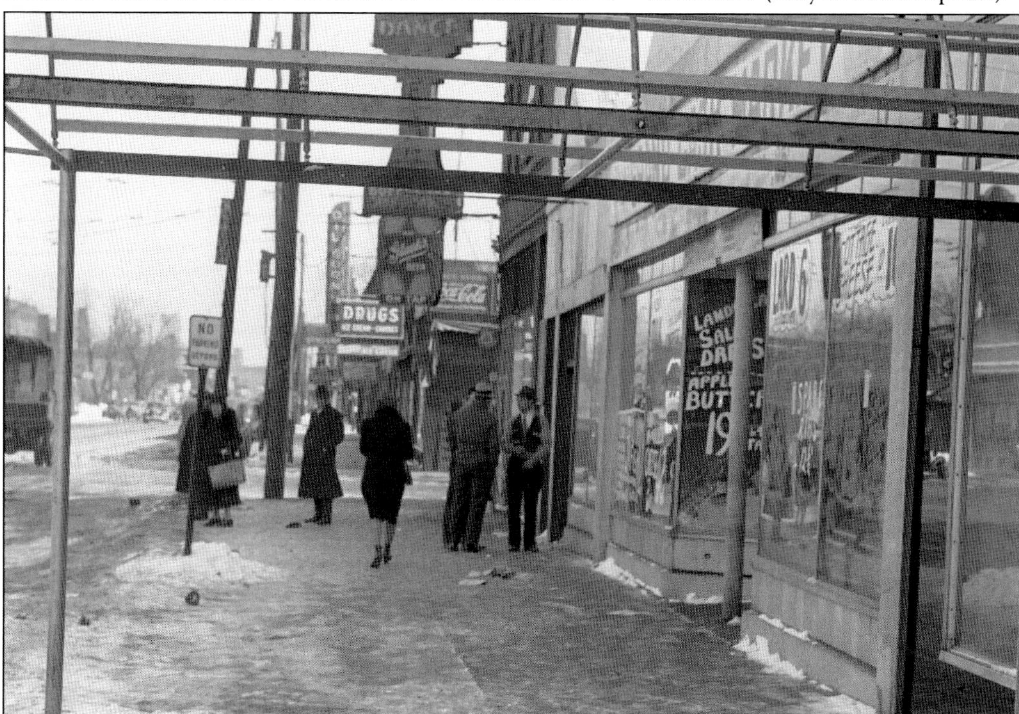

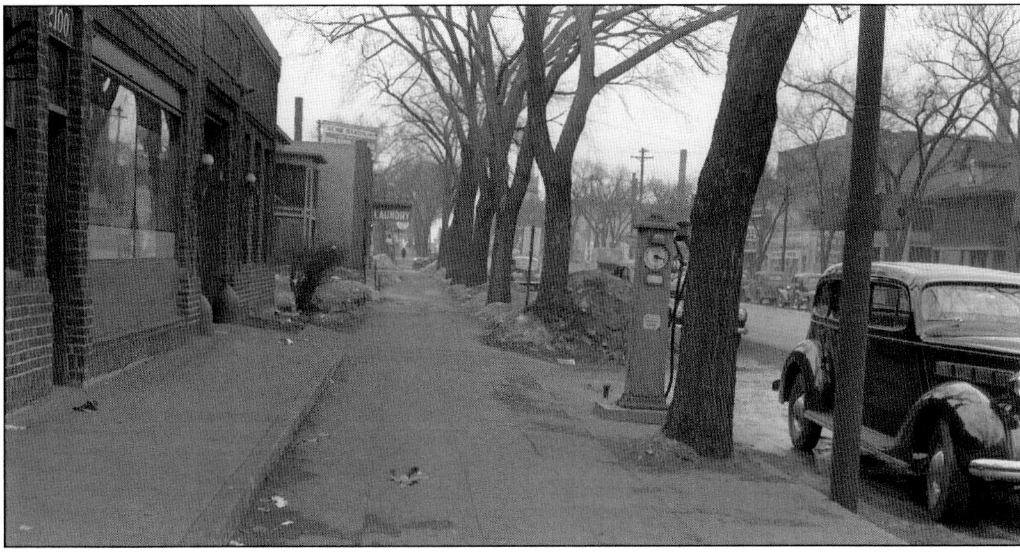

Shown here in 1944, the building at 2100 Lyndale Avenue was home to Harry W. Smith Ambulance, an ambulance company with a fleet of emergency vehicles based out of the Lyndale Avenue office. Note the gas pump on the street's curb, which was fairly common in dense commercial districts with older buildings such as the Harry W. Smith's 1919 building. (City of Minneapolis.)

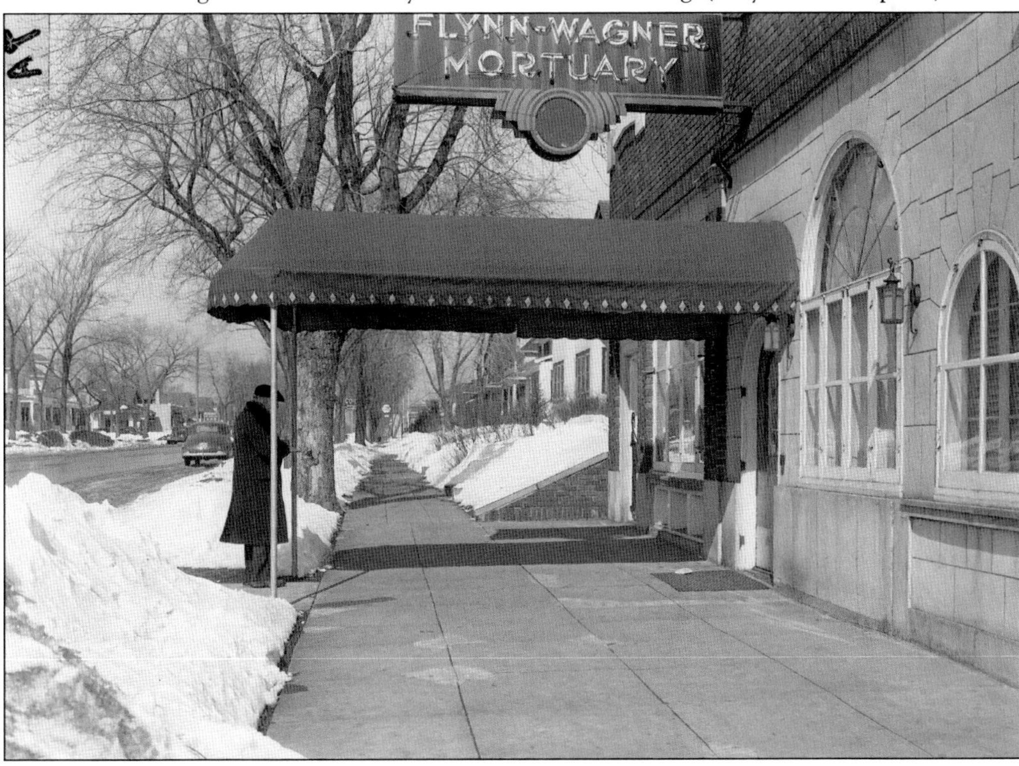

Raymond Flynn and Ernest Wagner opened the Flynn-Wagner Mortuary at 2707 Lyndale Avenue in 1926. In the late 1920s, the business moved to 3541 Lyndale Avenue. Flynn's son Lloyd would later join the business; at that point, it was renamed Flynn and Son Funeral Home and retained that name until it closed in the late 1970s. This photograph dates to around 1941. (City of Minneapolis.)

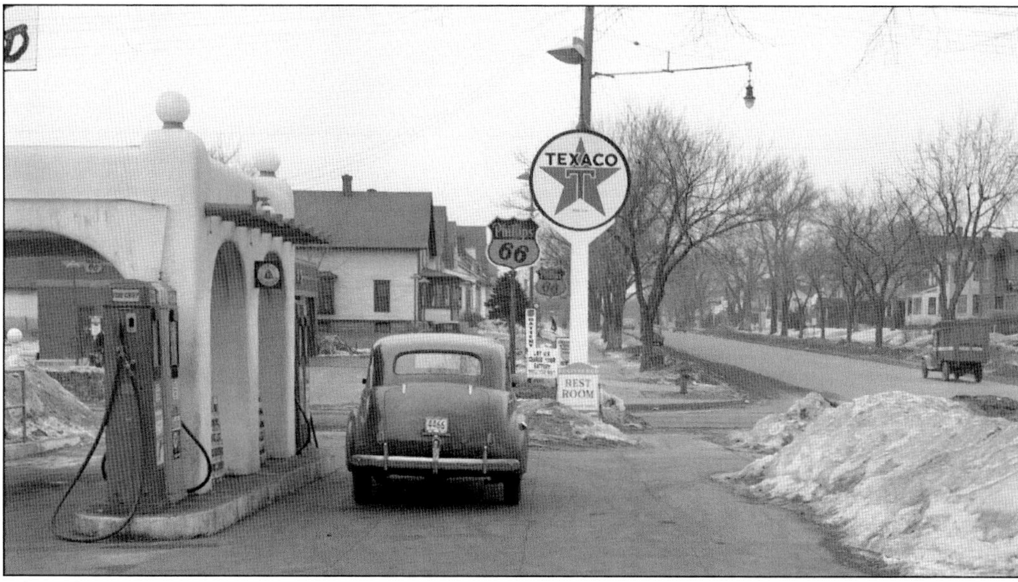

The Thirty-sixth Street and Lyndale Avenue intersection has long been home to auto-service stations. The building housing Texaco, at 3600 Lyndale Avenue, was built as a gas station in 1922. Next door in 1924, at 709 West Thirty-sixth Street, was a repair garage that today houses the Parent's Auto and Tire Center. This 1941 photograph shows the Texaco station and the Phillips 66 station across Thirty-sixth Street. (City of Minneapolis.)

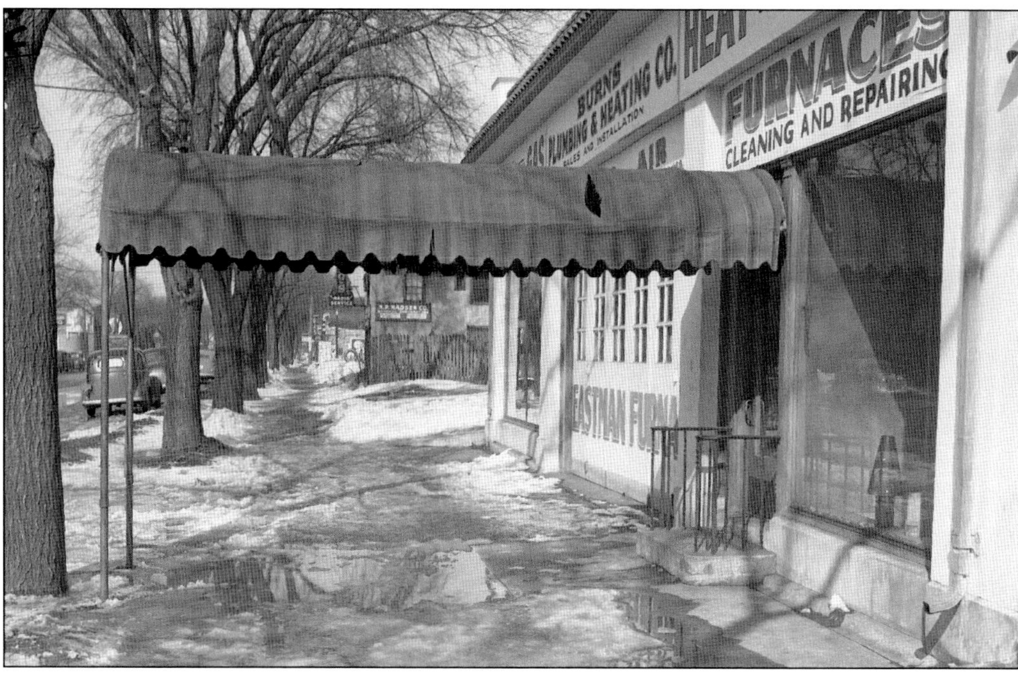

Eastman Furnace Company, at 2831 Lyndale Avenue, shared space with Burns Plumbing and Heating Company and Terry Manufacturing Company, which produced chimney drafts. This 1941 photograph shows an awning from the door over the sidewalk toward the street, which was a common practice during that time. The building would become the home of George Cook Construction in 1950. (City of Minneapolis.)

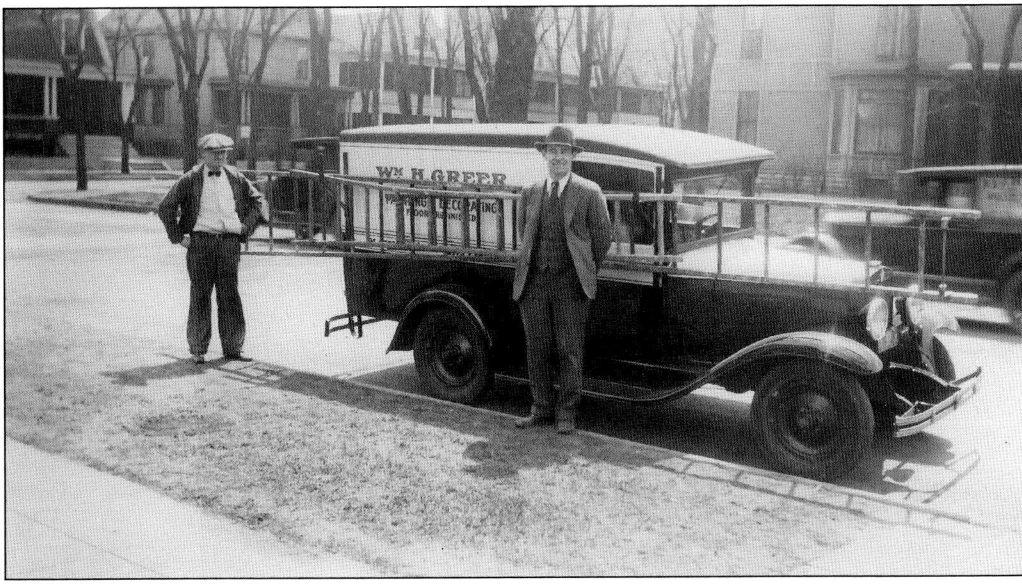

When Salem English Lutheran Church decided to give its parsonage, located at 610 West Twenty-eighth Street, a fresh coat of paint in 1933, there was no need to look far for the right man for the job. William Greer, shown here with his truck, worked out of nearby shop at 2713 Lyndale Avenue. (SELC.)

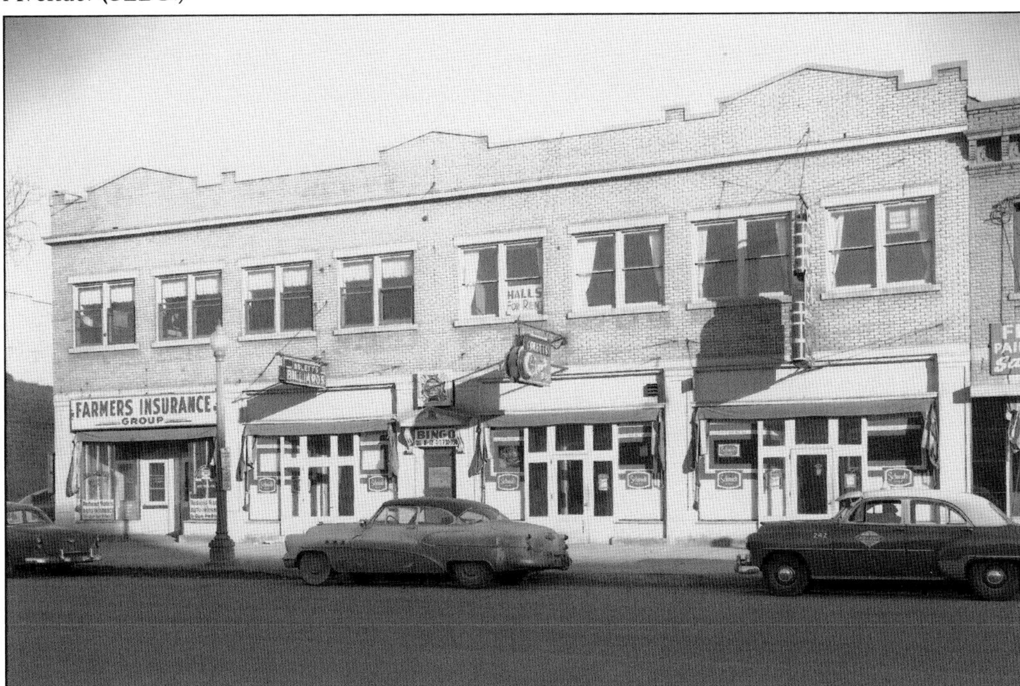

In 1955, John Murphy's accounting firm, Farmer's Insurance Group, USS Yorktown VFW post, and Russell "Buzz" Arlett's tavern and billiards were located at 2945–2951 Lyndale Avenue, shown here. Arlett was a famous minor-league baseball player who played for the Minneapolis Millers in the mid-1930s and was known for setting records for his home run–hitting abilities. The building is now home to the Jungle Theater. (Minnesota Historical Society.)

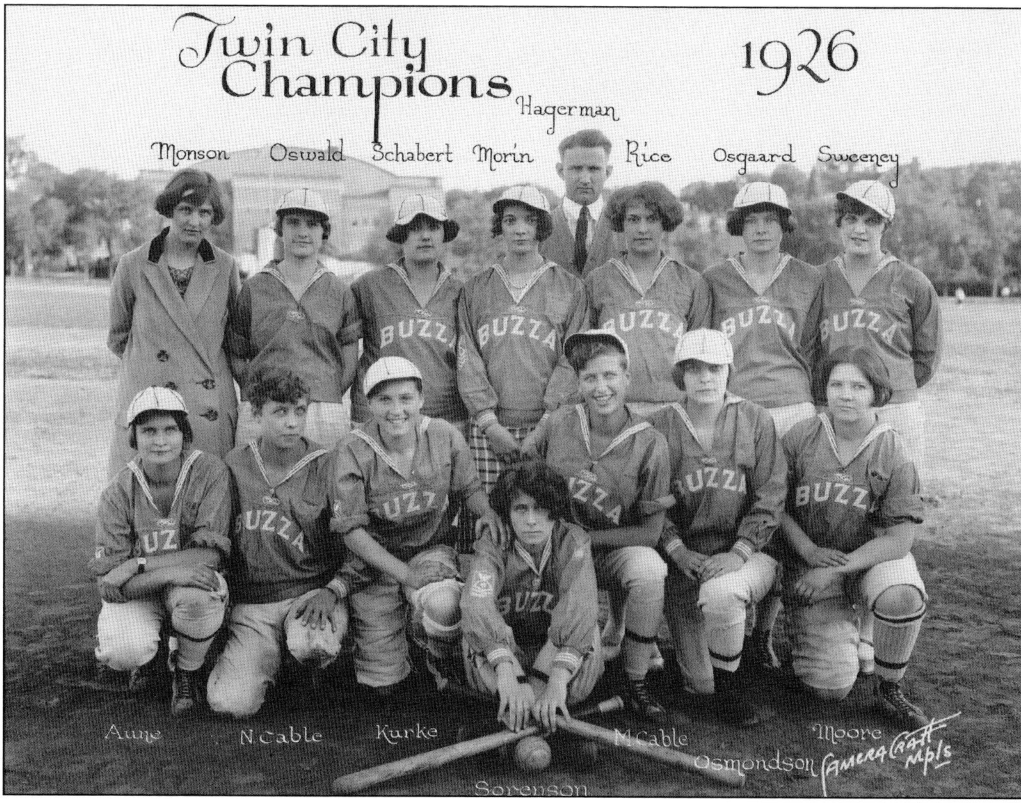

Like many bigger companies in the city, the Buzza Card Company hosted several company sports teams, including the Buzza Hornets, a men's baseball team, and the Bees, a women's softball team. In July 1926, the Bees, shown here, defeated the team from Dayton's and won the division title. The Hornets had similarly good luck, beating the Northern Fire Apparatus Company to claim victory. (Hennepin County Library; photograph by Camera Craft.)

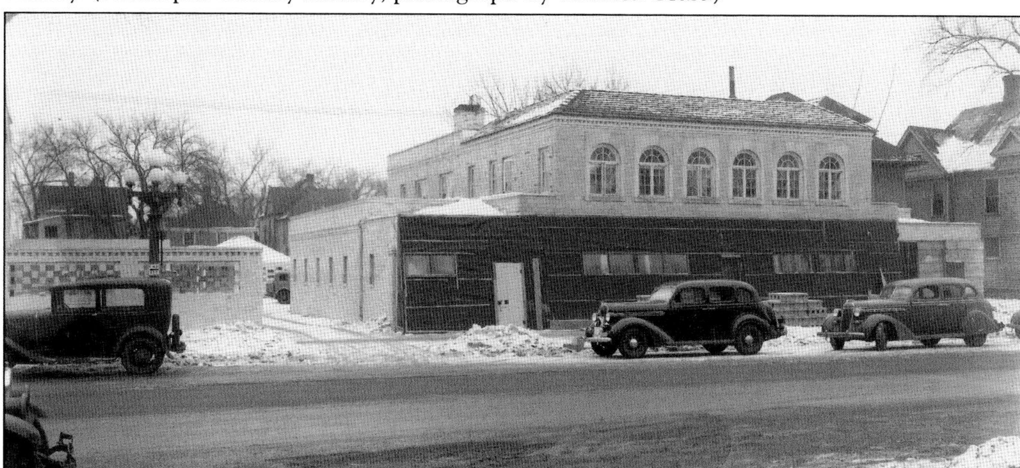

The construction of 3015–3019 Lyndale Avenue, just south of Lake Street, was completed in 1937. By 1938, the building included several physicians' offices, Swenson's Food Market, the Solderlin Plumbing and Heating Company, and six apartments on the upper floors, with all but one rented. The building still stands today. (Hennepin County Library; photograph by H. E. Vanderwater.)

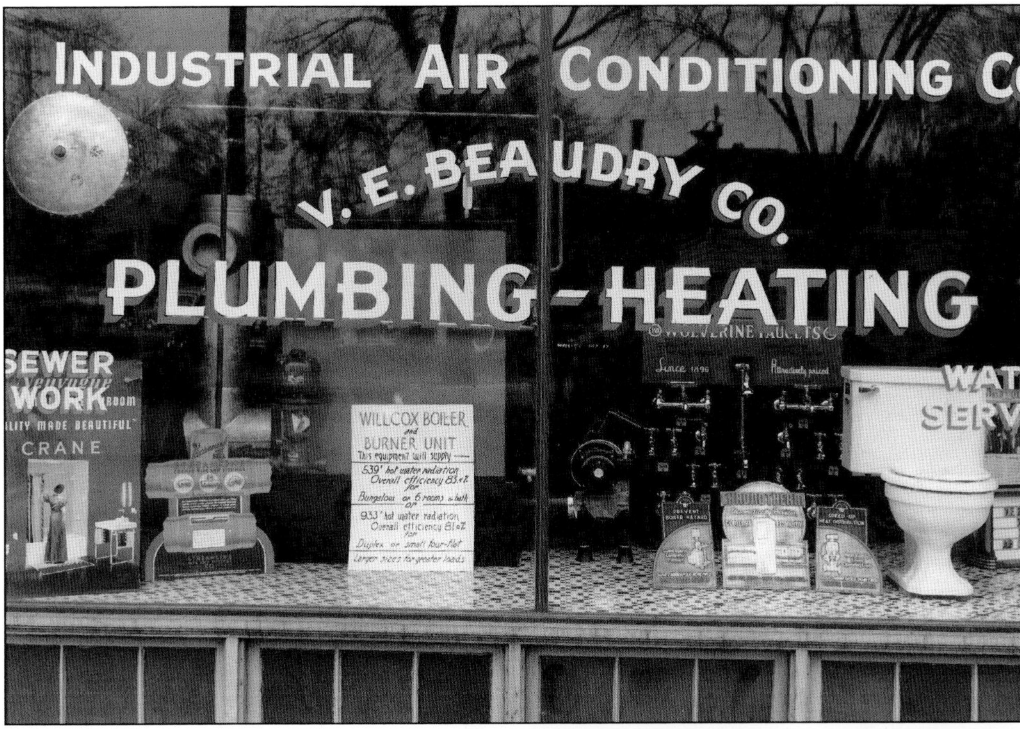

V. E. Beaudry Company, located at 504 West Lake Street, served the heating, plumbing, and air-conditioning needs of local homes and businesses. During the early 1930s, Victor Beaudry ran a plumbing business at Bryant Avenue and Thirty-sixth Street. By the late 1940s, the business had become the Beaudry Plumbing and Heating Company and had moved yet again, this time to an expanded location at 2901 Lyndale Avenue. (Hennepin County Library.)

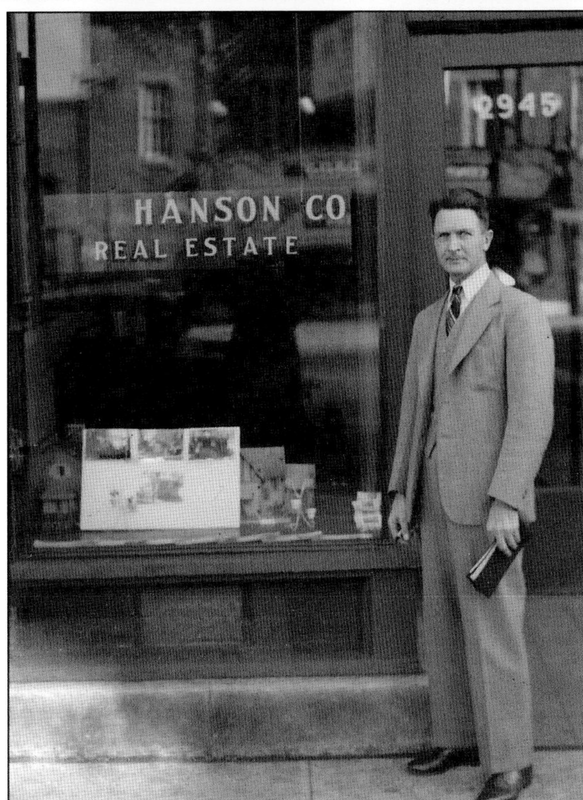

The Hanson Company, at 2945 Lyndale Avenue, is shown here in 1939. Someone connected with Salem English Lutheran Church took the photograph. In 1950, the congregation purchased a commercial property known as "Hanson's Store," at 2741 Lyndale Avenue. The unidentified man in the photograph is presumably Mr. Hanson. (SELC.)

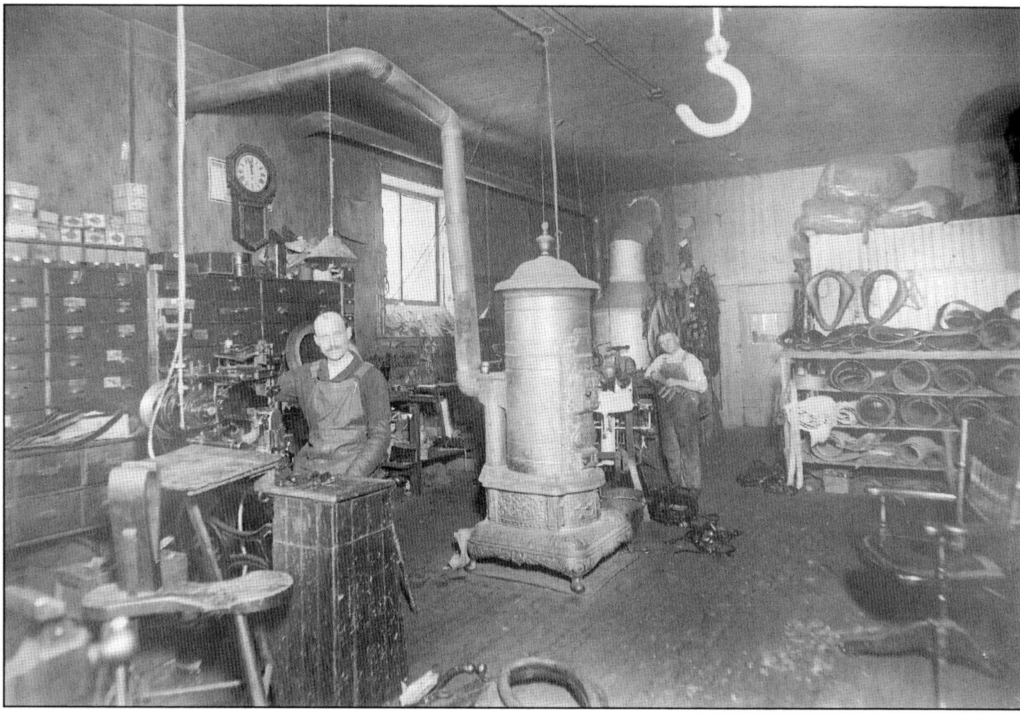

Emil Schatzlein (left) took time out in 1920 to pose for this photograph of his saddle shop at 609 West Lake Street (home to the current Dulano's). Schatzlein began his business immediately after arriving in Minneapolis from California in 1907. Initially his business primarily served working horses and their owners; these included south Minneapolis market farmers as well as the neighborhood's plentiful delivery teams. (Schatzlein Saddle Shop.)

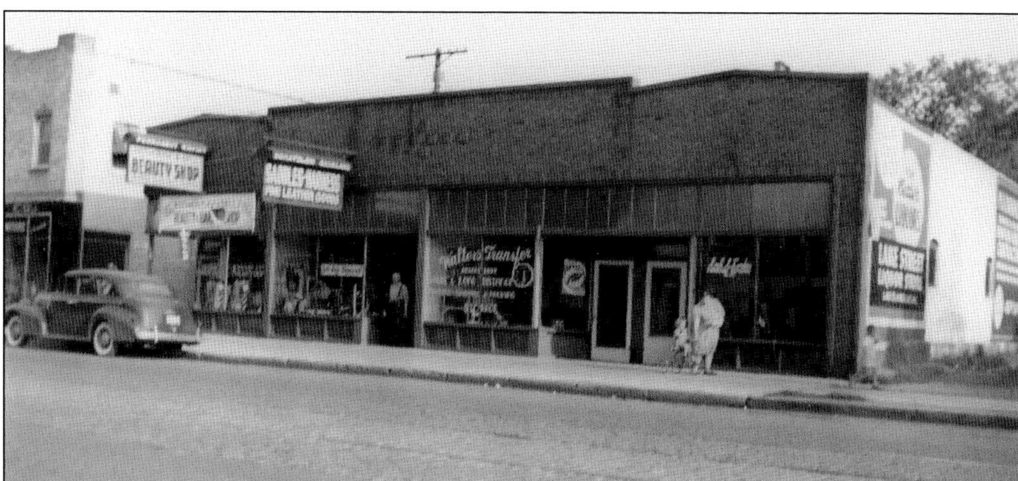

In 1936, Emil Schatzlein moved his business to this building at 421 West Lake Street. Here he stands in the doorway of his store. The 1930s had been a rough decade; the family had lost much of their savings when the Calhoun State Bank failed. Business had improved by the 1940s, the presumed date of this photograph, although survival in an era of automobiles required flexibility. (Schatzlein Saddle Shop.)

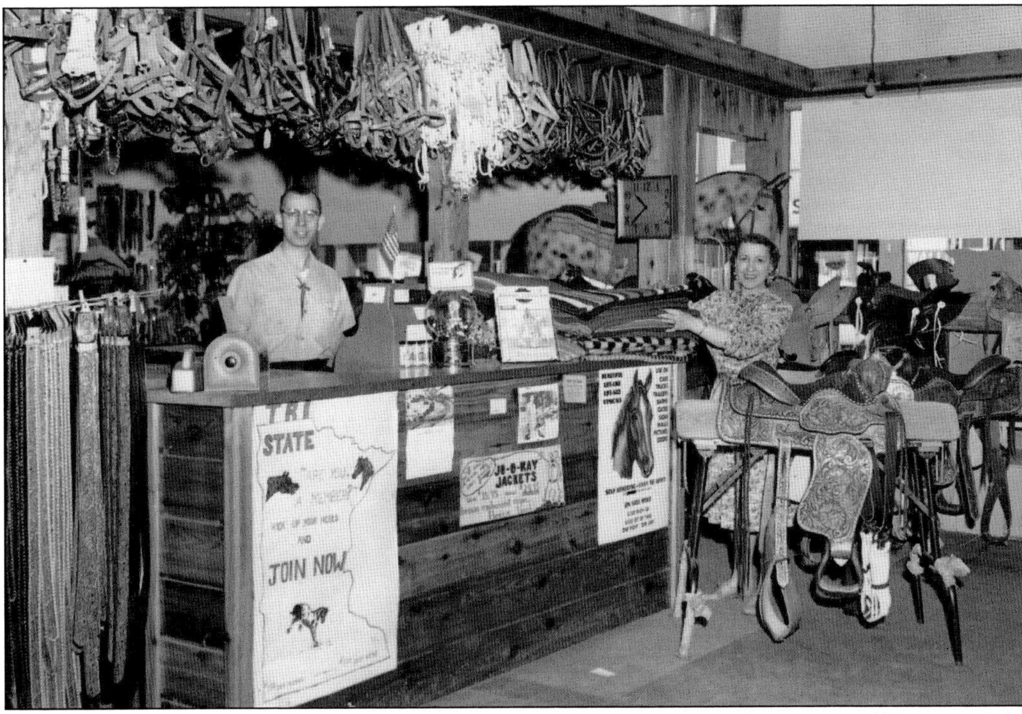

By 1963, the year of this photograph, Schatzlein's Saddle Shop had grown to fill most of the storefronts in the 421 West Lake Street Building. The items sold had evolved over the years; the saddles and accessories hanging here were not intended for the working horses of earlier generations. Emil Schatzlein died in 1958, but second-generation owners Jerry and Millie Schatzlein, shown here, continued the family business. (Schatzlein Saddle Shop.)

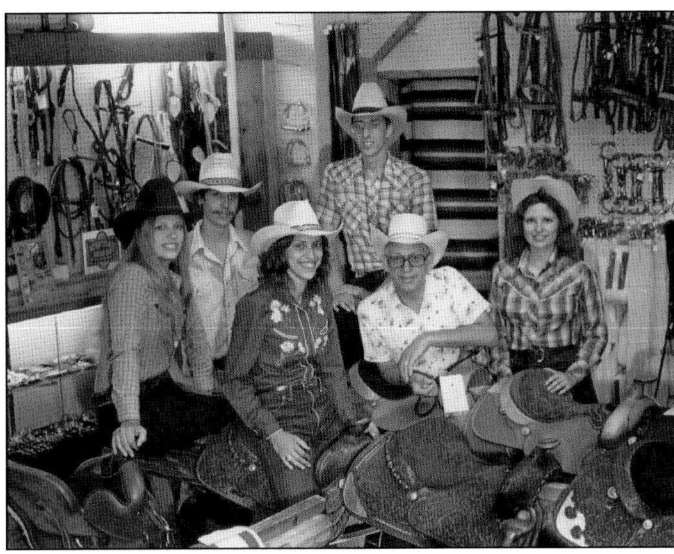

The 1980 release of the John Travolta movie *Urban Cowboy* marked another milestone in the ongoing evolution of Schatzlein's Saddle Shop. Seen here in 1981 are, from left to right, Janet, Paul, Peggy, Gary, Jerry, and Linda Schatzlein show off the store's selection of clothing and accessories available to Lyn-Lake's own urban cowboys. The store was sometimes so packed with enthusiastic shoppers that it was difficult to maneuver through the aisles. (Schatzlein Saddle Shop.)

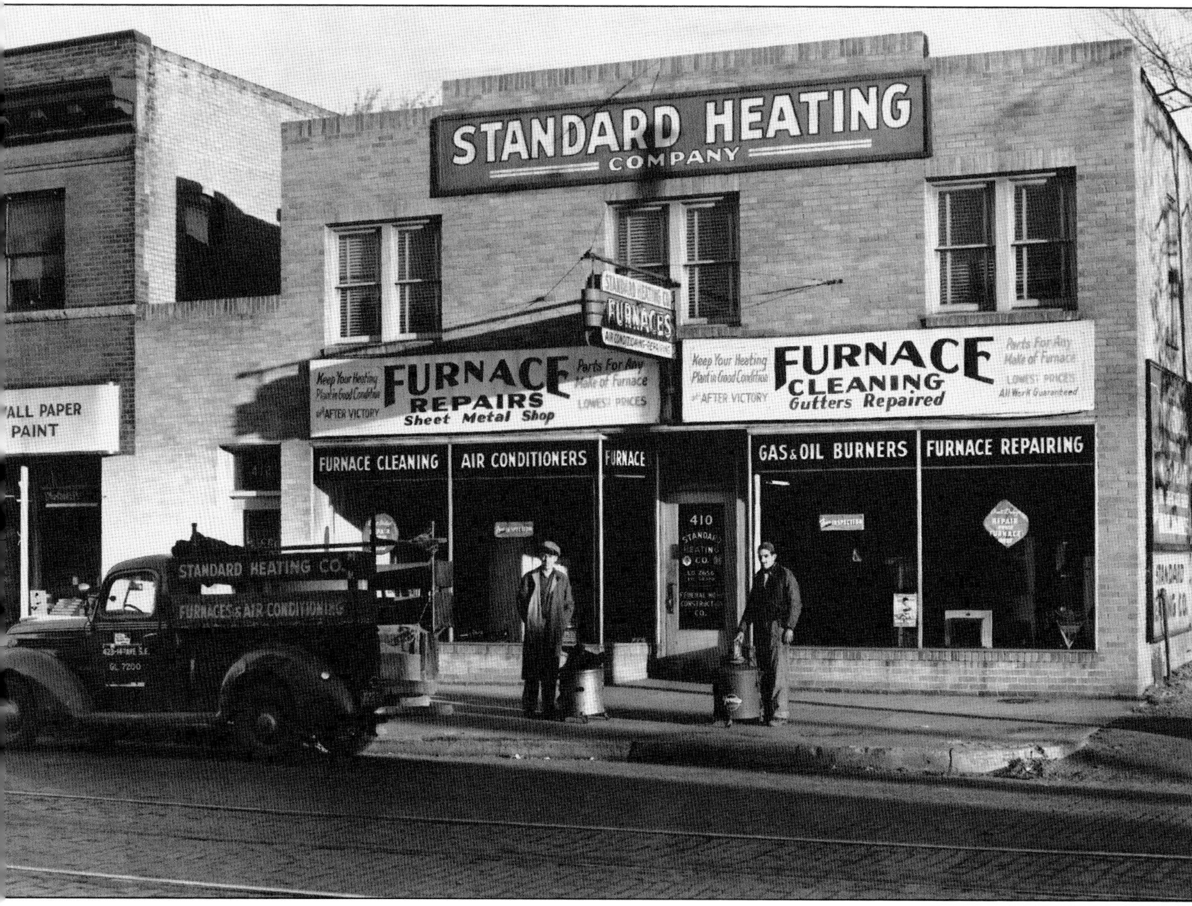

Although Anthony Ferrara started Standard Heating Company in 1924, the business did not move into these larger quarters at 410 West Lake Street until the fall of 1941. This 1941 photograph of the new space shows a building that came complete with new showrooms for the various gas-, oil-, and coal-powered heating and cooling systems both sold and serviced. For its grand opening in the new space, customers could purchase a new furnace ranging from $69.50 to $189.50 or have their furnace cleaned for $3.95. By 2009, Standard had long outgrown the Lyn-Lake space; current owners and brothers Ted and Todd Ferrara first looked at expanding or relocating within the neighborhood but could not find adequate property. Ultimately they moved to a new building at Plymouth Avenue and Second Street North, a location not in the neighborhood but still within city limits. (Standard Heating and Air Conditioning.)

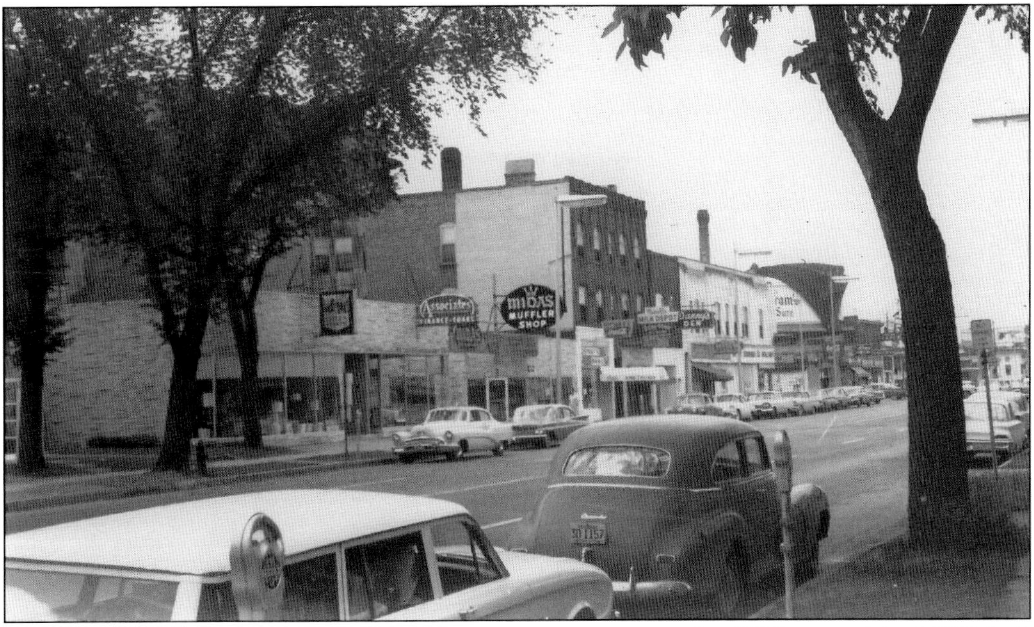

The diversity of both business and building types is apparent in this 1960 view of the 3000 block of Lyndale Avenue. By the 1960s, Lyn-Lake was home to many car-oriented businesses, such as the Midas Muffler Shop shown here. Restaurants and bars also filled the commercial district: Danny's Den, Muralt's Café, and Peggy's Barbeque are all visible to the north of the Midas store. (City of Minneapolis.)

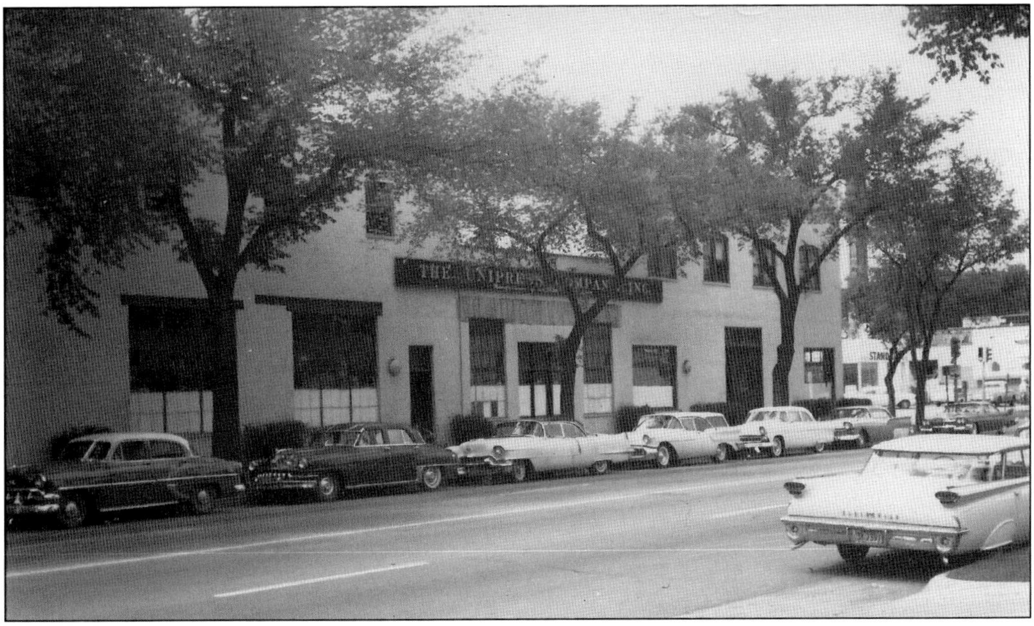

The Unipress Company, located at 2800 Lyndale Avenue, manufactured and sold specialized laundry equipment. It also operated Midland Laundry Equipment out of the site, advertised as "distributors of nationally known laundry and dry-cleaning equipment, also factory rebuilt equipment." The laundry industry was undergoing great changes, with large numbers of washing machines now purchased for home use. (City of Minneapolis.)

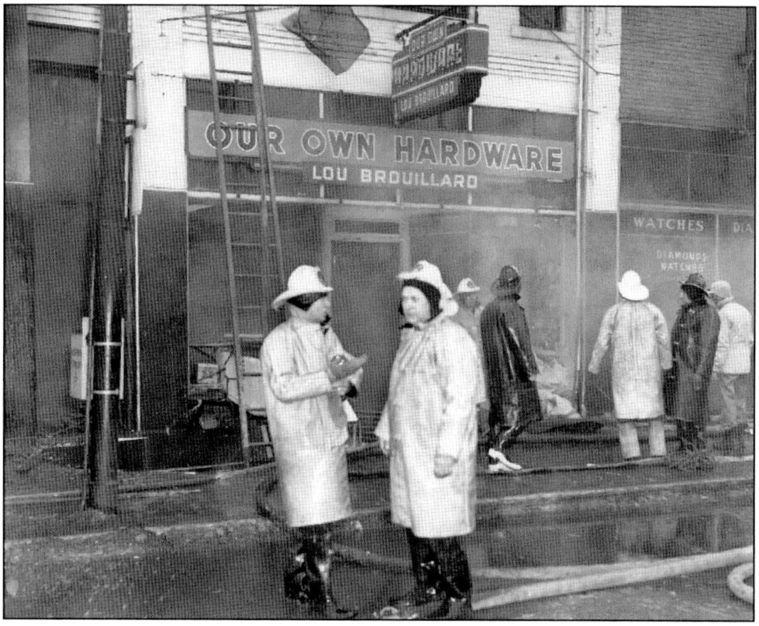

Lou Brouillard's Our Own Hardware store, previously known as Calhoun Hardware, was one of several damaged during the 1950 Wilharm Pharmacy Building fire. Hardware stores were like markets—there was one of these practical and essential stores in nearly every commercial node, and Lyn-Lake was no exception. Our Own Hardware was a Twin Cities–based cooperative buying group. (Hennepin County Library.)

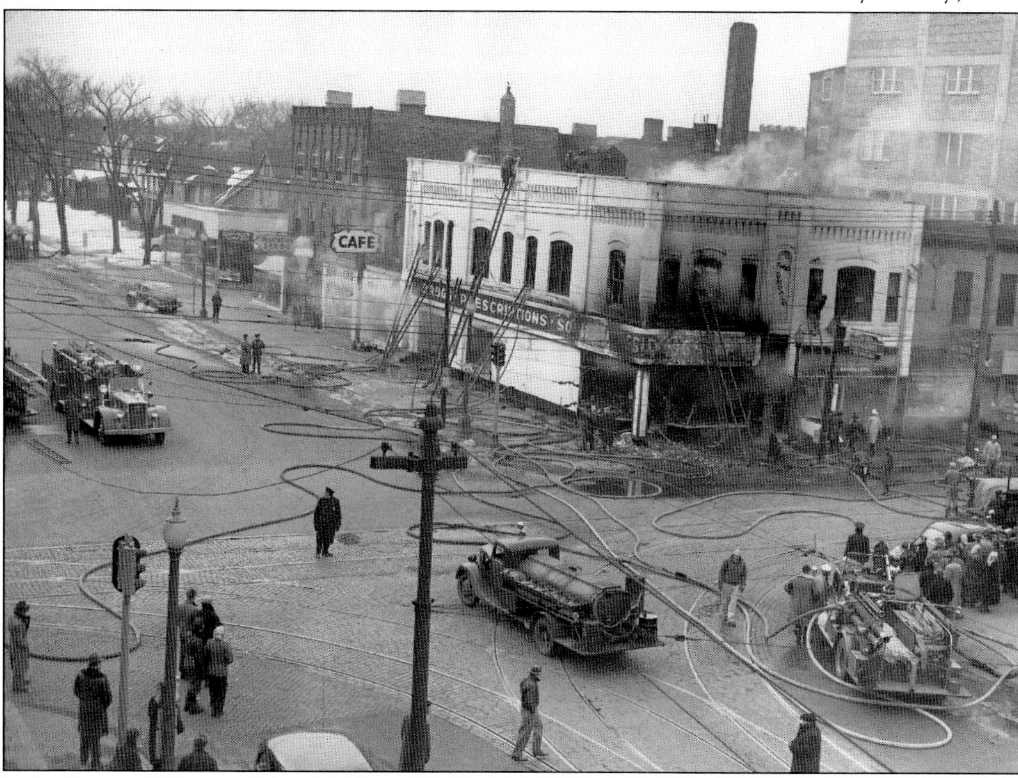

In 1950, the Wilharm Pharmacy Building, located on the southwest corner of Lake Street and Lyndale Avenue, survived a fire that left it damaged but intact. Visitors to Lyn-Lake today will recognize this view, even if the specific stores have changed. Visible in the photograph are a service station, the Plantation Barbeque, Don and Ed's Dinette, Brouillard Hardware, Thurston's Jewelry, and the Wilharm Pharmacy. (Hennepin County Library.)

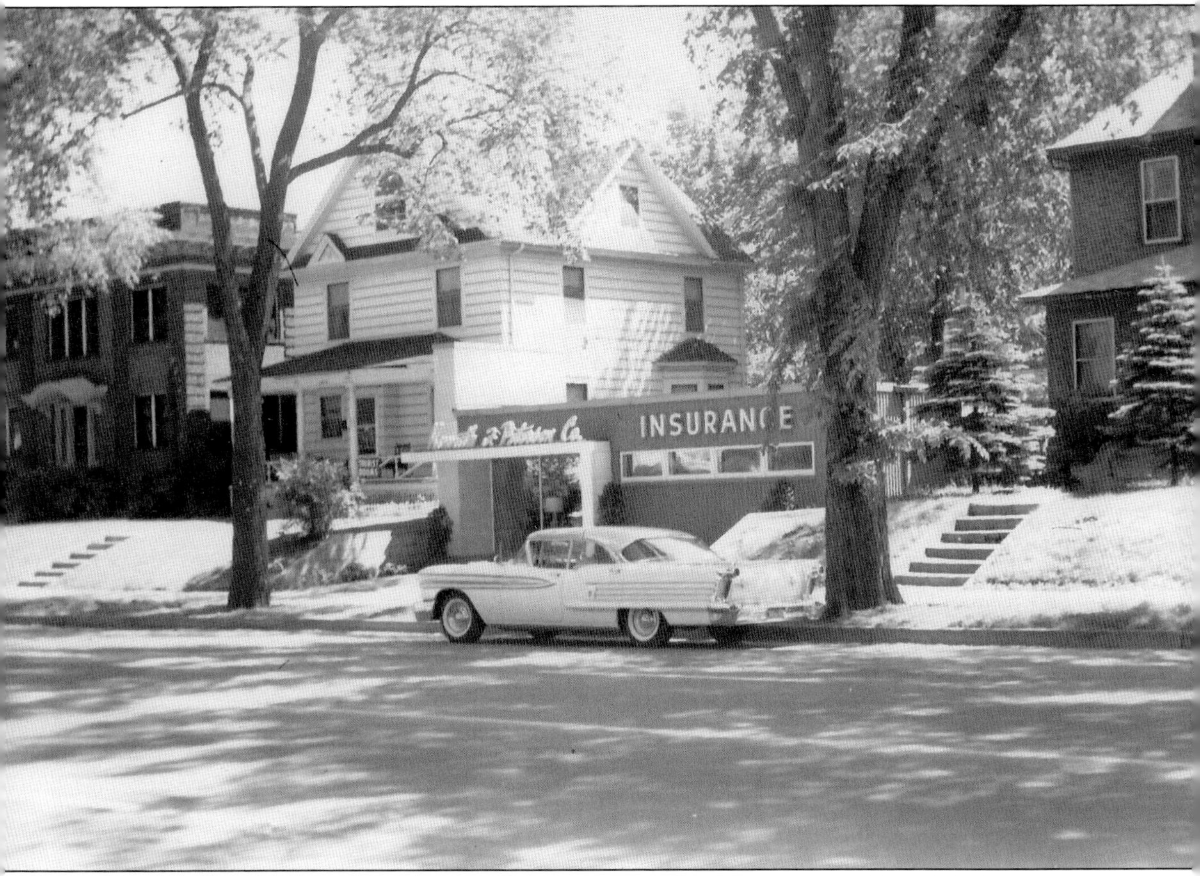

The 1960 home of the Kenneth F. Peterson insurance company, at 2441 Lyndale Avenue, was a sleek one-story commercial building constructed in 1948. Peterson's neighbor to the north, Elizabeth Lindor, also provided commercial services. The sign on her porch advertised, perhaps optimistically, the availability of "tourist rooms." This photograph was taken in July 1960, so she may have been trying to attract Aquatennial business. The Aquatennial is an annual multi-day festival in the summer featuring outdoor events and activities in Minneapolis, such as boat races, sand castle contests, parades, and more. She might also have read the information put out by various city booster organizations lauding the emergence of Minneapolis as a tourist destination. "Minneapolis, Gateway to Minnesota's Land of 10,000 Lakes," cheered that year's city directory, going on to note that "the year 1960 has seen a large influx of visitors to Minneapolis," with increasing numbers attending the "period of fun and frolic" that was the annual Aquatennial festival. While not located in a lake neighborhood, Lyndale Avenue was within walking or easy public transportation distance to most Aquatennial sites. (City of Minneapolis.)

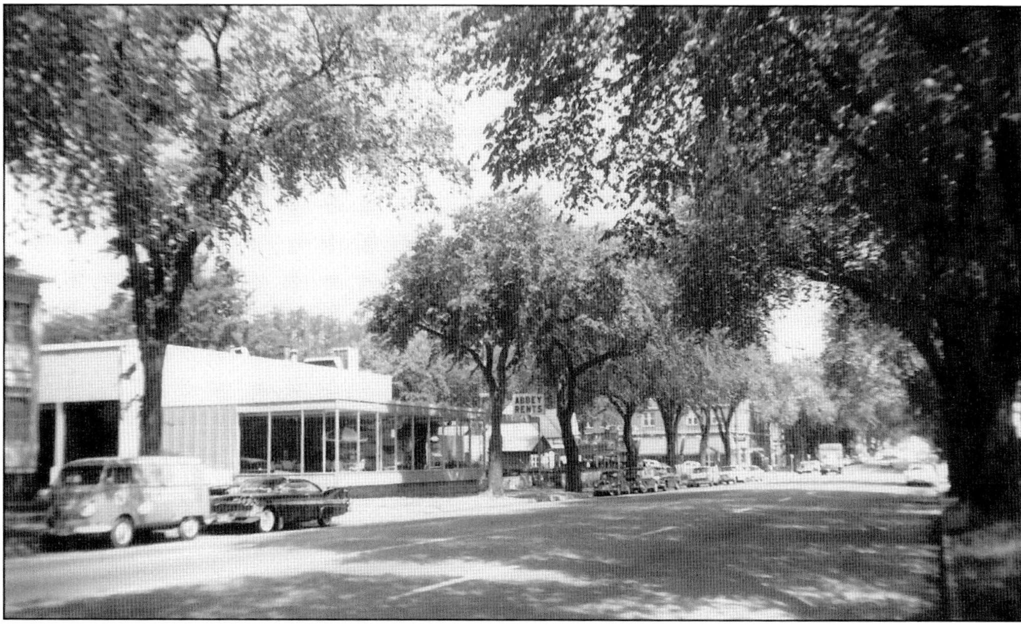

This photograph, taken in the summer of 1960, was taken from the east side of Lyndale Avenue looking northwest toward Twenty-second Street. Abbey Rents, on the left at 2220 Lyndale Avenue, was a hospital equipment rental company. Its modern building, constructed just four years earlier, stood in stark contrast to the older, traditional brick commercial buildings like the one visible at the Twenty-second Street intersection. (City of Minneapolis.)

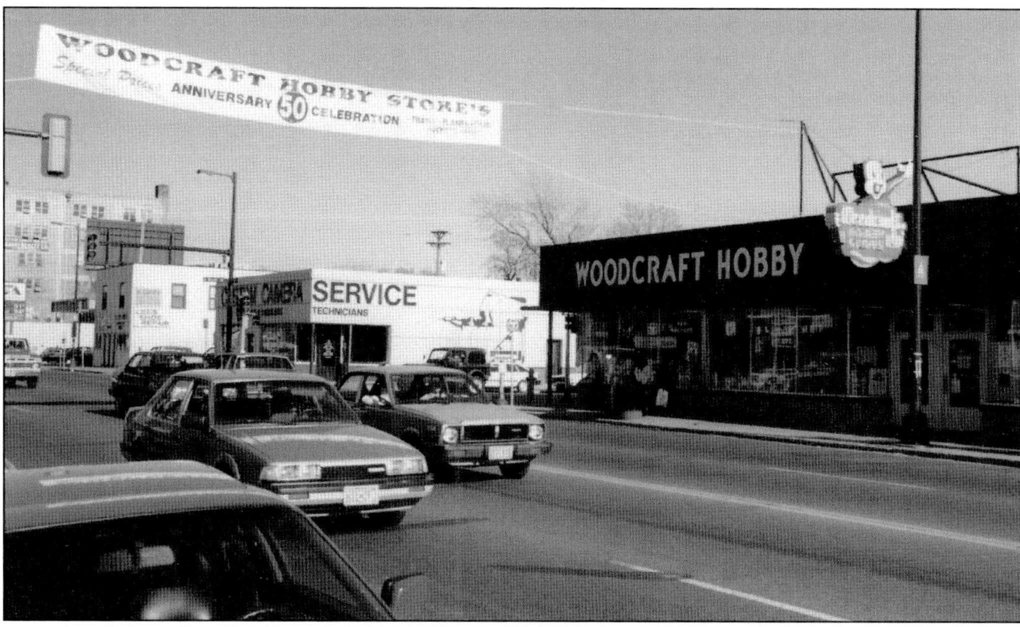

Woodcraft founder Claude Newman's son Paul began his 40 years of work at Woodcraft Hobby in 1954. Paul purchased a portion of the business from his father in the early 1970s, and by 1983 both property and business was his. The store closed in 1994, as the result of a shrinking market for traditional hobby products and Paul's need for a new adventure. This photograph dates to around 1988. (Paul Newman.)

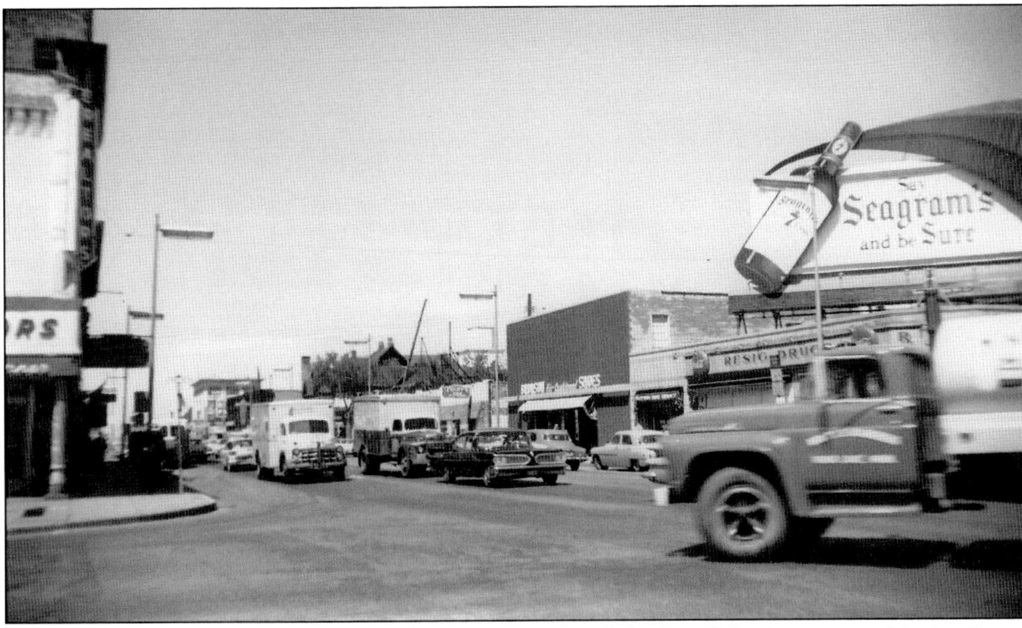

Bronson's Shoes, at 710 West Lake Street, was one of the Lyndale Avenue and Lake Street intersection's long-lasting businesses. Charles Bronson started the shoe store in 1928; after buying the patent for air-cushioned shoes, he expanded his business to "Bronson Shoes," which was now available nationwide. Twenty-two people worked out of this building filling orders from around the country, as well as manning the retail store. (City of Minneapolis.)

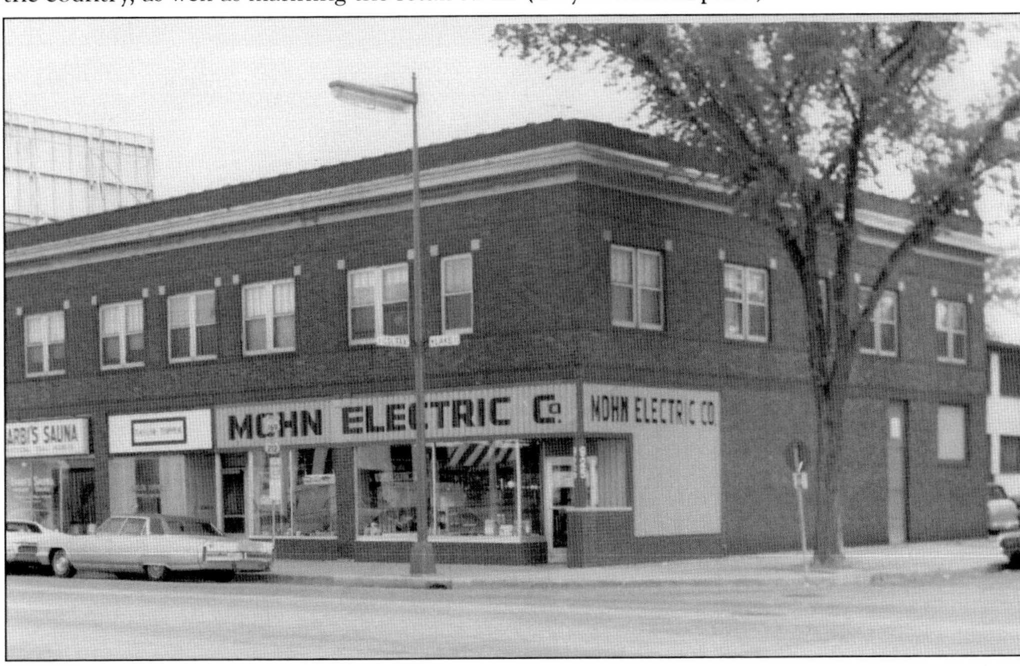

Carroll Mohn started the Mohn Appliance Company at Hennepin and Lagoon Avenues in 1945 and moved into this building at the corner of Colfax Avenue and Lake Street in 1969. Current owner Mark Hildreth purchased the building and the lamp and lighting business, by then known as Mohn Electric Company, in 1977. This photograph likely dates to that time. (Mohn Electric Company.)

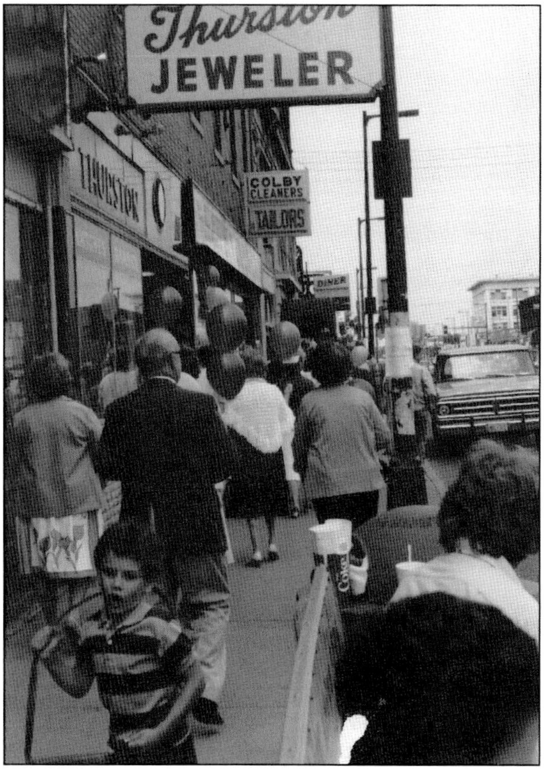

Members of the nearby Lyndale United Church of Christ are seen participating in a procession along Lake Street in this undated photograph. To the left is Thurston's Jewelers, one of the oldest businesses in the district. Founded in 1910, the jewelry store was known for both its jewelry as well as its optometry department. Current owner Lloyd Drilling is the third owner of the business, which still can be found in its original 705 West Lake Street location. (LUCC.)

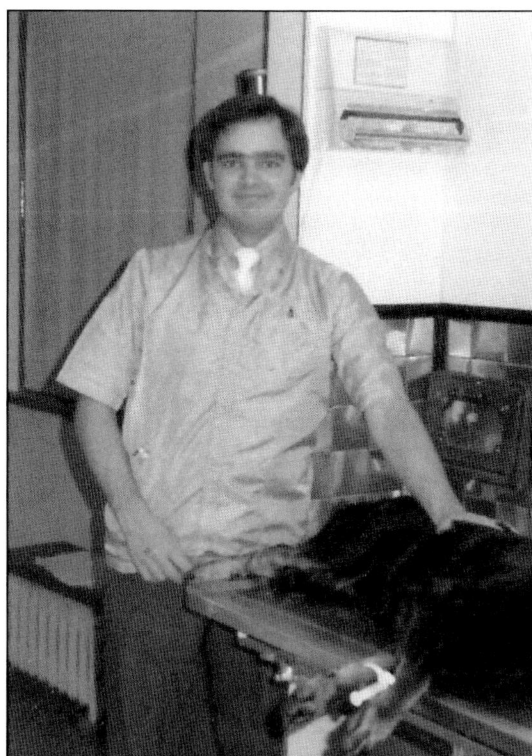

Many Lyn-Lake pet owners are familiar with the Lyndale Animal Hospital, at 2554 Lyndale Avenue, as well as with Dr. Leonard Schnack. Schnack, now retired, first came to Lyndale Animal Hospital in 1970. He is shown here with a dog in 1974. Both the business and the building have a distinguished and long history; the 1936 structure was the first animal hospital built in Minneapolis. (Leonard Schnack.)

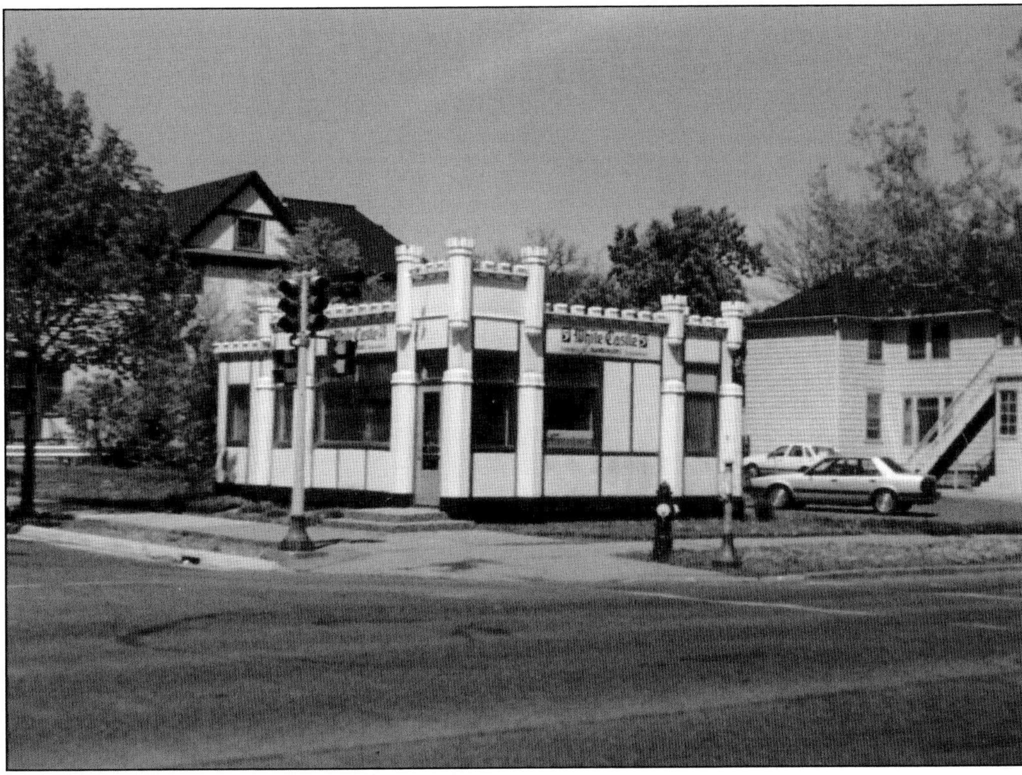

This White Castle building, prefabricated and movable, arrived at Thirty-third Street and Lyndale Avenue in 1984 from its earlier home on Central Avenue, and, before that, Washington Avenue. It has never been used as a restaurant in its current location. Lyn-Lake didn't have a White Castle, but it did have a White Tower; a branch of that chain opened at Lake Street and Lyndale Avenue in 1928. (Hennepin History Museum.)

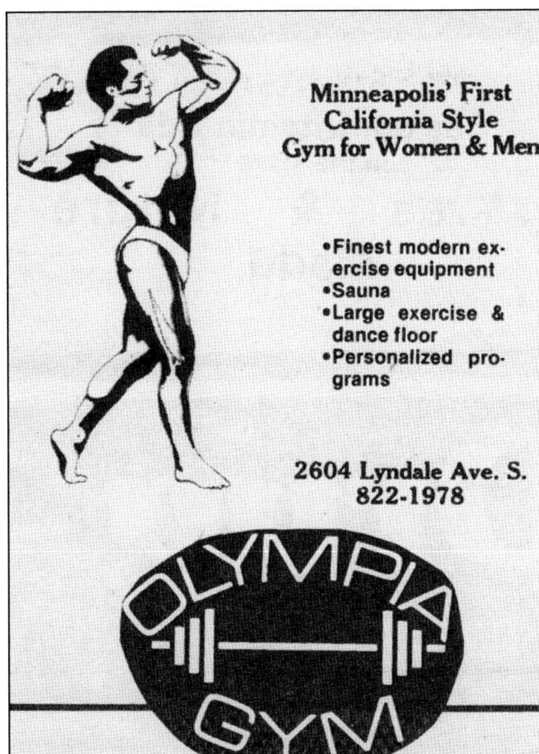

The Olympia Gym, at 2604 Lyndale Avenue, opened in 1980 to serve the needs of the Twin Cities' most serious weight lifters. Owner Ken Sherman, a competitive bodybuilder, extensively remodeled the building and filled it with the best equipment available. It was inspired by Arnold Schwartzenegger's World Gym, and while beginners were welcome, the primary clientele was made up of those who were serious about building some serious muscles. (Hennepin County Library.)

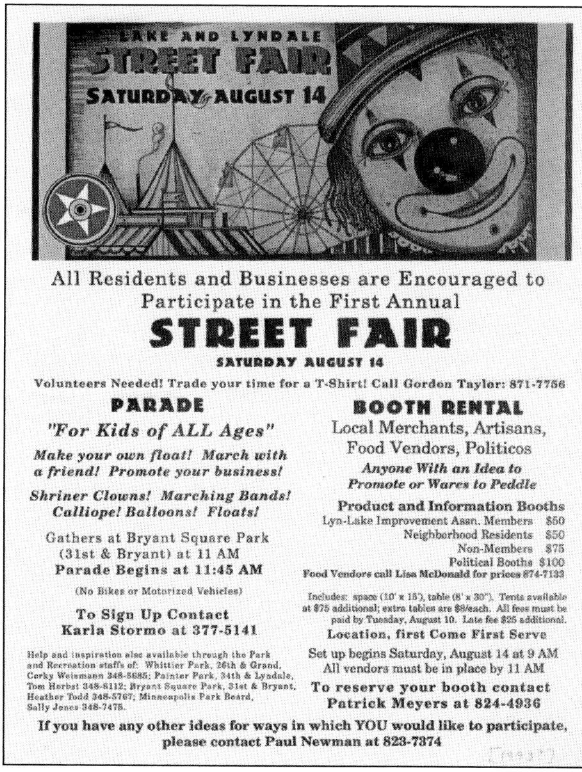

This poster advertises what would become the first-ever Lyn-Lake Street Festival. The August 1993 event was billed as a small town–inspired "summer holiday," complete with a parade and plentiful activities for families. It was sponsored by the Lyn-Lake Improvement District but drew on volunteers from a diverse array of neighborhood organizations, businesses, and residents. (Hennepin County Library.)

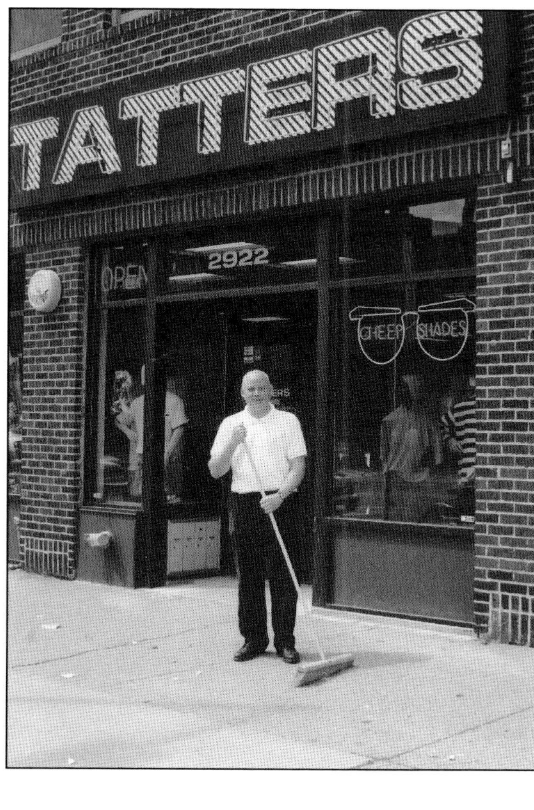

Vintage clothing store Tatters has been around for more than 25 years now. In 1984, Platters, a record shop, was added to the second floor of the 2922 Lyndale Avenue location. Platters resulted from customers' many questions about where to buy the music played in the store. This 1991 photograph was taken during the annual Lyn-Lake Clean Sweep. Tatters has since relocated to 2928 Lyndale Avenue. (Paul Newman.)

Three

Food and Drink

Lyn-Lake has long had a reputation as being a center for both eating and drinking. At one point, its many "3.2 joints" lined both Lake Street and Lyndale Avenue, serving many thirsty residents as they returned home from work. Places like the CC Club, located at Twenty-sixth Street and Lyndale Avenue, have become legends, enjoying national icon status for those interested in the Minneapolis music scene. Beginning in the 1990s, coffee houses began to enter in great numbers, and now it is difficult to go far without encountering at least one place to purchase a shot of espresso.

During the 1970s and 1980s, an increasing number of ethnic restaurants moved into the area: Greek, Ethiopian, Caribbean, Vietnamese, Italian, and a number of other restaurants served up breakfast, lunch, and dinner to hungry diners from both the neighborhood and beyond.

Markets, butchers, dairies, soda fountains, and other assorted stores provided the necessities—and indulgences—of life to generations of Lyn-Lake residents. And when the co-op movement got going, Lyn-Lake was right in the heart of things; the local co-op the Beanery was involved in the infamous "co-op wars," while the Wedge has gone on to become a national leader as well as neighborhood favorite.

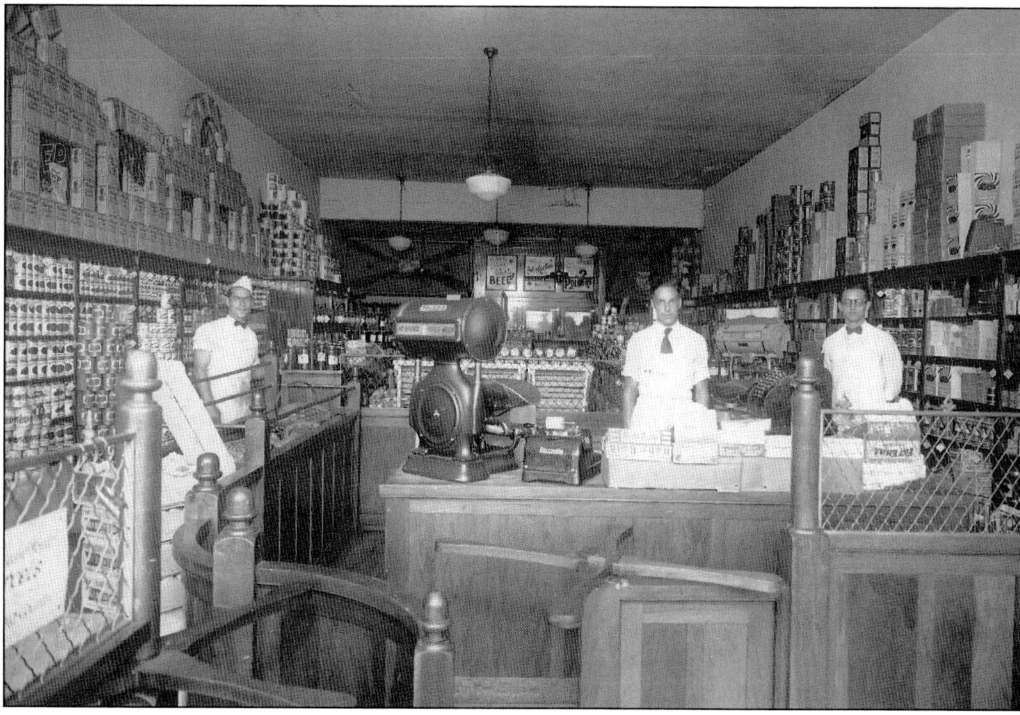

At the Piggly Wiggly, located at 2407 Lyndale Avenue and shown here in 1930, one could purchase a Baby Ruth candy bar, Kellogg's Corn Flakes, Quaker Oats, or select from their "choicest corn-fed beef." A large can of Sweet Girl Tomatoes cost 20¢, and a box of Jell-o went for 8¢. This Piggly Wiggly opened in the early 1920s and became another grocery store in the early 1930s. (Hennepin County Library.)

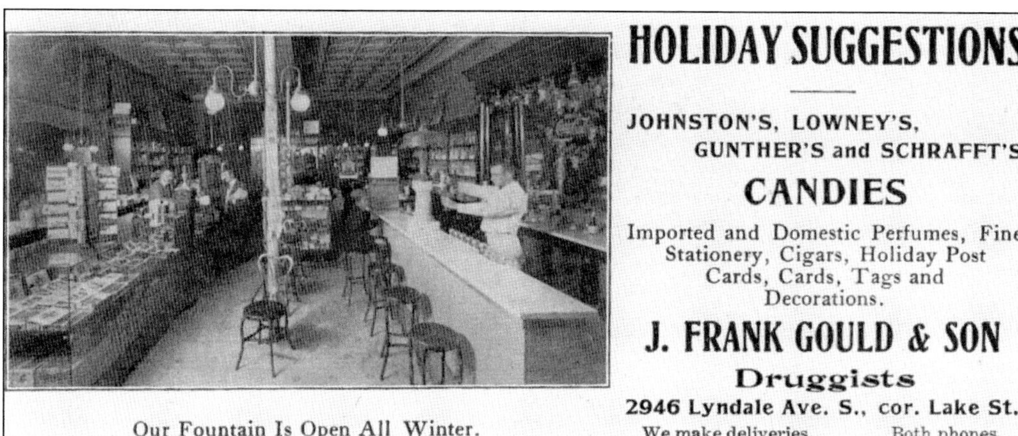

J. Frank Gould was often referred to as Lyn-Lake's "pioneer grocer." His store, at 2946 Lyndale Avenue, was one of the most prominent 19th-century businesses at the Lake Street and Lyndale Avenue intersection. In addition to groceries, the market offered full druggist services as well as a soda fountain. This advertisement appeared in the nearby Lyndale Congregational Church's weekly publication. (LUCC.)

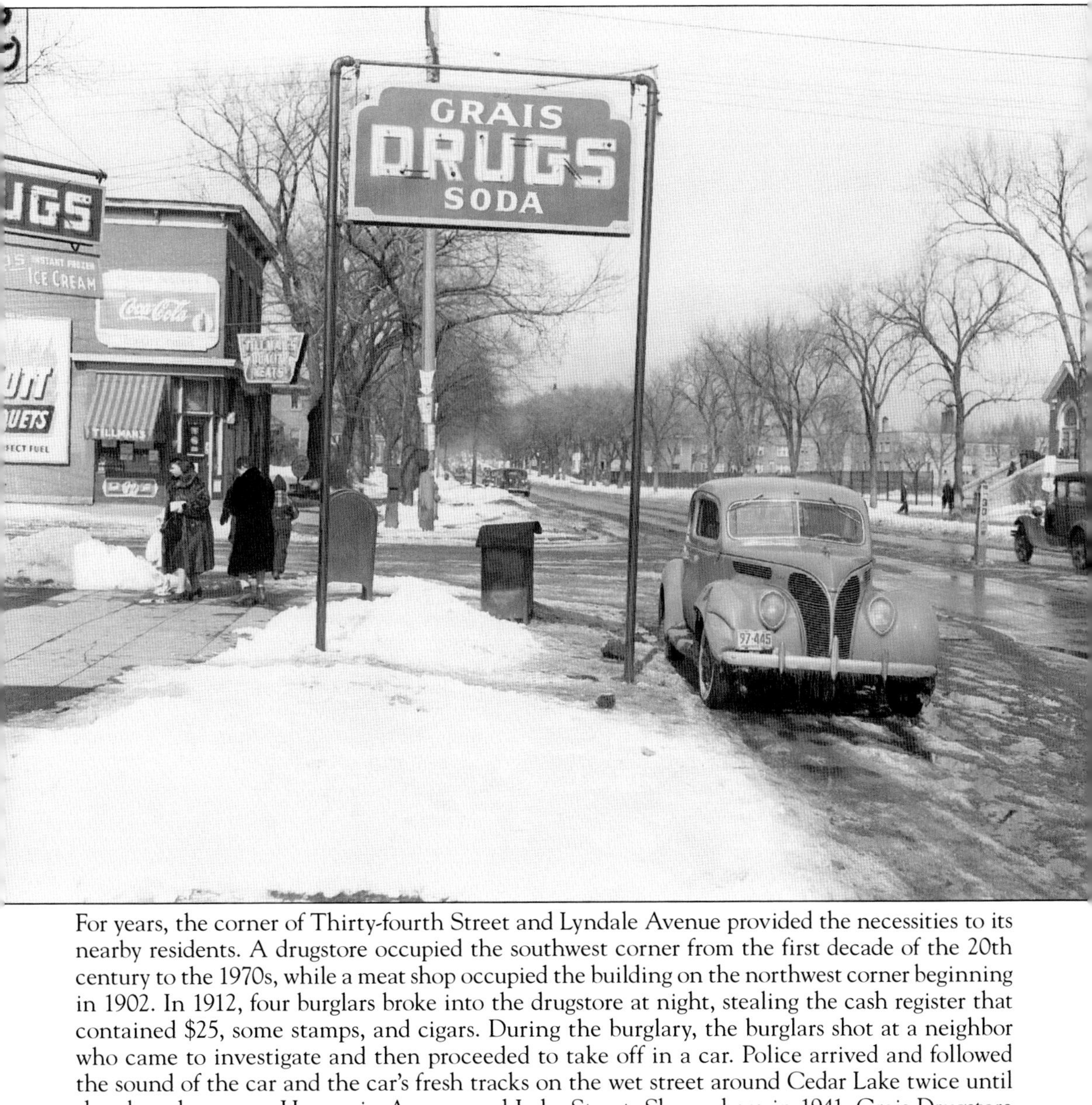

For years, the corner of Thirty-fourth Street and Lyndale Avenue provided the necessities to its nearby residents. A drugstore occupied the southwest corner from the first decade of the 20th century to the 1970s, while a meat shop occupied the building on the northwest corner beginning in 1902. In 1912, four burglars broke into the drugstore at night, stealing the cash register that contained $25, some stamps, and cigars. During the burglary, the burglars shot at a neighbor who came to investigate and then proceeded to take off in a car. Police arrived and followed the sound of the car and the car's fresh tracks on the wet street around Cedar Lake twice until they lost them near Hennepin Avenue and Lake Street. Shown here in 1941, Grais Drugstore was opened at 3400 Lyndale Avenue in 1931 by Sam and Arnold Grais. This store was their first of what would become a chain of drugstores in the Twin Cities. Tillman Meats opened in the first decade of the 20th century and later joined Donald Olson as the business transformed into Olson's Food Market. (City of Minneapolis.)

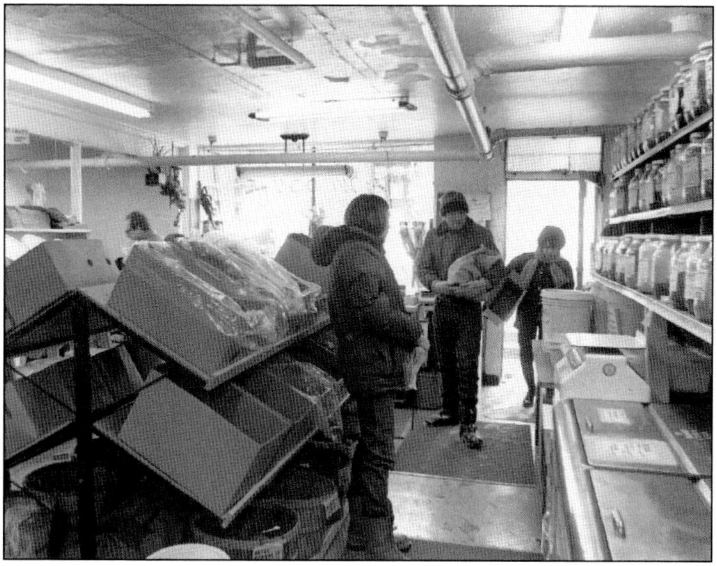

Started in 1974 by a group of neighbors, the Wedge Community Foods co-op was first located at 715 West Franklin Avenue and sold a limited selection of dairy products, frozen vegetables, and fish along with unrefined bulk foods and fresh produce. Its members were interested in health, environmental issues, and social justice. That period saw growth in co-ops as an outgrowth of the new-left political movement. (Jeremy Nichols.)

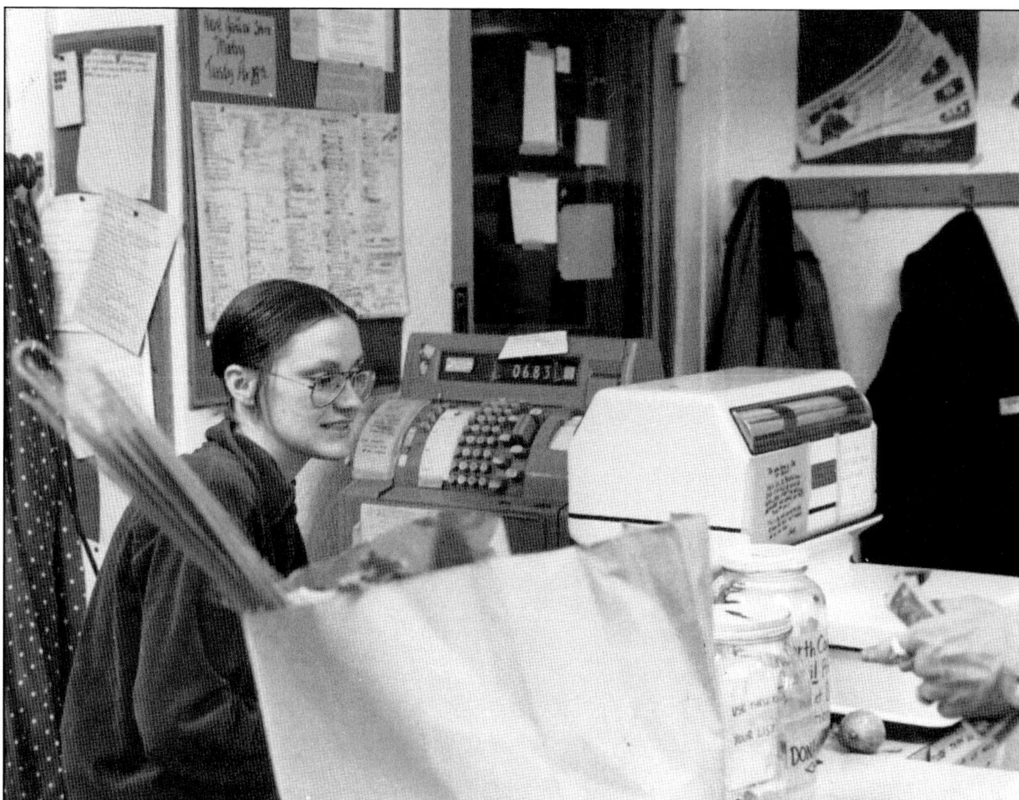

As a member-owned enterprise, the Wedge co-op's policies changed based on its members input. The Wedge at one time did not carry meat or ice cream with sugar. As the co-op continued to see its members purchase ice cream elsewhere, the co-op introduced Häagen-Dazs ice cream. Today the Wedge boasts that it had the first USDA certified organic meat department in the country. (Jeremy Nichols.)

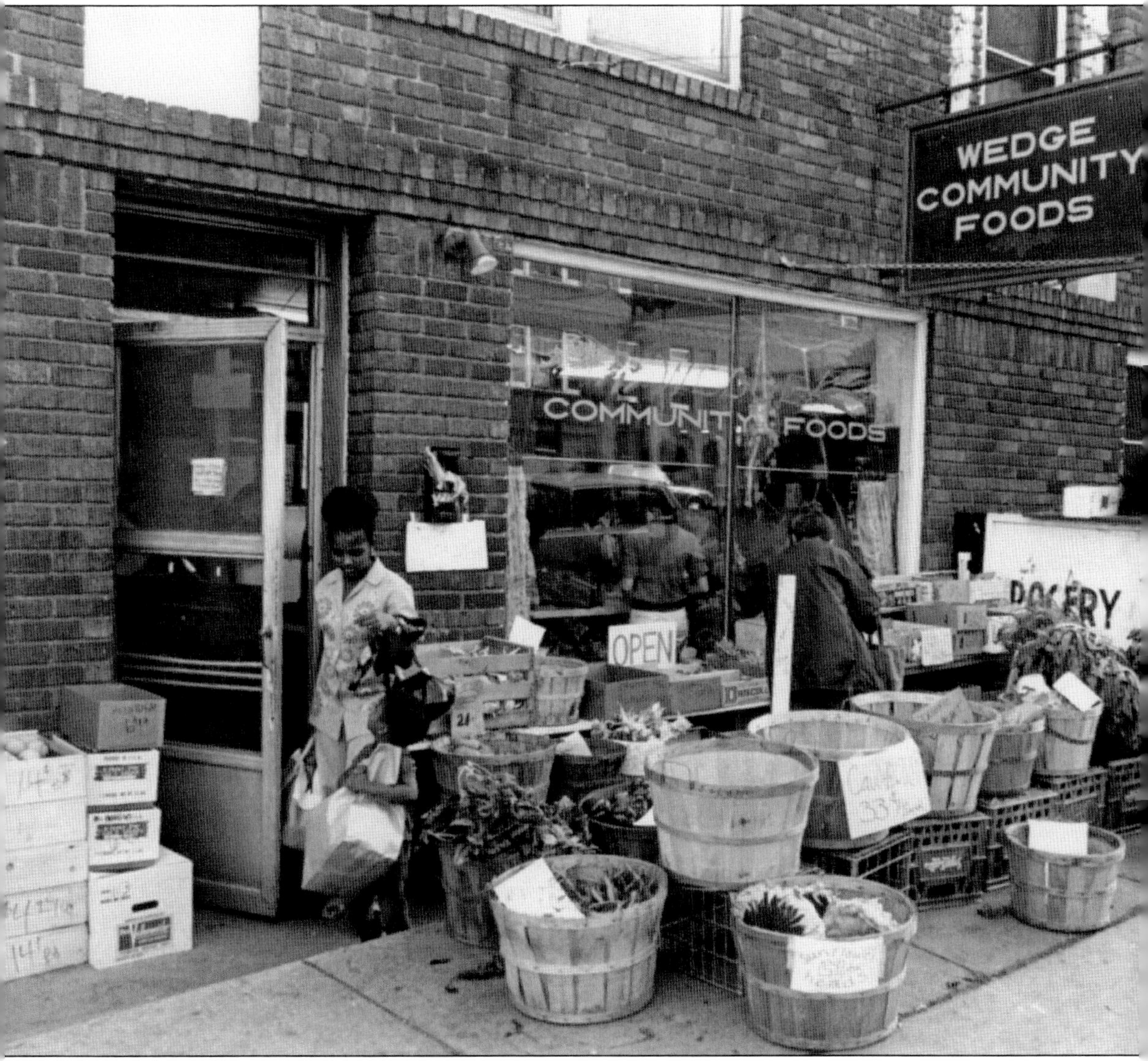

As interest in the co-op increased, the Wedge outgrew its space and moved to an old 7-Eleven on Lyndale Avenue just south of Franklin Avenue. Membership and sales continued to grow, and by 1991 the co-op's membership coordinator, Elizabeth Archerd, said that it was "a supermarket by industry standards . . . operating out of a convenience store." In 1992, the Wedge tripled its space in a new building adjacent to the 7-Eleven. Dan Foley, the general manager of the co-op in 1992, said that the expansion was a "reflection of the community needs" as "it was so crowded, people couldn't shop there. The customers wanted more selection, more room, more hours, more service, and healthy, natural foods and organic foods." Not everyone was happy with the expansion. Prior to opening, vandals dumped buckets of paint in the store and tried to it up by opening propane gas tanks. However, the community embraced the store, and the Wedge saw memberships increase from 550 to 6,000 between 1991 and 1998. (Jeremy Nichols.)

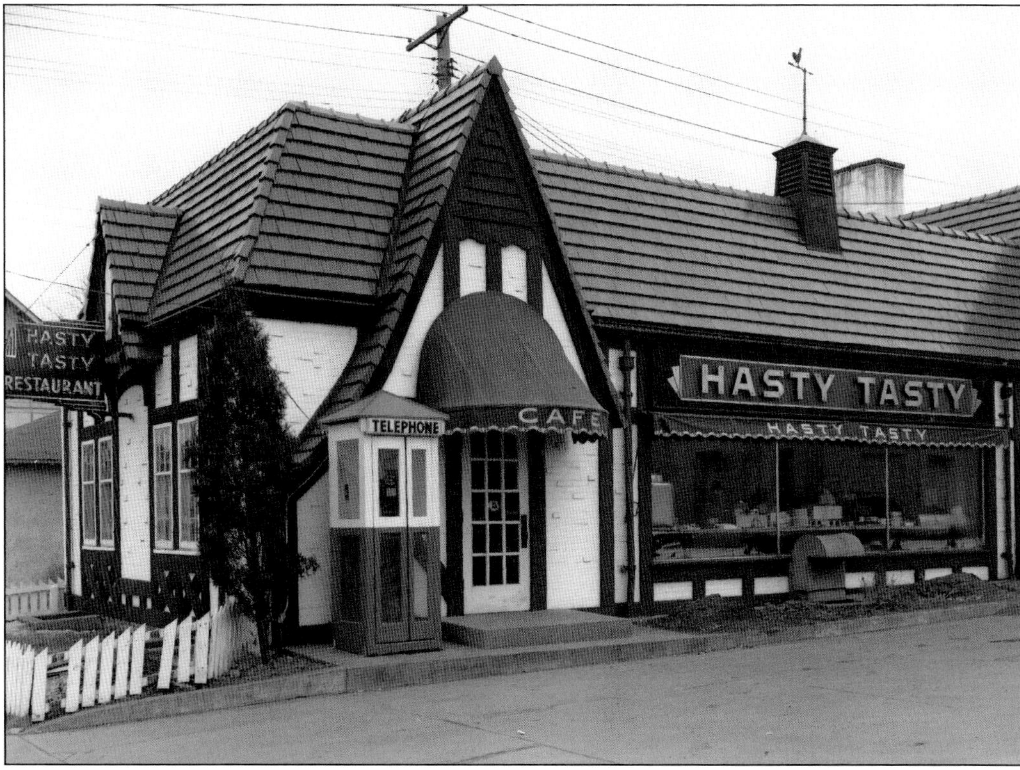

This Hasty Tasty, located at 3601 Lyndale Avenue, was part of a small but popular chain of local cafés with headquarters in the heart of nearby Uptown. A third location was at Fiftieth Street and France Avenue. In addition to its restaurants, Hasty Tasty offered catering services. This photograph was taken in 1953. (Minnesota Historical Society; photograph by Norton and Peel.)

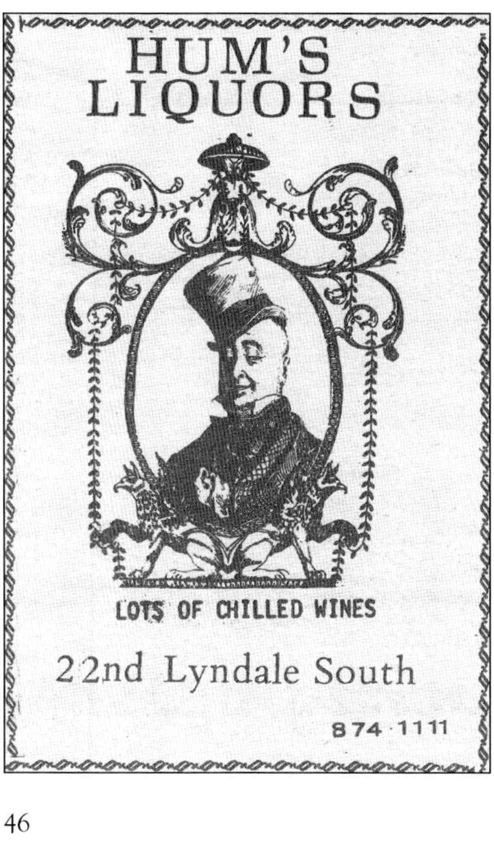

Hum's Liquor, located at 2126 Lyndale Avenue, has been a neighborhood institution since Al Hum and David Mackey opened the store in the mid-1960s. Hum's has witnessed firsthand both the neighborhood's ups and downs; in 1972, rising crime impacted Hum's directly when Minneapolis police officer and part-time Hum's employee Inno Suek was shot and killed during a store robbery. This advertisement ran in *The Wedge* in January 1976. (Hennepin County Library.)

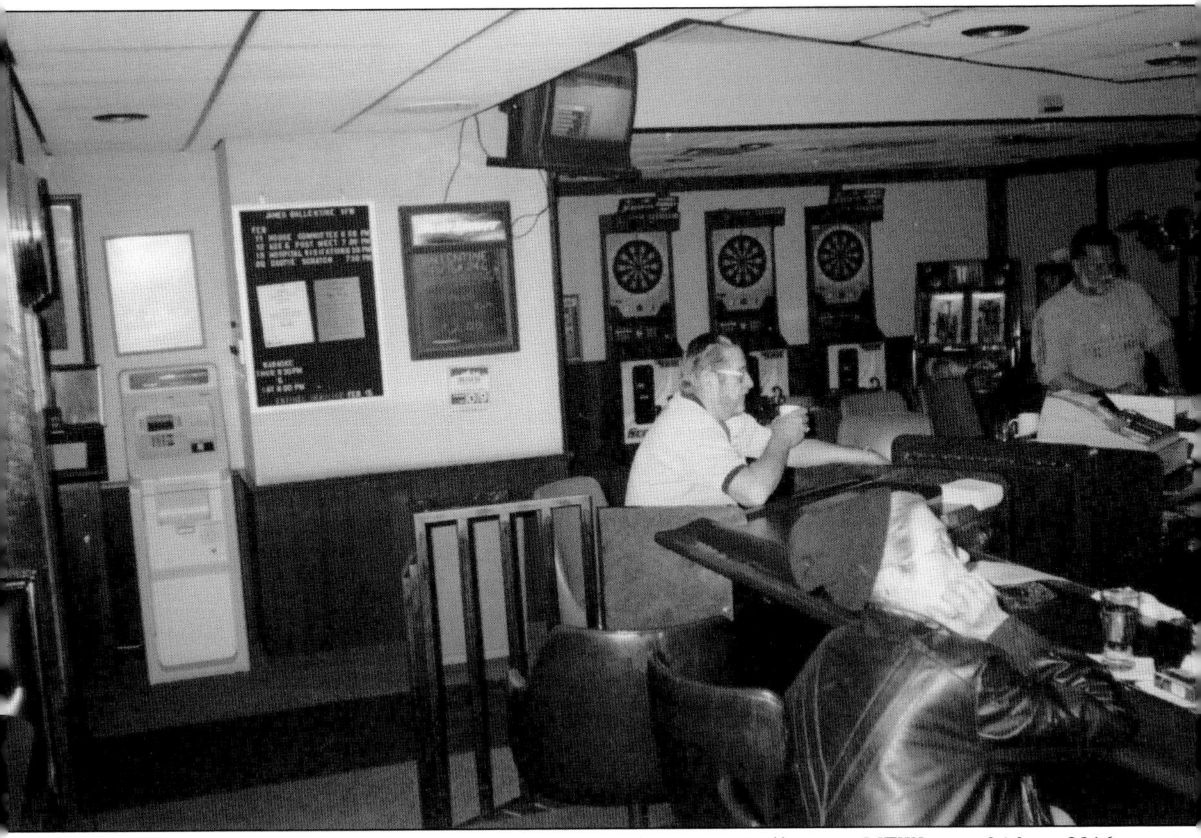

On the surface, this unassuming lounge space at the James Ballentine VFW post 246, at 2916 Lyndale Avenue, may appear like the hundreds of other VFW lounges across Minnesota and the country. And of course the bar, shown here on a cold February day in 2002, does have the essential basics: cheap beer, snacks, and pull-tabs. But the Ballentine, also known informally as the "Uptown VFW," has grown to enjoy a local and even national reputation as more than just another watering hole. In 2010, the post, along with nearby bar CC Club, made *Esquire*'s list of the best bars in America. *Esquire* cited the cheap beer, the diverse audience consisting of both retired veterans and the neighborhood's young hipsters, and "the best karaoke the Cities have to offer." The original members of the 86-year-old post might recognize the community spirit behind events like the VFW-sponsored 2010 block party, albeit surprised at the names of the contemporary bands playing, like Rogue Valley and F*ck Knights. (LNA; photograph by Matthew Allen.)

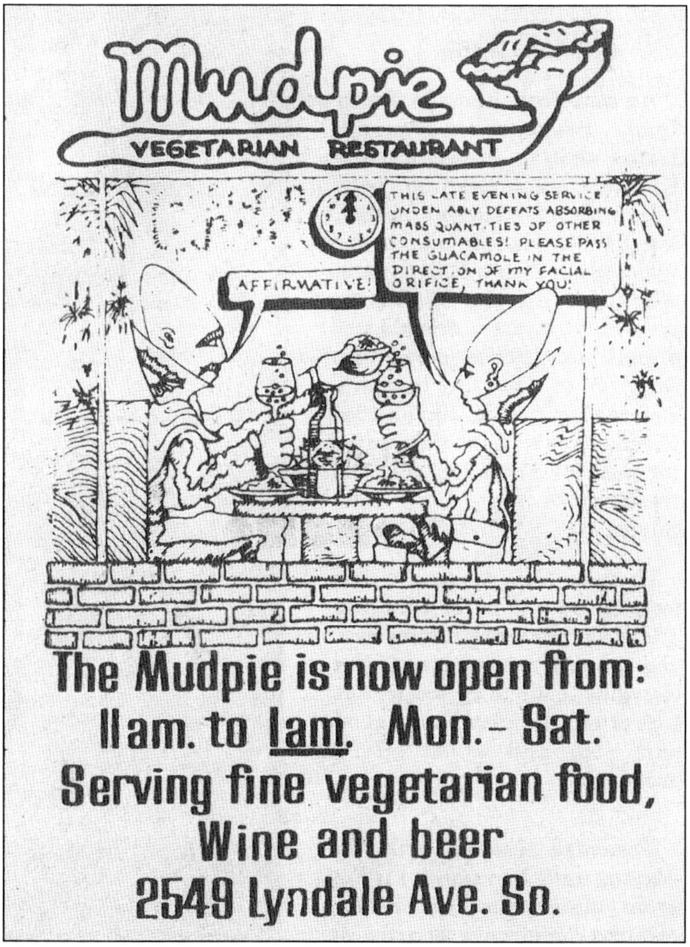

The Mudpie Vegetarian Restaurant, at 2549 Lyndale Avenue, opened its doors in 1972. Owner and chef Robbie Stair sought to provide vegetarians with improved restaurant options while simultaneously proving to local carnivores that vegetarian fare could be both filling and tasty. He succeeded, and by 1979, the year in which this advertisement appeared in *The Wedge*, the restaurant had approximately 30 people on staff and could seat up to 100 diners. (Hennepin County Library.)

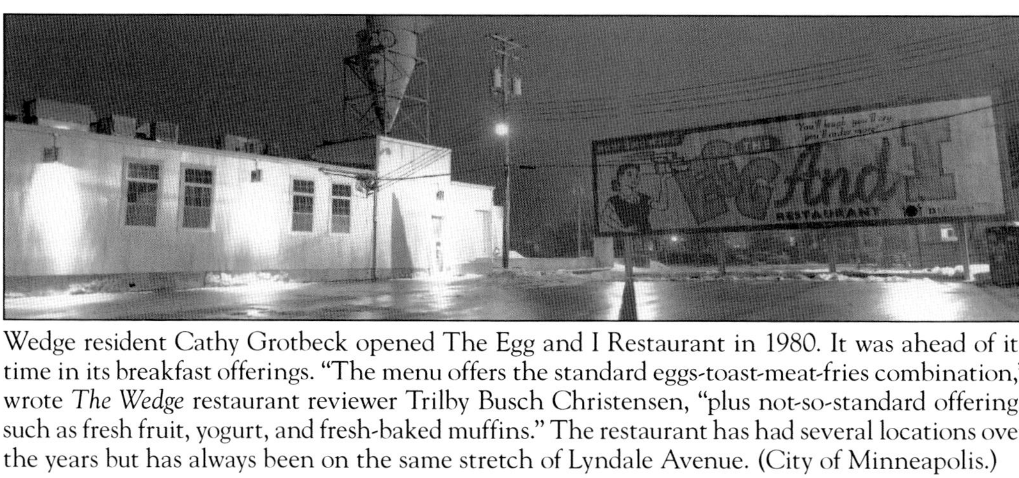

Wedge resident Cathy Grotbeck opened The Egg and I Restaurant in 1980. It was ahead of its time in its breakfast offerings. "The menu offers the standard eggs-toast-meat-fries combination," wrote *The Wedge* restaurant reviewer Trilby Busch Christensen, "plus not-so-standard offerings such as fresh fruit, yogurt, and fresh-baked muffins." The restaurant has had several locations over the years but has always been on the same stretch of Lyndale Avenue. (City of Minneapolis.)

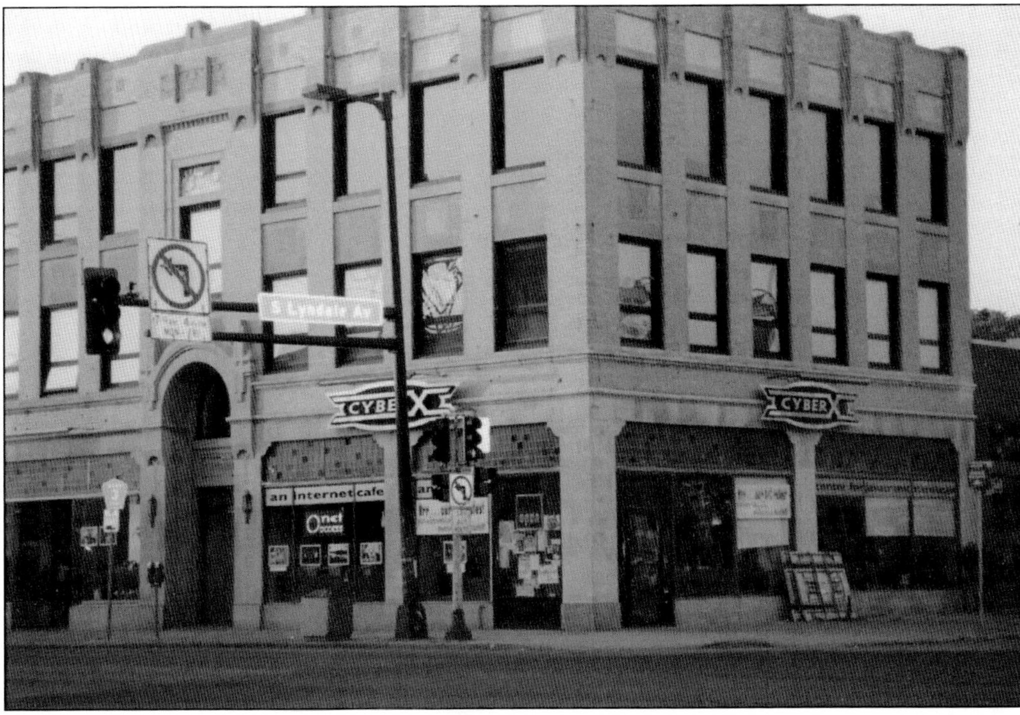

When the CyberX Internet Café, located at the corner of Lyndale Avenue and Lake Street, opened in 1995, its coffee- and energy drink–swilling patrons could use one of five networked computers for $7 an hour, with half an hour free with the purchase of a drink. CyberX closed in 2001, and today no café is complete without Wi-Fi. (LHENA.)

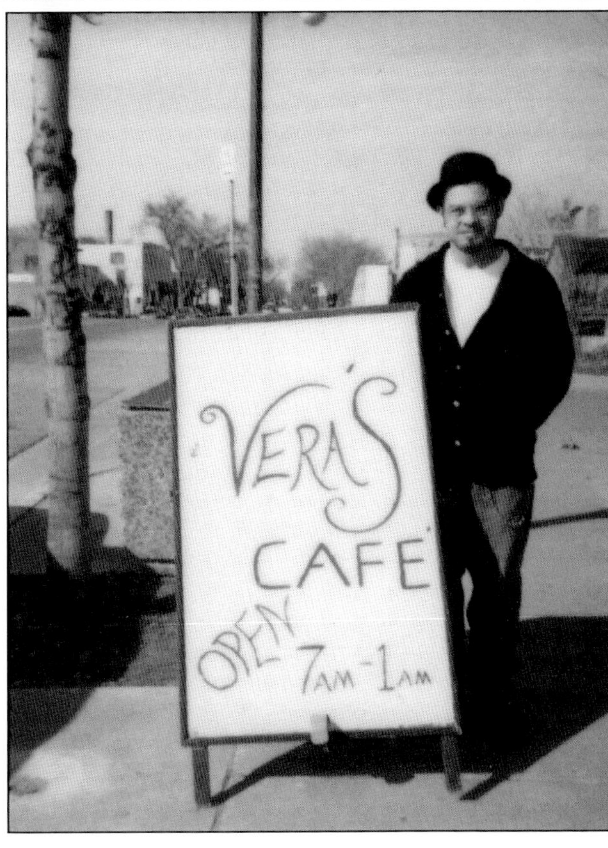

Vera's Café owner Wayne Butzer poses outside of the restaurant, located at 2901 Lyndale Avenue. Befitting a neighborhood known for its large numbers of lesbian, gay, bisexual, and transgender (LGBT) residents, Butzer estimated between 60 and 70 percent of his customers were gay, with an overall "100-percent gay-friendly crowd." Vera's closed in 2009 after nearly a decade in business; Butzer blamed the 2007 reconstruction of Lyndale Avenue for an ultimately crippling disruption of business. (LHENA.)

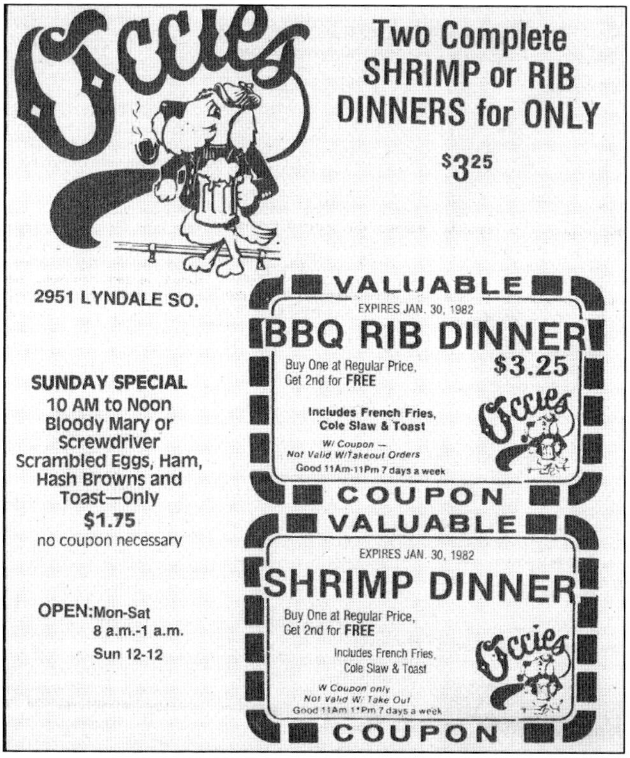

Pat Blumenthal, owner of the Poodle on East Lake Street, purchased Occie's in 1980. This advertisement dates from 1982, when it was published in the *Whittier Globe*. In 1987, Blumenthal remodeled the restaurant and renamed it Zandy's. When that did not take off, he remodeled it yet again, revamped the menu, and turned it into Knickers. (Hennepin History Museum.)

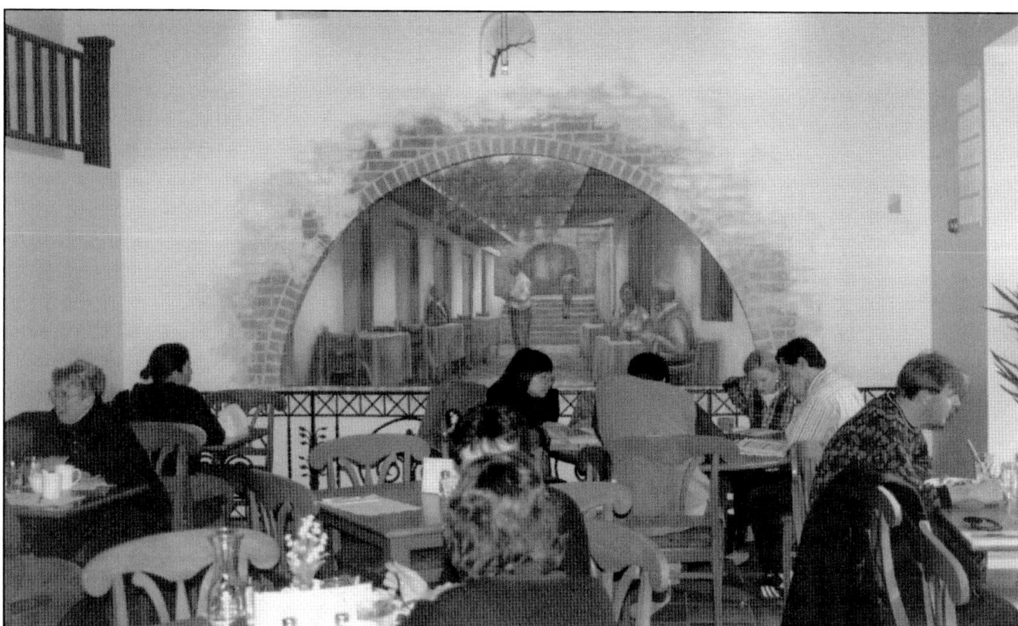

Alkif and Denise Arambadjis's It's Greek to Me restaurant, an anchor business at Lake Street and Lyndale Avenue, is pictured here in 1997 shortly after its reopening, which followed an ambitious remodeling. The changes included this interior courtyard, intended to evoke the pleasures of a Greek courtyard during even the coldest of Minnesota winters. The restaurant's 1982 opening helped to cement Lyn-Lake's reputation as a dining destination. (LNA.)

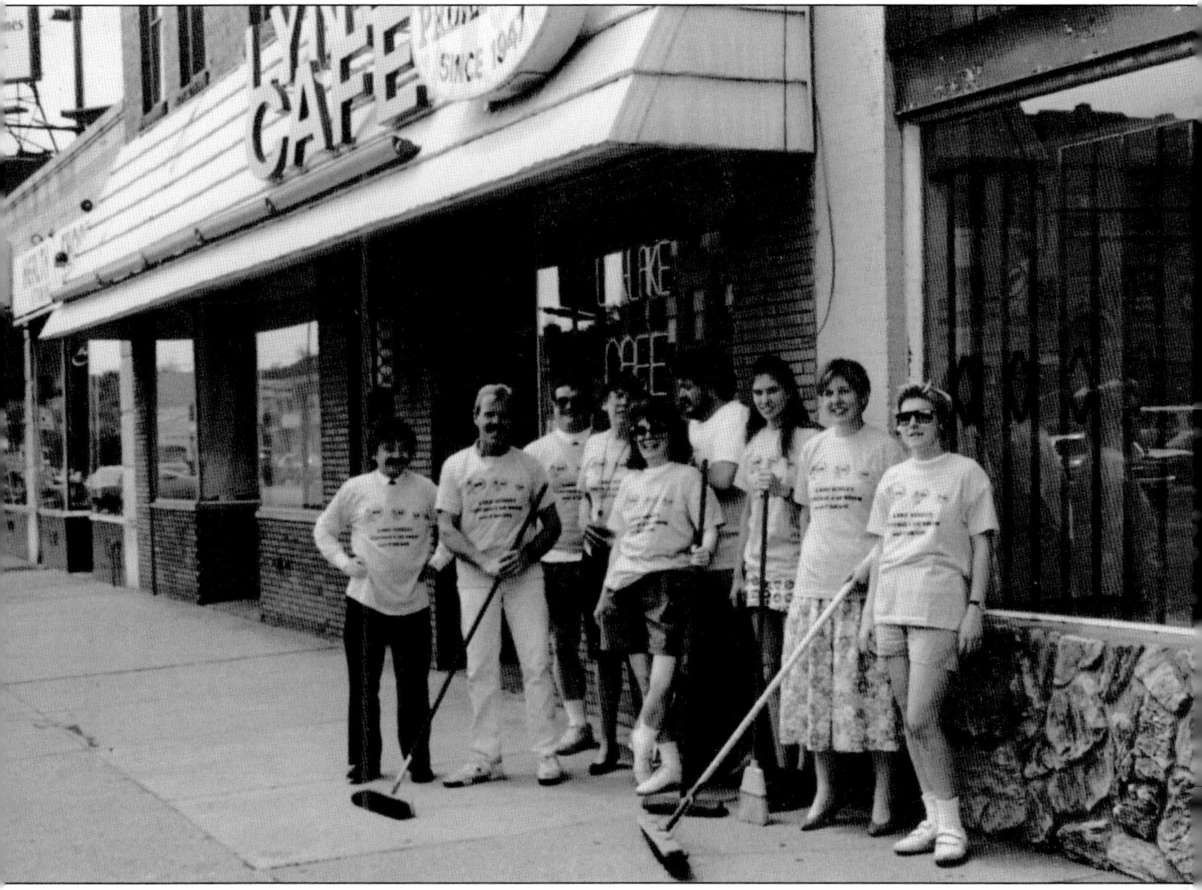

The Lyn-Lake Café opened in 1947 at the northeast corner of Lyndale Avenue and Lake Street. It was known for its traditional home-style American cooking and especially its locally famous prime rib. It was a local hangout and meeting place for many local organizations and a favorite spot for locals to sit and watch the world pass by. In 1978, then-owner Mike Mueller, already very active in the neighborhood and intersection, helped to found the Lyn-Lake Businessmen's Association. This photograph was taken in 1991 during the annual Lyn-Lake Clean Sweep, an annual event organized by the Lyn-Lake Business Association, the predecessor to Mueller's earlier Lyn-Lake Businessmen's Association. The following year, the café was purchased by Phillipos, Bruck, and Andenet Getachew; the brothers were drawn to the café for its sense of community. They continued to offer American staples and added dishes from their native Ethiopia. Unfortunately for local residents, the Lyn-Lake Café had closed by 1994. (Paul Newman.)

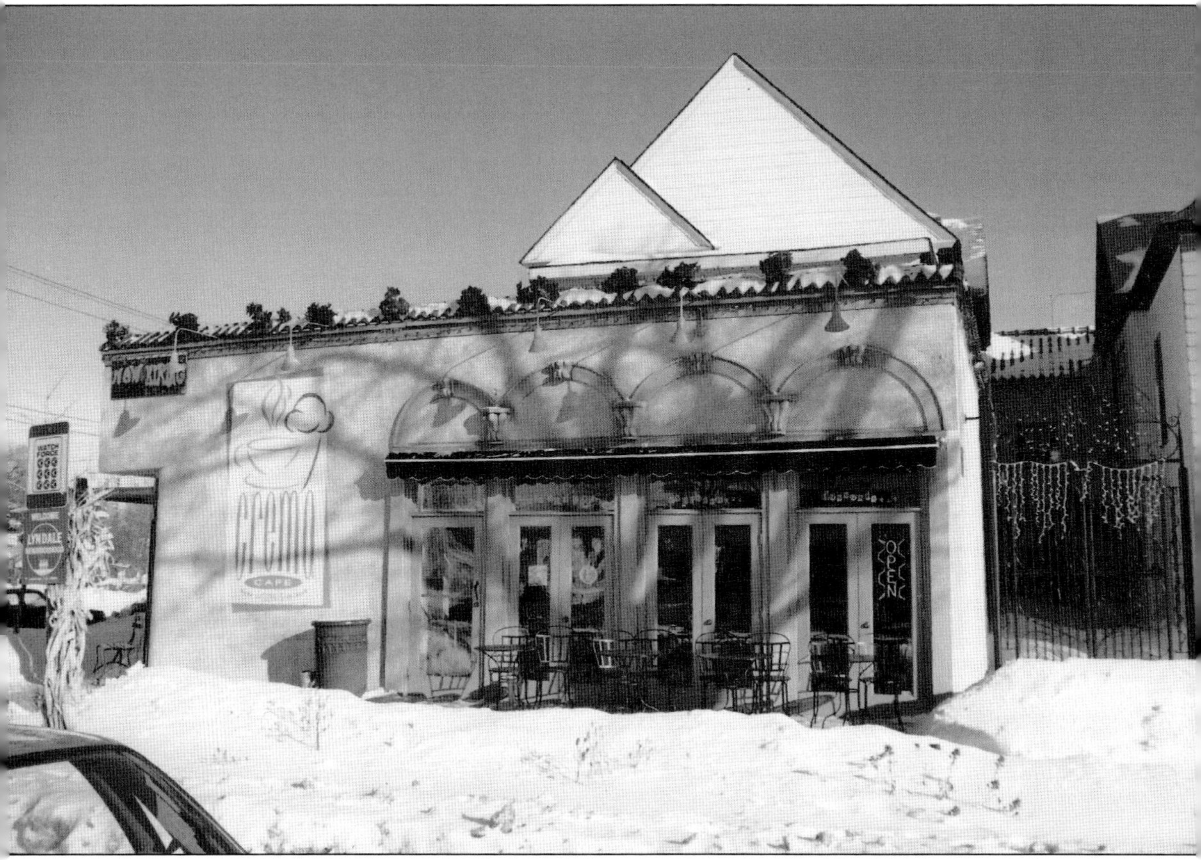

While Crema Café on Thirty-fourth Street and Lyndale Avenue did not open until 1994 (shown here in 1997), its roots go back much further. Sonny's Ice Cream founder, Sonny Siron, opened a malt shop on Nicollet Avenue in 1945 and then later moved to this location across from what was at the time Lyndale School. He raised his family in the building and built a local gourmet ice cream empire in the downstairs factory. In 1994, Siron's son Ron, along with his partner, Carrie Gustafson, opened Crema Café to share Sonny's Ice Cream with the public. The couple did most of the work themselves, including excavating nearly seven dumpsters of dirt in order to create a level space for the storefront. Crema Café's design was inspired to evoke feelings of the Italian countryside, a nation famous for its ice cream. Italy was also the source of inspiration for Gustafson's entrance into the ice cream world. Sonny Siron died in 2007, but Ron and Carrie continue in the family footsteps. The café remains open, and Sonny's Ice Cream is still manufactured on-site. (LNA.)

Four

Community

Lyn-Lake is an informal neighborhood that consists of portions of the following four formal Minneapolis neighborhoods: CARAG, LHENA (the Wedge), Whittier, and Lyndale. Each of these four neighborhoods has its own organizational structure to mobilize volunteers and actively engage the community, each has its own newspaper, and each has a history that has developed, in part, along shared patterns of connections to the main corridors of Lyndale Avenue, Lake Street, and the Twenty-ninth Street railroad trench. Together these four different areas make up the greater Lyn-Lake area.

These different "micro-areas" are further bound together by shared amenities that help forge a shared sense of community. Parks and playgrounds have provided places for both children and adults to play; police have walked the beat and worked with residents to combat crime and promote community policing programs; and organizations of all sorts have given local residents a place to meet fellow neighbors while having fun, giving back to the community, or both. This chapter is dedicated to some of the many ways in which Lyn-Lake's community has made a neighborhood out of individuals and has helped to create a sense of belonging and identity within the larger city.

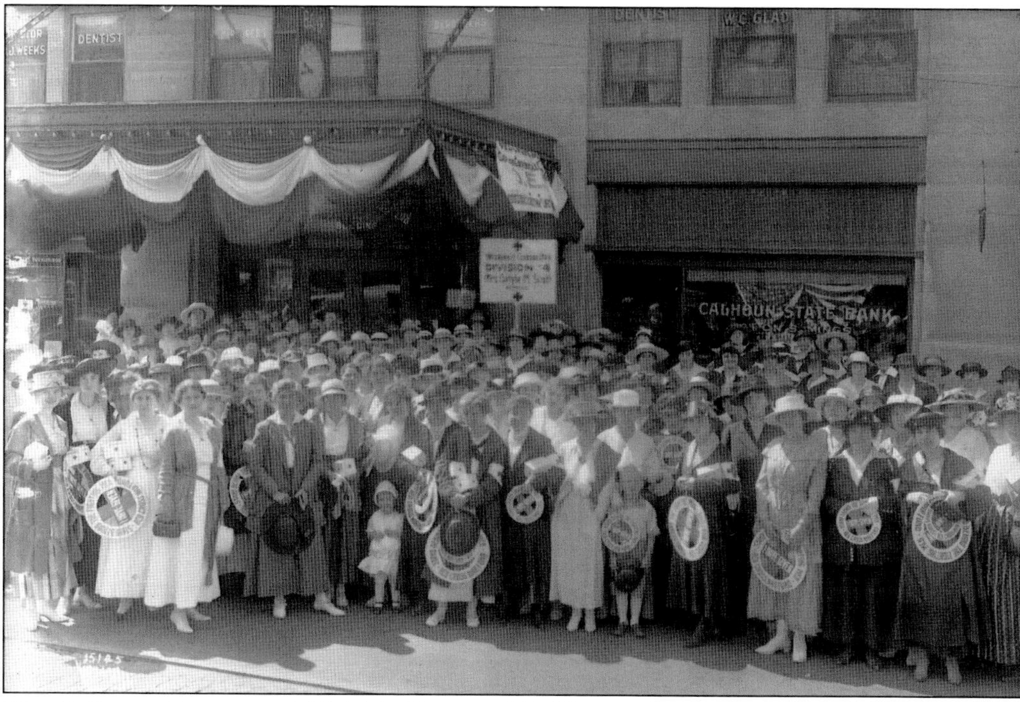

The Calhoun Commercial Club Building, at 711 West Lake Street, was the lynchpin of the Lyndale-Lake intersection, the neighborhood, and the first-floor tenant Calhoun State Bank, which was the favored financial institution of many local residents. In June 1917, these Red Cross Women's Auxiliary volunteers staged a promotional rally outside of the bank to solicit donations to the Red Cross War Fund. (Hennepin County Library; photograph by C. J. Hibbard.)

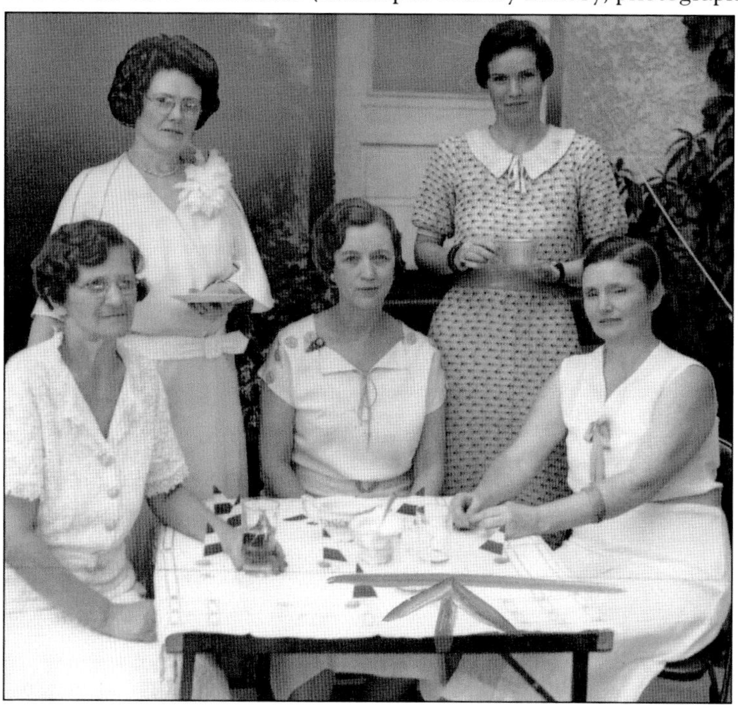

Groups and clubs played an important role in the lives of many Lyn-Lake residents. These members of the Abraham Lincoln Circle of the Grand Army of the Republic (GAR), an organization for the female descendants of Union soldiers, pose for a photograph at a September 1936 garden social held at the home of Mayme Ude, located at 3233 Garfield Avenue. (Hennepin Count Library; photograph by the *Minneapolis Times*.)

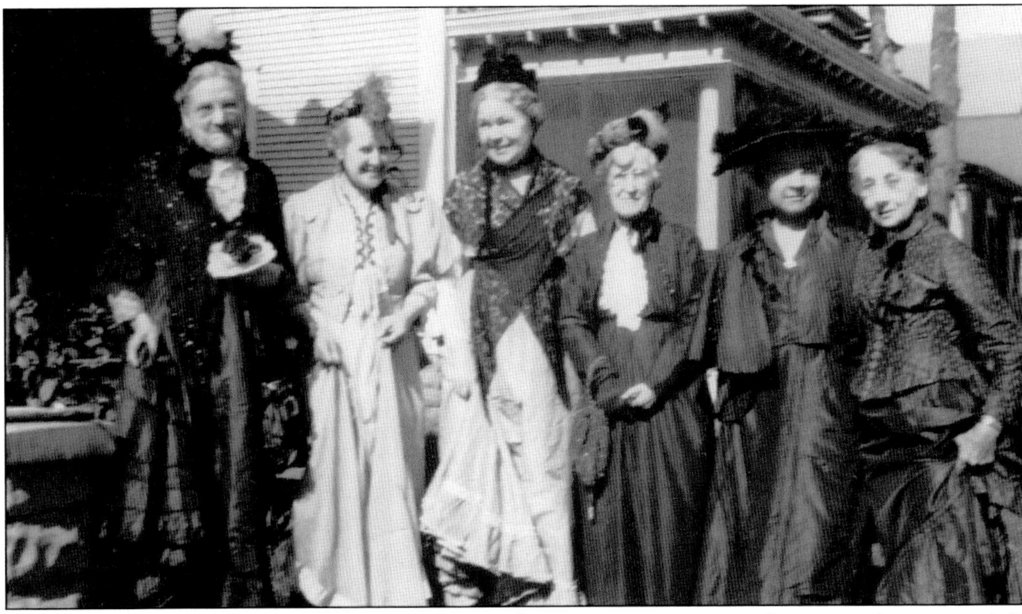

"Women have done their share in the building of communities, cities and nations; this is especially true of this district," declared the 1926 *Lake Street Guide*. "The women of this community are as well, if not the best organized in the city" and "all interested in either Church or Social Societies" as well as politics and business. These women, dressed for a vintage fashion show, embody that community spirit. (LCC.)

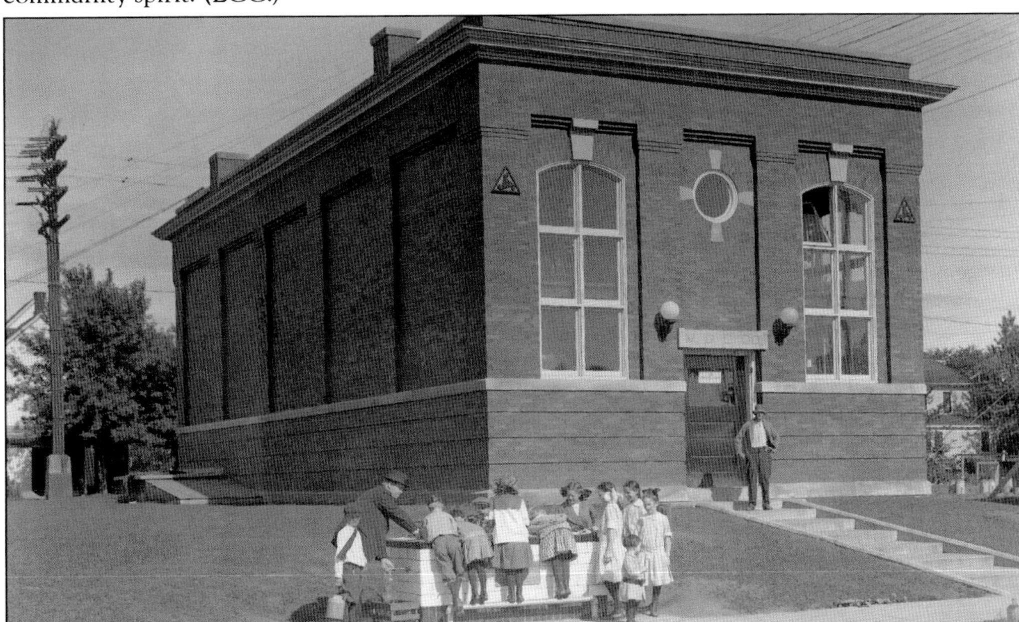

In 1915, General Electric installed a drinking fountain in front of its newly completed substation on the corner of Garfield Avenue and Thirty-third Street. The artesian well was of great interest to the neighbors, especially the local children. The fountain featured white tile with an inset plaque proclaiming that the fountain was a gift to the residents of Minneapolis. This photograph was taken in June 1915. (Hennepin County Library.)

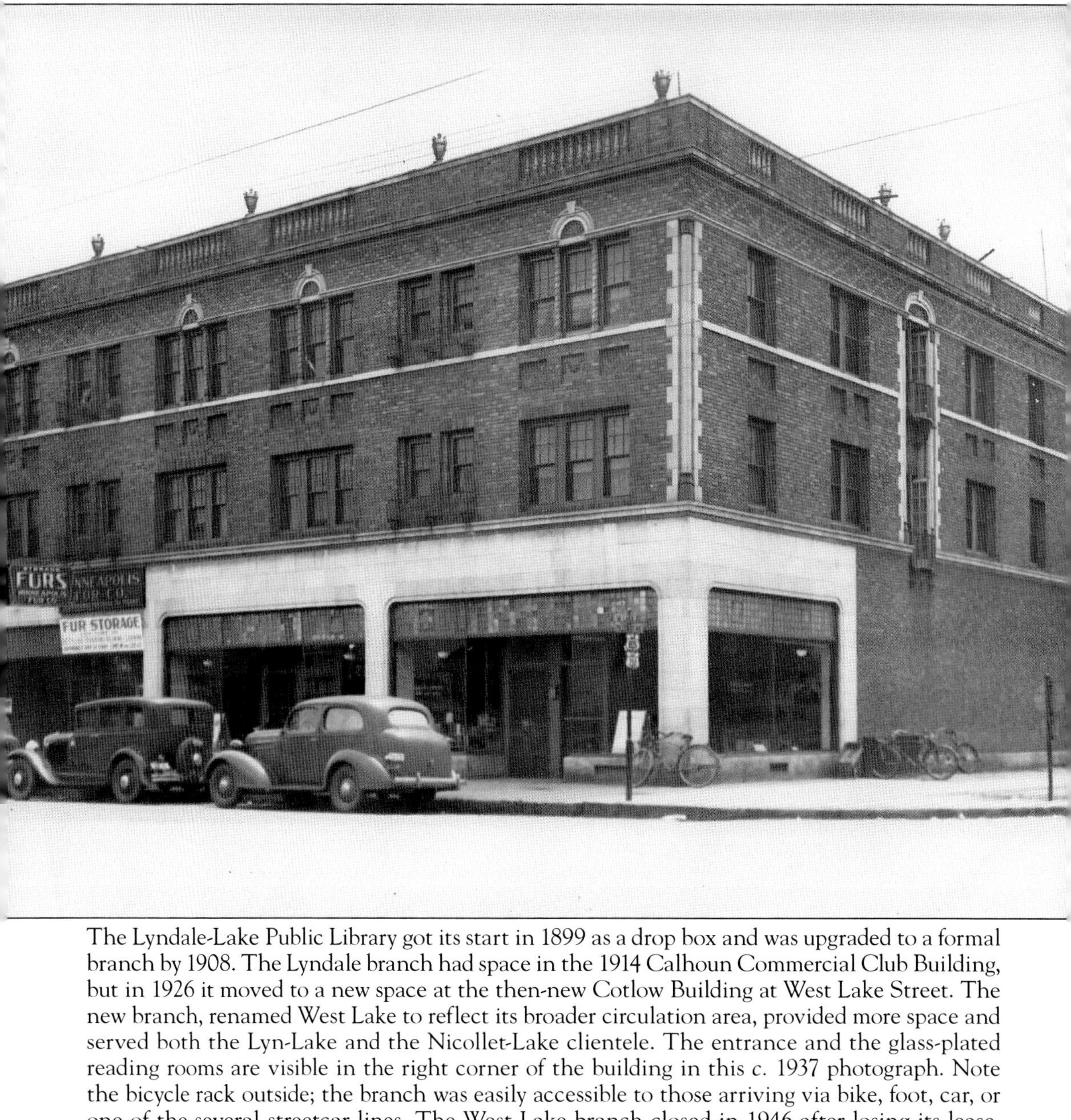

The Lyndale-Lake Public Library got its start in 1899 as a drop box and was upgraded to a formal branch by 1908. The Lyndale branch had space in the 1914 Calhoun Commercial Club Building, but in 1926 it moved to a new space at the then-new Cotlow Building at West Lake Street. The new branch, renamed West Lake to reflect its broader circulation area, provided more space and served both the Lyn-Lake and the Nicollet-Lake clientele. The entrance and the glass-plated reading rooms are visible in the right corner of the building in this c. 1937 photograph. Note the bicycle rack outside; the branch was easily accessible to those arriving via bike, foot, car, or one of the several streetcar lines. The West Lake branch closed in 1946 after losing its lease. The Minneapolis Public Library ultimately did not replace it, having decided that the Walker branch on Hennepin Avenue could adequately serve the broader circulation area. (Hennepin County Library.)

During World War I, Rev. Warren L. Bunger of the Lyndale Congregational Church requested a leave of absence to become the church representative in the army's YMCA. While serving in Europe, he met with many men and women from the neighborhood, both Lyndale church members and non-members alike. There was not a block in the neighborhood that was left untouched by the war. (LUCC.)

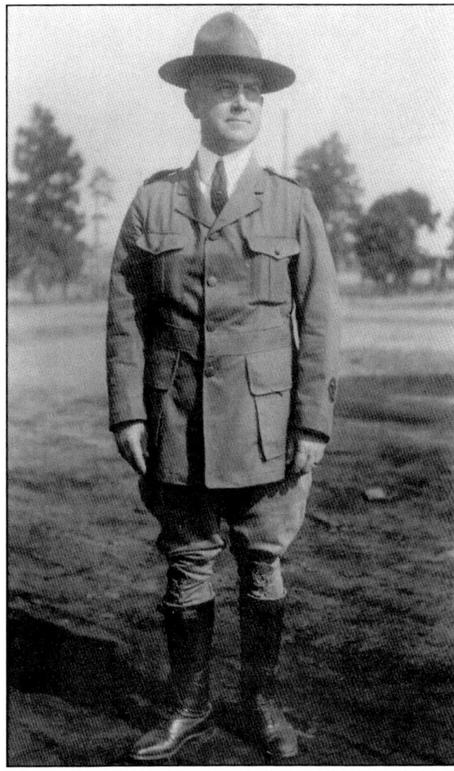

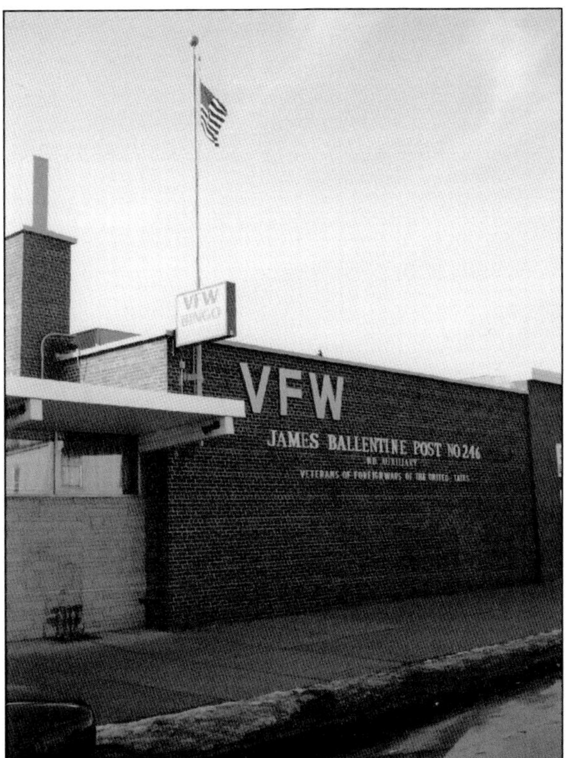

While the James J. Ballentine post 246 of the Veterans of Foreign Wars was founded in 1919, its current building dates back only to 1954. The building, located at 2916 Lyndale Avenue, was designed by architects Brandhorst and Leadholm and contained multiple meeting rooms, a lounge, office space, and a kitchen. It has not changed dramatically since then. This photograph dates to 2002. (LHENA; photograph by Matthew Allen.)

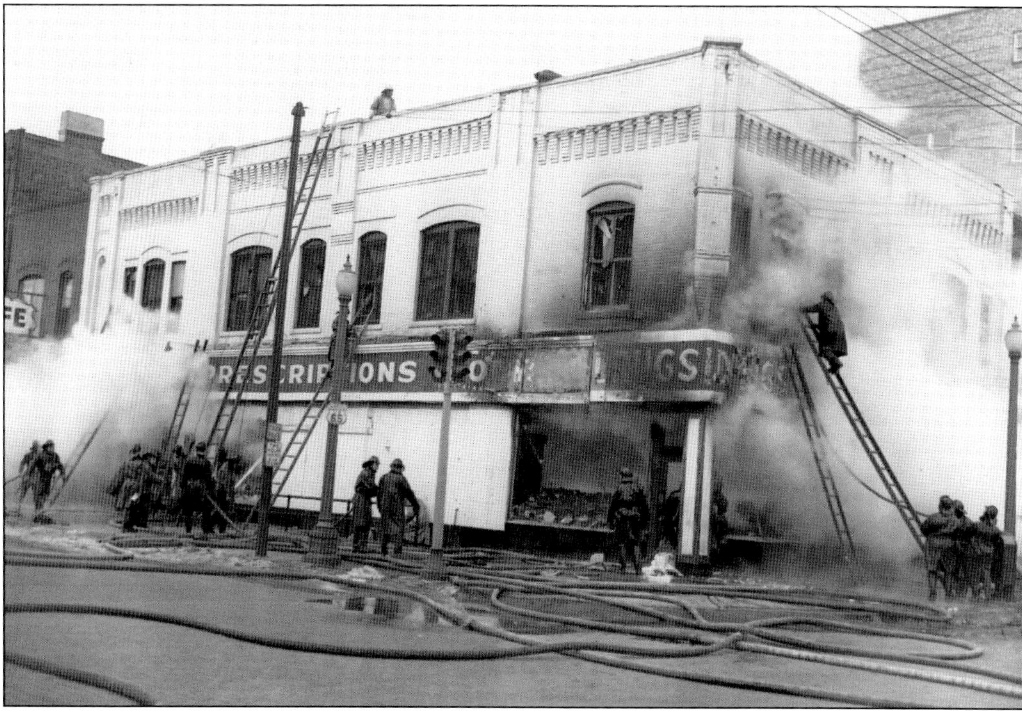

The residents of the apartments in the upper floors of the Wilharm Pharmacy Building, on the southwest corner of Lake Street and Lyndale Avenue, were lucky to escape this 1950 fire uninjured. Policeman William Peltola was nearby when the fire broke out and rescued six young children and their mother from one unit. The building survived, although both stores and homes suffered extensive smoke and water damage. (Hennepin County Library.)

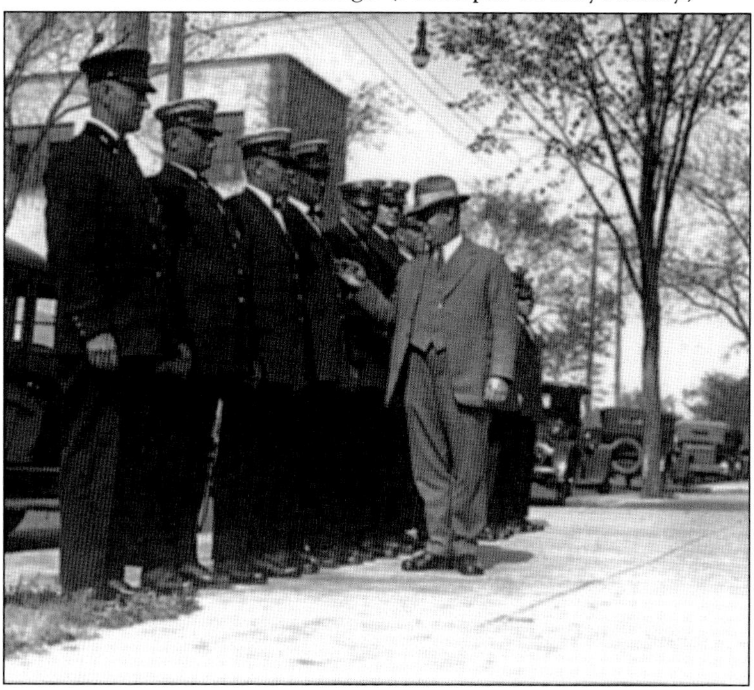

Minneapolis chief of police Frank Brunskill had a role in one of Lyn-Lake's most notorious bank robberies. In 1917, three armed men entered the Calhoun State Bank, forced employees into the vault, then left with $7,900 in cash. Then-detective Brunskill was put in charge of the investigation, which ultimately spanned multiple states. Here Chief Brunskill inspects officers in the Fifth Precinct near the Bryant Avenue station in 1925. (MPD.)

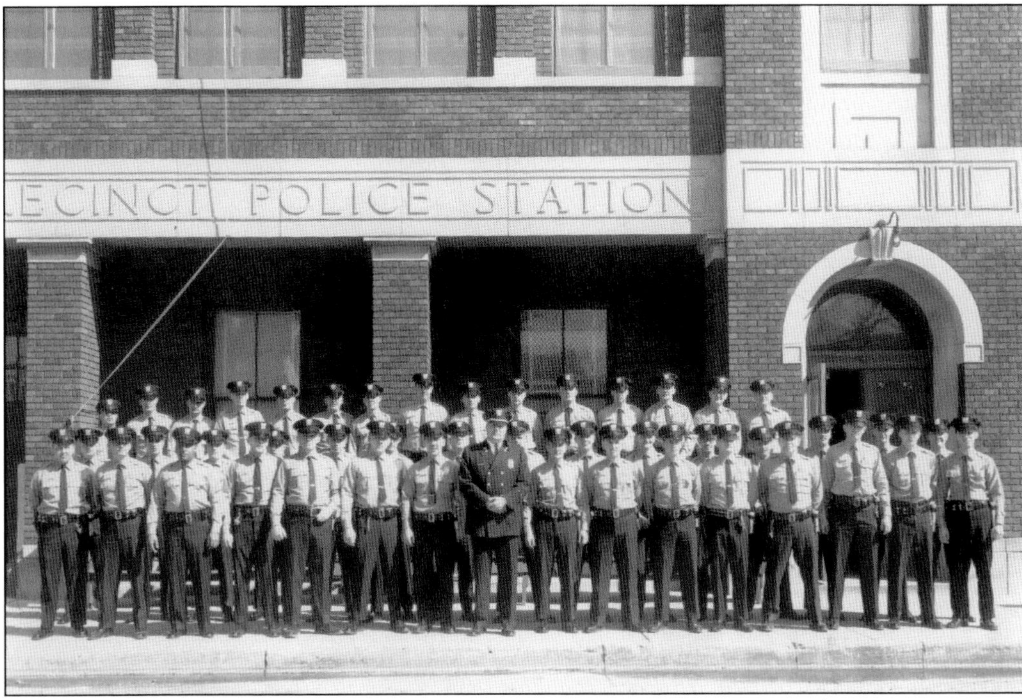

Minneapolis' Fifth Precinct Station was located at Twenty-ninth Street and Bryant Avenue, in the heart of Lyn-Lake. When the station was built in 1920, local politicians proclaimed it the "finest precinct station in the Northwest." For years, the Minneapolis Police Band practiced in the second-floor auditorium, while officers put in practice at a basement shooting range. These rookie officers are pictured here in 1966. (MPD.)

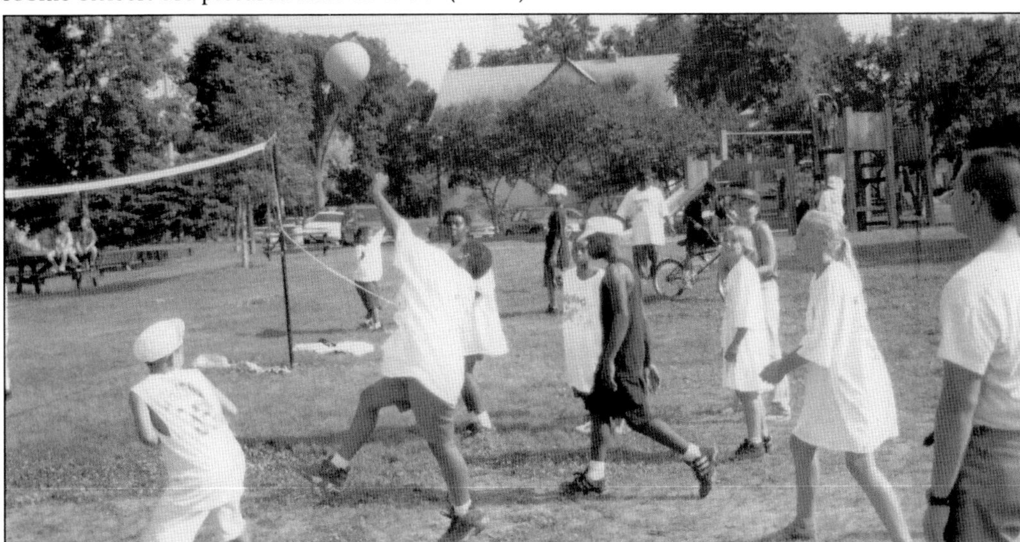

As part of the 1996 "Kickin' it with Cops" community outreach program, Lyn-Lake youth are seen joining local police for a volleyball game at Painter Park. The 1990s were a rough period, crime-wise, in Minneapolis, and Lyn-Lake residents and businesses struggled to combat rising crime rates within the neighborhood. Programs like "Kickin' it with Cops" helped strengthen community and police relationships, in this case with a focus on children and teenagers. (LNA.)

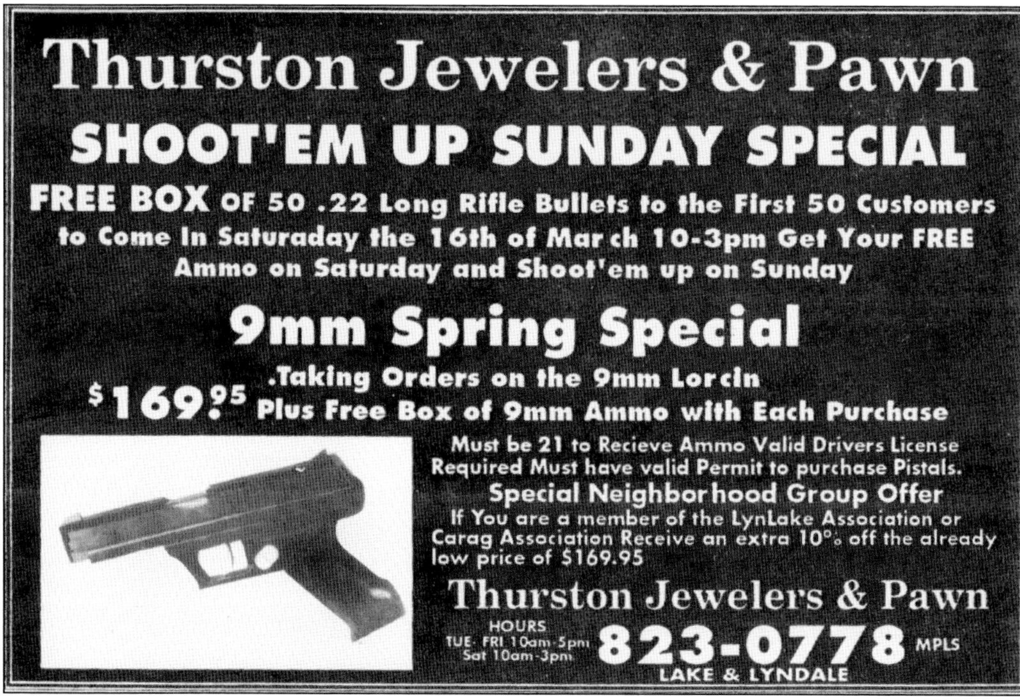

This March 1996 advertisement in the *Lake Area News* was placed by Thurston's owner, Lloyd Drilling, as a protest against the actions of several neighborhood groups. He had offered to give up his gun sales license in return for an expanded pawnshop license, but the business association and three out of the four surrounding neighborhood organizations still recommended against the license expansion. Drilling accused them of being elitist. (Hennepin County Library.)

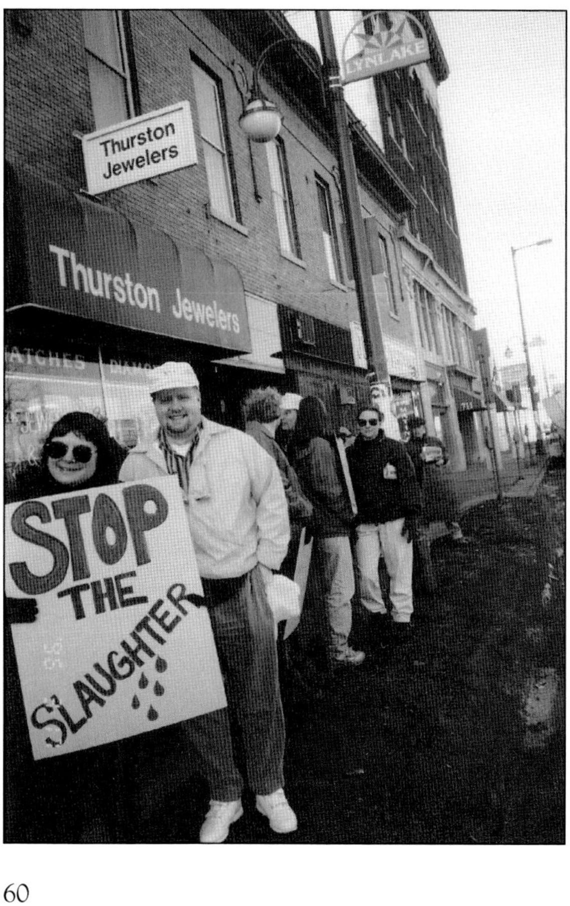

The Thurston's controversy came less than a year after the *New York Times* dubbed Minneapolis "Murderapolis." Despite Lyn-Lake's "hip" factor, high crime rates still plagued portions of the neighborhood. Around 50 people took to the streets in front of the Thurston's Jewelry storefront on Lake Street in protest the "Sunday Special" and what they considered to be Drilling's cavalier attitude toward violence in the community. (LNA.)

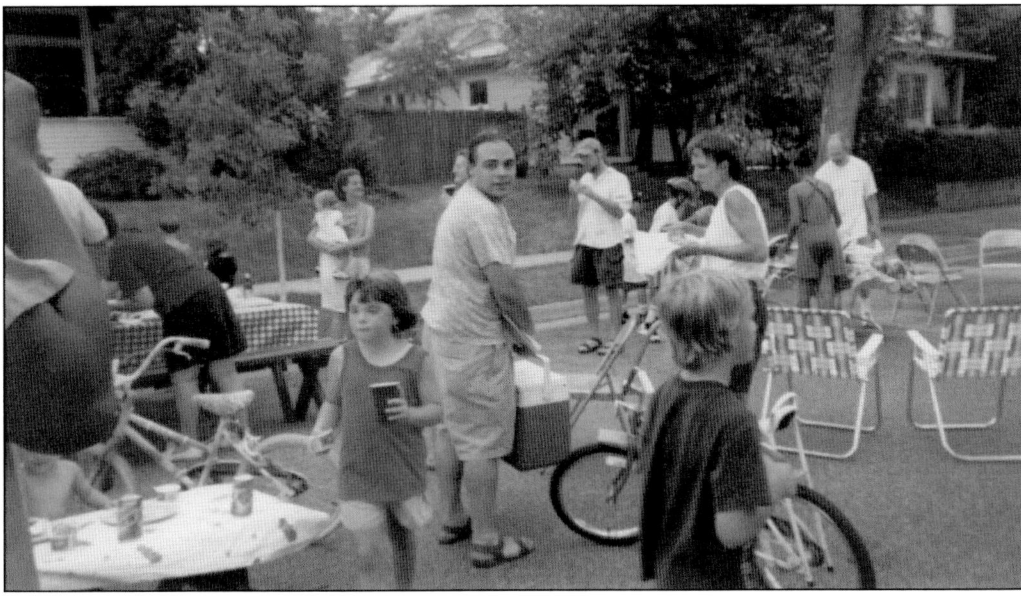

Lyndale Neighborhood coordinator Joe Barisonzi is seen passing out Sonny's Ice Cream, produced locally in a factory on the corner of Thirty-fourth Street and Lyndale Avenue, at a August 1996 National Night Out party on the 3400 block of Pleasant Avenue. The following year, Barisonzi won a prestigious national award for his community leadership efforts. Today Lyndale Neighborhood serves as a national model for its innovative approaches to community revitalization. (LNA.)

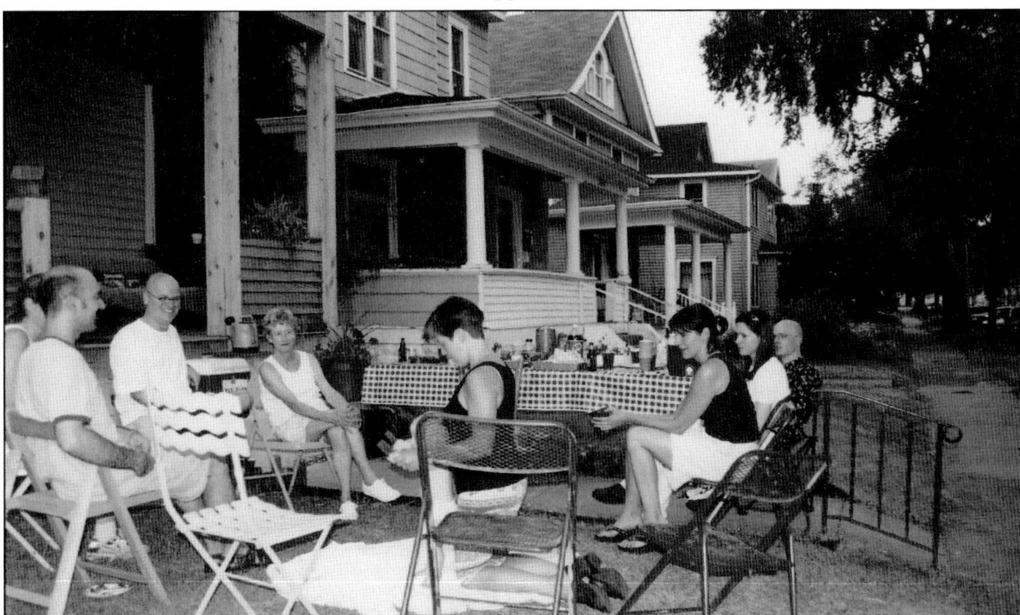

This August 7, 2001, party, held on the 2700 block of Aldrich, was one of 825 formal National Night Out block parties held in the city and one of dozens in the Lyn-Lake area aimed to build community connections and improved safety. Minneapolis was ranked the number one National Night Out city in the nation for 2001, the second time in two years that Minneapolis topped the list. (LHENA.)

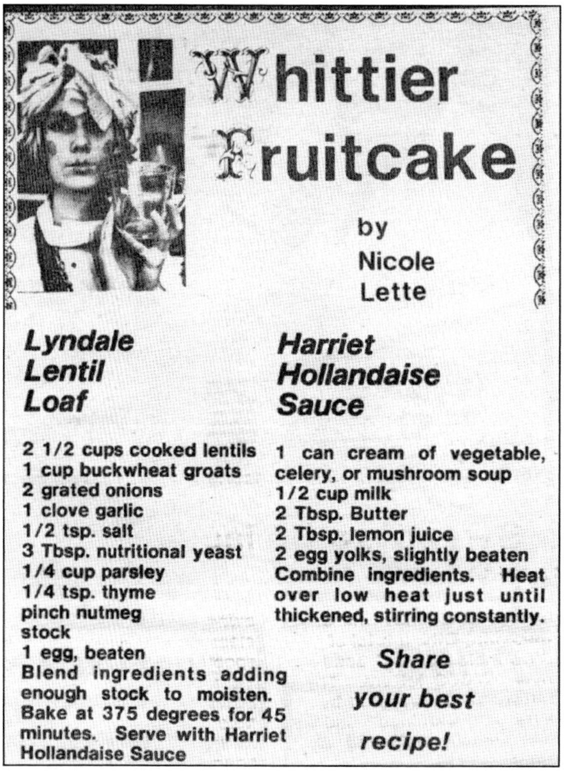

Whittier Fruitcake

by
Nicole
Lette

Lyndale Lentil Loaf

2 1/2 cups cooked lentils
1 cup buckwheat groats
2 grated onions
1 clove garlic
1/2 tsp. salt
3 Tbsp. nutritional yeast
1/4 cup parsley
1/4 tsp. thyme
pinch nutmeg
stock
1 egg, beaten
Blend ingredients adding enough stock to moisten. Bake at 375 degrees for 45 minutes. Serve with Harriet Hollandaise Sauce

Harriet Hollandaise Sauce

1 can cream of vegetable, celery, or mushroom soup
1/2 cup milk
2 Tbsp. Butter
2 Tbsp. lemon juice
2 egg yolks, slightly beaten
Combine ingredients. Heat over low heat just until thickened, stirring constantly.

Share your best recipe!

The "Whittier Fruitcake" was a monthly recipe column by Nicole Lette in the neighborhood newspaper, the *Whittier Globe*. This recipe for Lyndale Lentil Loaf and the accompanying Harriet Hollandaise Sauce ran in May 1977. The *Whittier Globe* offered readers a wide range of articles, from candid police columns to interviews with residents to coverage of serious issues facing the neighborhood. Controversial at times, the *Globe* has been published since 1976. (Hennepin County Library.)

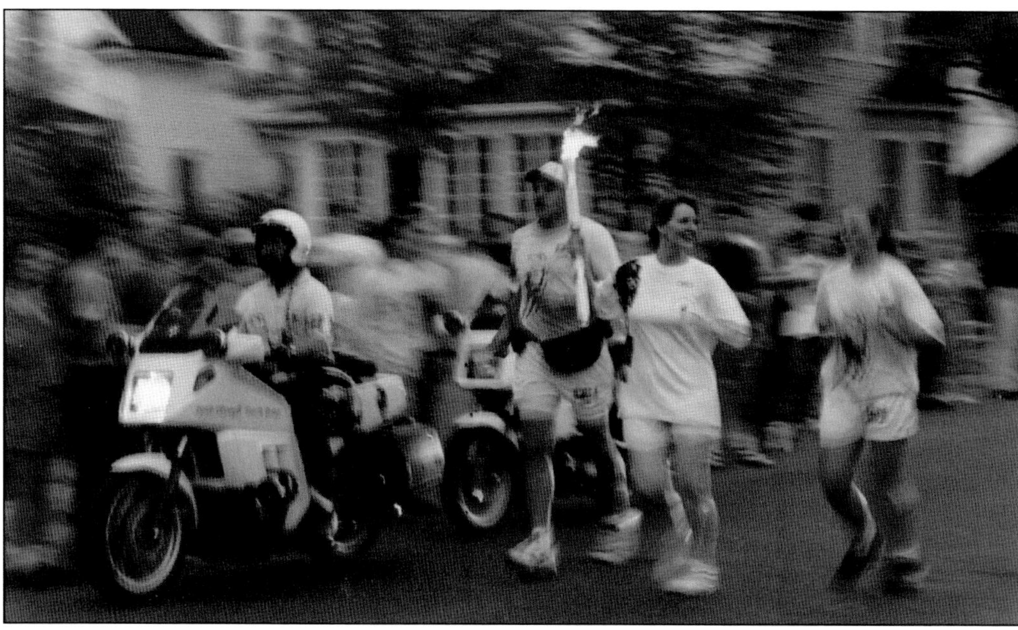

In early June 1996, the Olympic torch passed through Minneapolis en route to the Atlanta Olympic Games' July 19 opening ceremony. The torch skirted the southern edges of the greater Lyn-Lake area; the runners came north along Nicollet Avenue, turned west on Thirty-sixth Street, and headed toward Lake Calhoun. This runner and his escorts pass through the Lyndale neighborhood portion of the run. (LNA.)

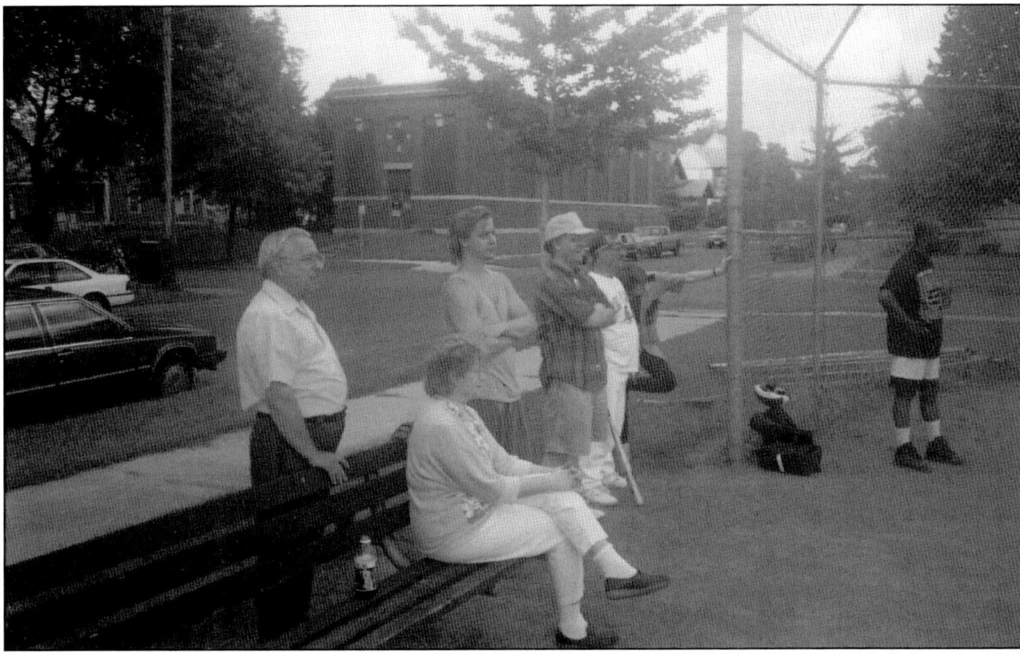

The Lyndale Neighborhood Association (LNA) has been around since the 1970s, but it took on a new significance in 1990 as crime, including homicide, rocked the neighborhood. LNA became an active force for improving the neighborhood, gaining national recognition in the process. Here a LNA softball team squares off against the Neighborhood Revitalization Program (NRP) team in Painter Park in 1994. (LNA.)

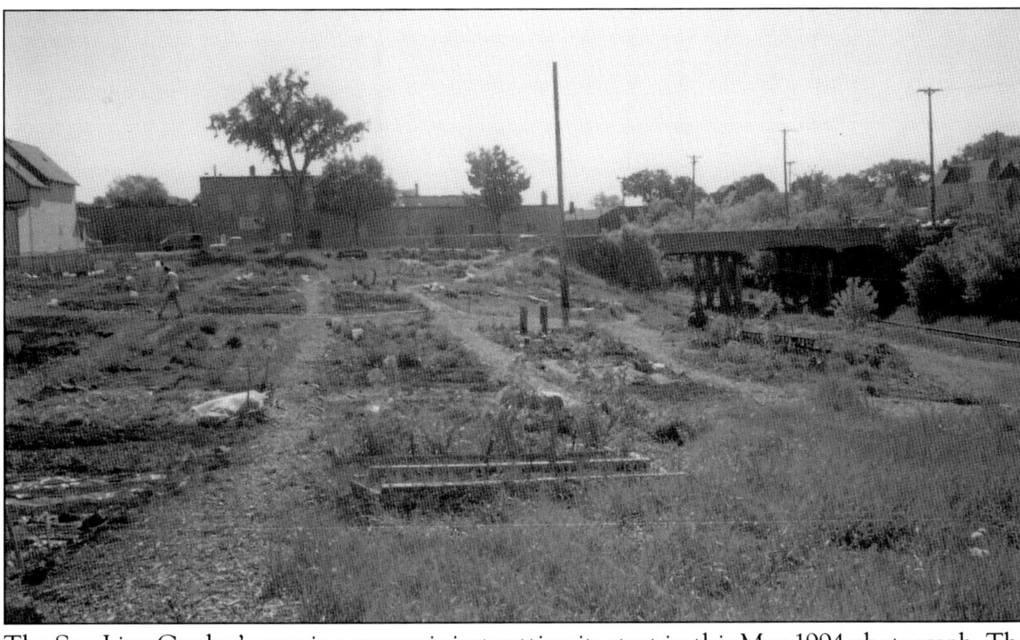

The Soo Line Garden's growing season is just getting its start in this May 1994 photograph. The community garden, located at 2845 Garfield on the site of demolished grain elevators, began in 1991 and is Minneapolis's second-oldest community garden. The garden has 80 plots, and its gardeners take great pride in their flowers, fruits, vegetables, and other plants. (LNA.)

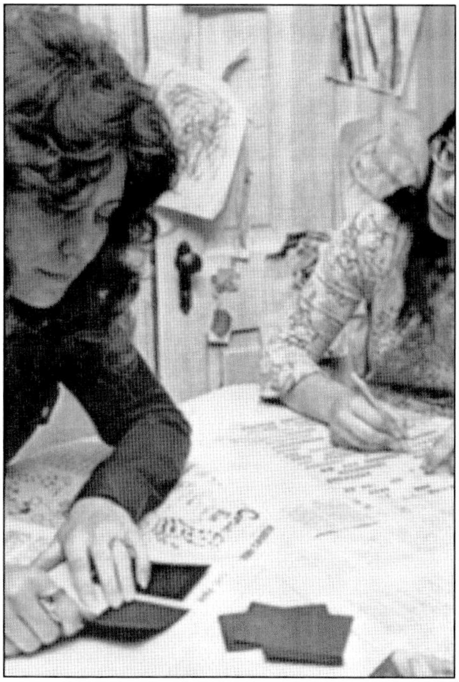

Lowry Hill East is home to the longest-running neighborhood newspaper in the city. In the November 1970 inaugural issue of *The Wedge*, the editors explained that the name was chosen to reflect the shape of the neighborhood, as well as "our search for a *tool* with which to promote communication with our neighbors." Here Lorraine Scott (left) and Rita Martinez put together a 1972 edition of the paper. (LHENA.)

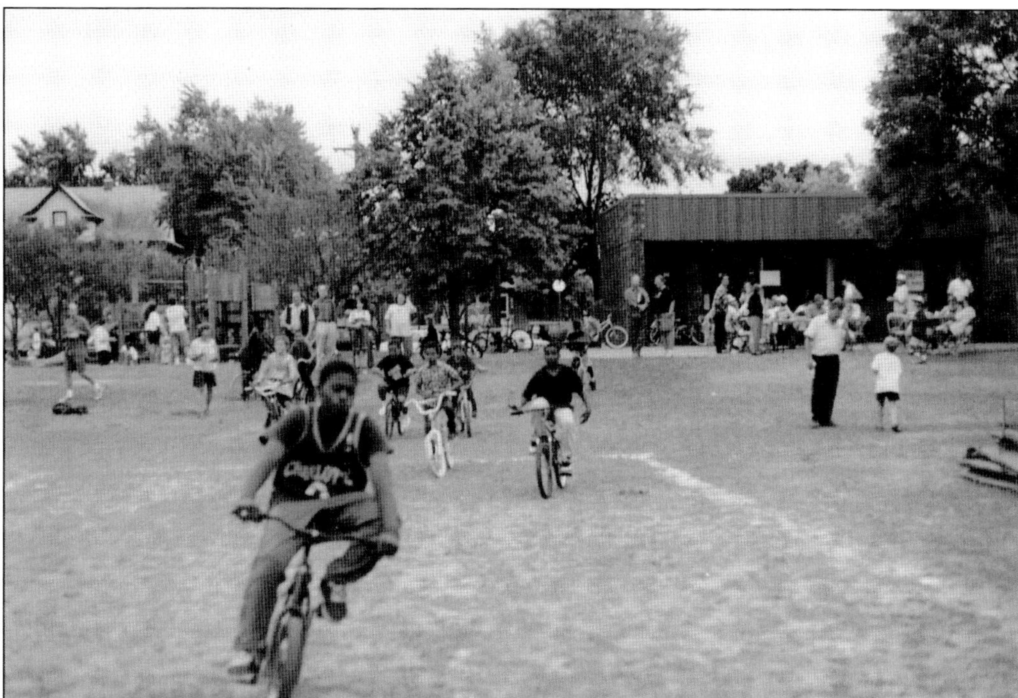

Ice cream socials are staples of the neighborhoods in the Lyn-Lake area. Here the Lyndale neighborhood celebrates its annual ice cream social in 1996. Unlike the other neighborhoods in the Lyn-Lake area, Lyndale benefited from having an ice cream factory literally right in its backyard. The Sonny's Ice Cream factory was, and still is, located directly across the street from the park's Thirty-fourth Street and Lyndale Avenue building. (LNA.)

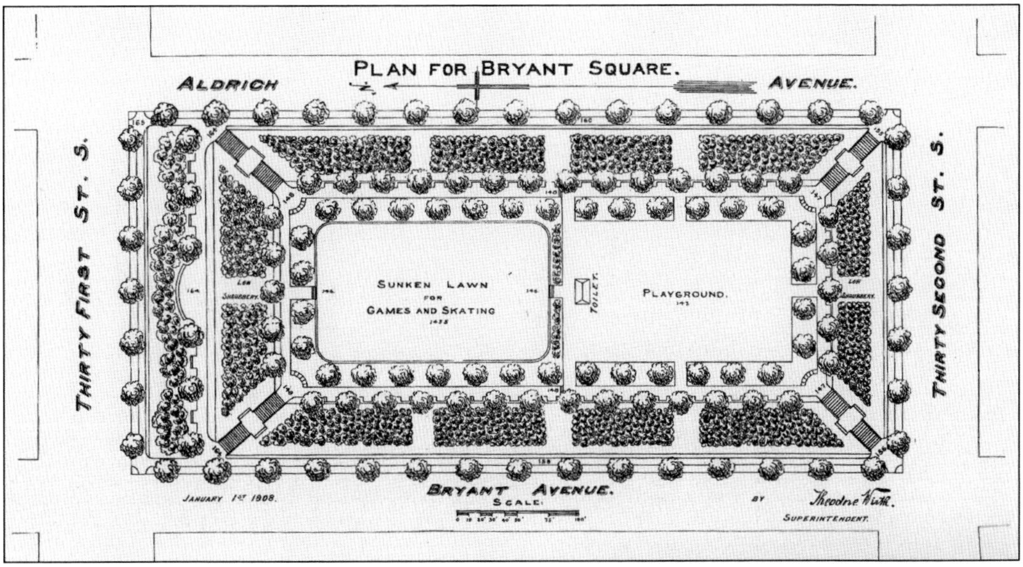

Bryant Square Park was purchased in 1904 but was unusable due to its deep swampy basin. In the 1908 park plan, the Park Commissioners stated, "[It] demonstrates that this unsightly square can be transformed into a very attractive sunken garden and playground if it can only be filled in." Doing so would require 16,000 cubic yards of filling, and at least some of it was expected to come in the form of garbage. (Hennepin County Library.)

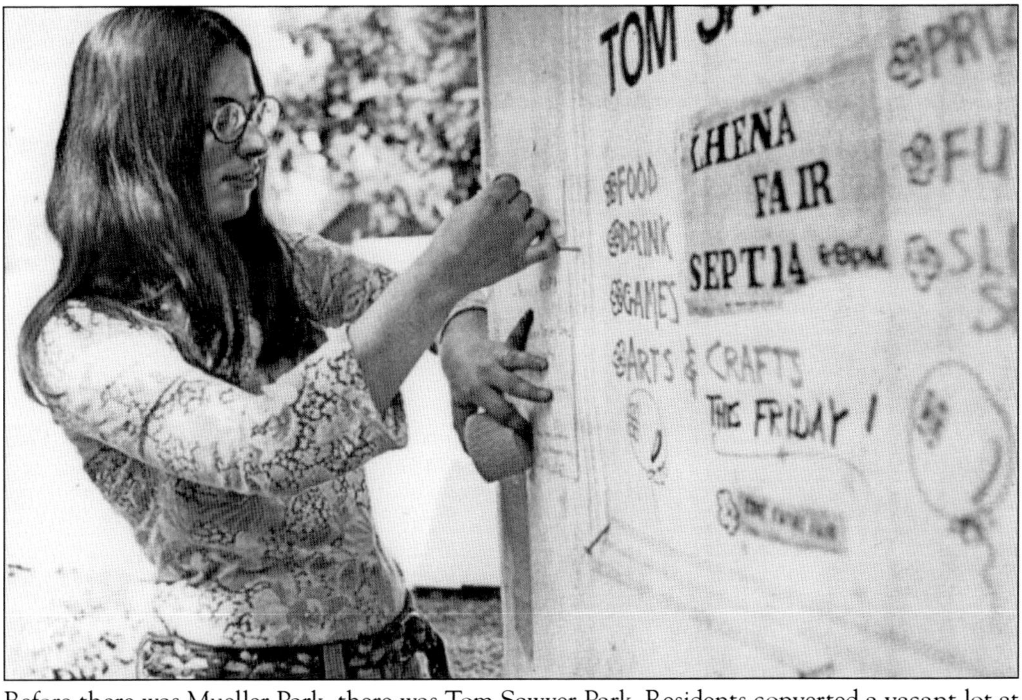

Before there was Mueller Park, there was Tom Sawyer Park. Residents converted a vacant lot at Twenty-seventh Street and Aldrich Avenue into a neighborhood gathering place in 1972, using donated materials and volunteer labor. Here local leader Rita Martinez posts a LHENA arts and crafts fair sign on the park's bulletin board. Use of Tom Sawyer tapered off after the official Mueller Park opened in 1976. (LHENA.)

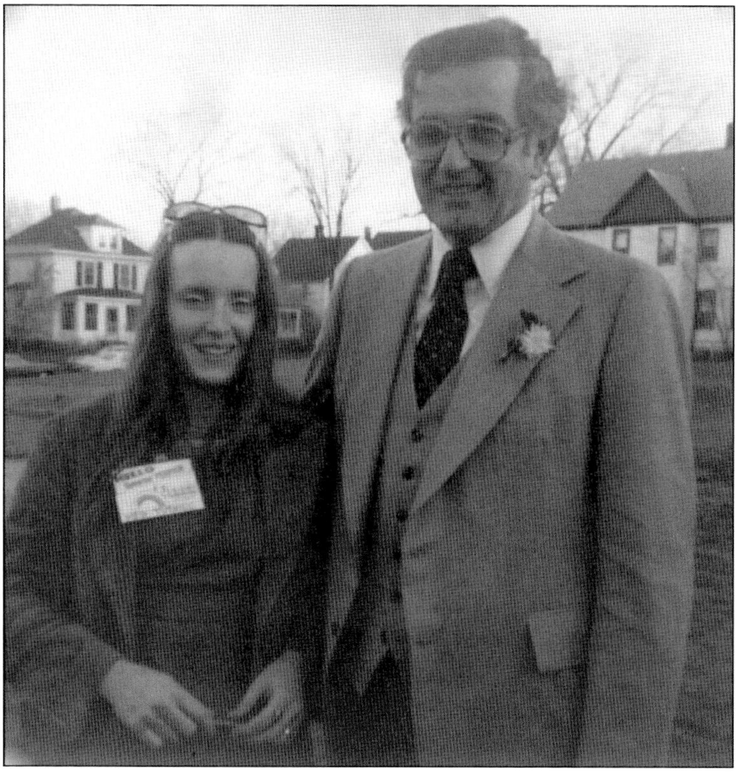

On November 2, 1977, Gov. Rudy Perpich visited the neighborhood to participate in the ceremony to rename the relatively new park and playground at Twenty-fourth Street and Bryant Avenue in honor of Wedge residents Bob and Herb Mueller. Here Perpich poses with local activist (and later city council member) Meg Tuthill. The governor returned to the neighborhood the following year as part of his 1978 state tour. (LHENA.)

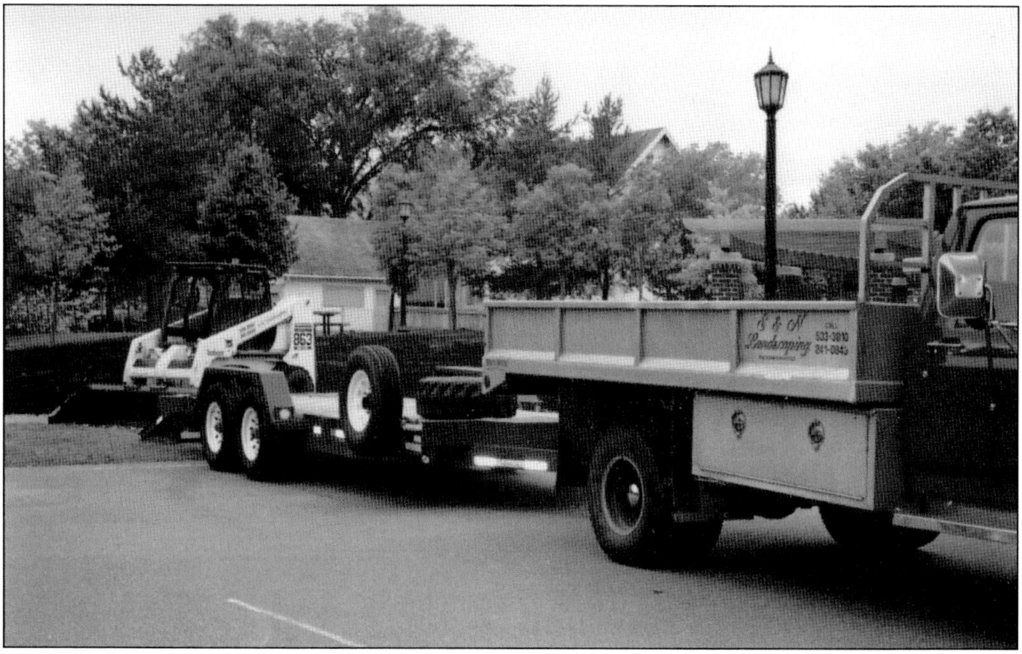

In September 2001, Mueller Park received new sod and grass, as well as a large truck filled with mulch for the park's plentiful shade trees. Volunteers showed up to meet Minneapolis Parks' Forestry Division staff, and together they spent several hours of hard labor to move and spread a dump truck's worth of steaming manure. (LHENA.)

Five

Arts and Culture

The Lyn-Lake area has developed a reputation for being an artistic hub of the Twin Cities. Arts organizations, galleries, and theaters began to move into the area in earnest in the 1990s, although the neighborhood had a thriving arts scene far before that. Commercial artists at the Buzza Card Company designed cards and posters for a national market during the 1920s and the 1930s, while nationally renowned musicians performed in neighborhood bars and clubs during the 1950s and 1960s. Artists looking for spacious, yet affordable, space moved into homes in the neighborhood and sometimes rented former industrial space in the buildings lining Twenty-ninth Street. During the 1980s, Lyn-Lake was a center for the punk and rock music scenes, with musicians and aspiring musicians prowling the aisles of records stores like the Oar Folkjokeopus, the Wax Museum, and any number of other vinyl stores. When the Jungle Theater moved to the area in 1991, it started a new wave of interest from the performing arts community, as well as arts organizations such as Intermedia Arts. Today Lyn-Lake aggressively markets itself as a community friendly to artists, both of the professional and the amateur variety. Arts in all of its forms are accepted and embraced, and vernacular artistic expression of both the sanctioned—art cars, for example—and the controversial—graffiti art—can be found in abundance.

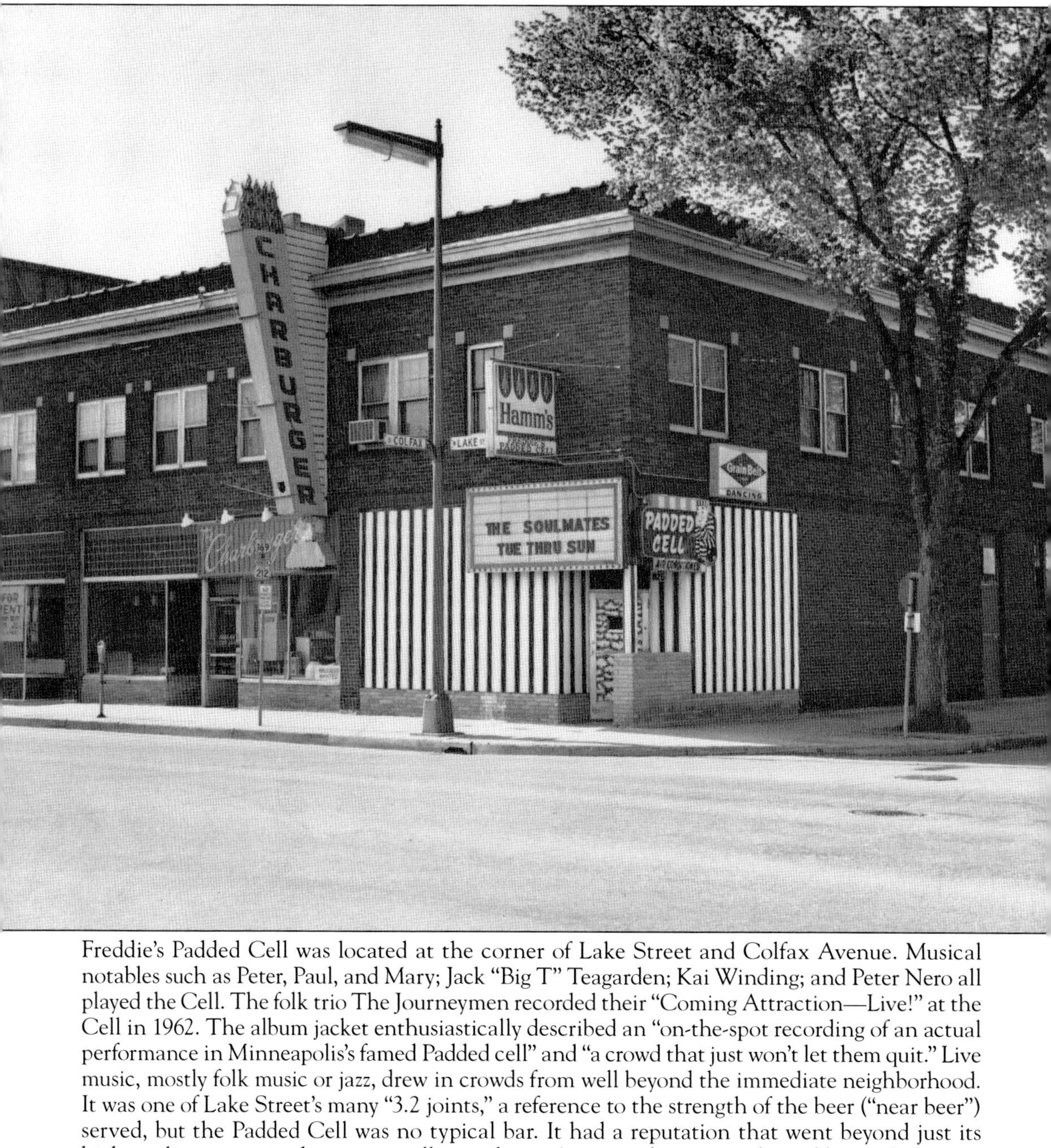

Freddie's Padded Cell was located at the corner of Lake Street and Colfax Avenue. Musical notables such as Peter, Paul, and Mary; Jack "Big T" Teagarden; Kai Winding; and Peter Nero all played the Cell. The folk trio The Journeymen recorded their "Coming Attraction—Live!" at the Cell in 1962. The album jacket enthusiastically described an "on-the-spot recording of an actual performance in Minneapolis's famed Padded cell" and "a crowd that just won't let them quit." Live music, mostly folk music or jazz, drew in crowds from well beyond the immediate neighborhood. It was one of Lake Street's many "3.2 joints," a reference to the strength of the beer ("near beer") served, but the Padded Cell was no typical bar. It had a reputation that went beyond just its high-quality acts or its distinctive jailhouse decor. Among other stories, legend has it that it was home to several monkeys until the city told the owner they had to go. This photograph was taken sometime around 1968. (Mohn Electric Company.)

Dulano's Pizza has been at 607 West Lake Street since the late 1960s. The building has a long past; its shell dates to the 19th century, and over the years it has been home to the Schatzlein Saddle Shop, a barbershop, and immediately prior to Dulano's arrival, the Torch Bar. Live music was a staple from the start, with a focus on bluegrass. (LNA.)

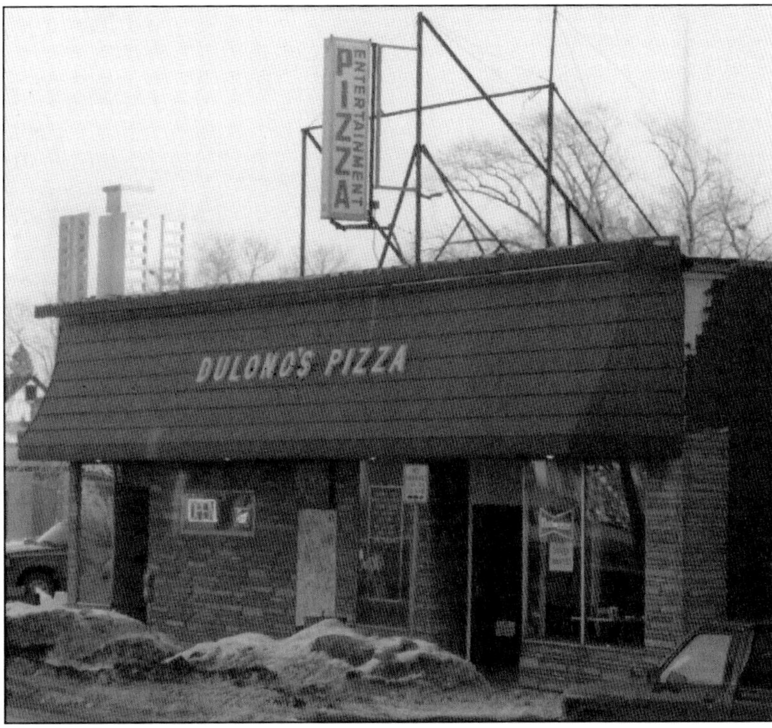

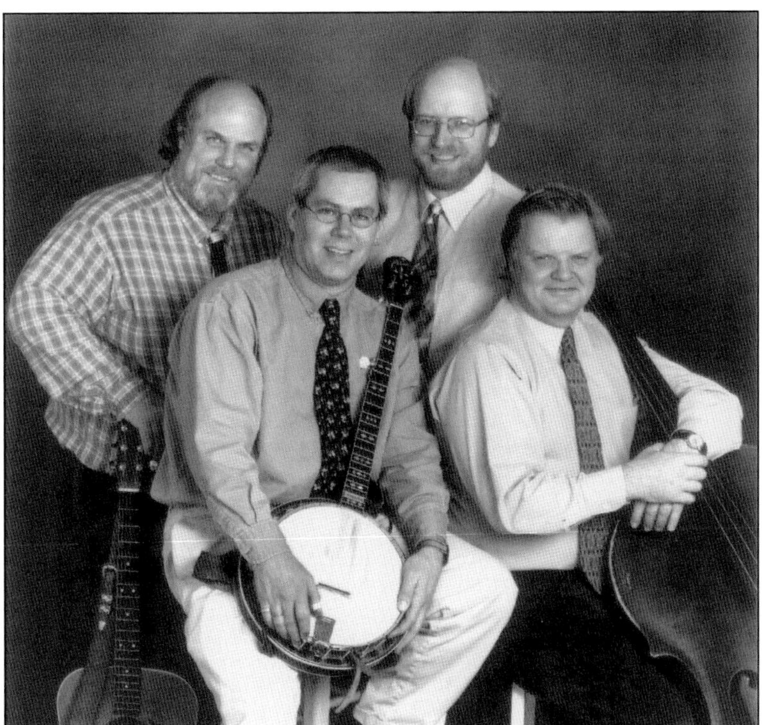

Minneapolis-based bluegrass band Middle Spunk Creek Boys was formed in 1968. They began playing at Dulano's in 1971 and have been regulars there ever since. In addition to the formal concert schedule, they also practiced at the restaurant several nights each month, which evolved into informal jam sessions with other bluegrass regulars. This photograph shows the band in 2002. (Middle Spunk Creek Boys; photograph by Cheryl Walsh Bellville.)

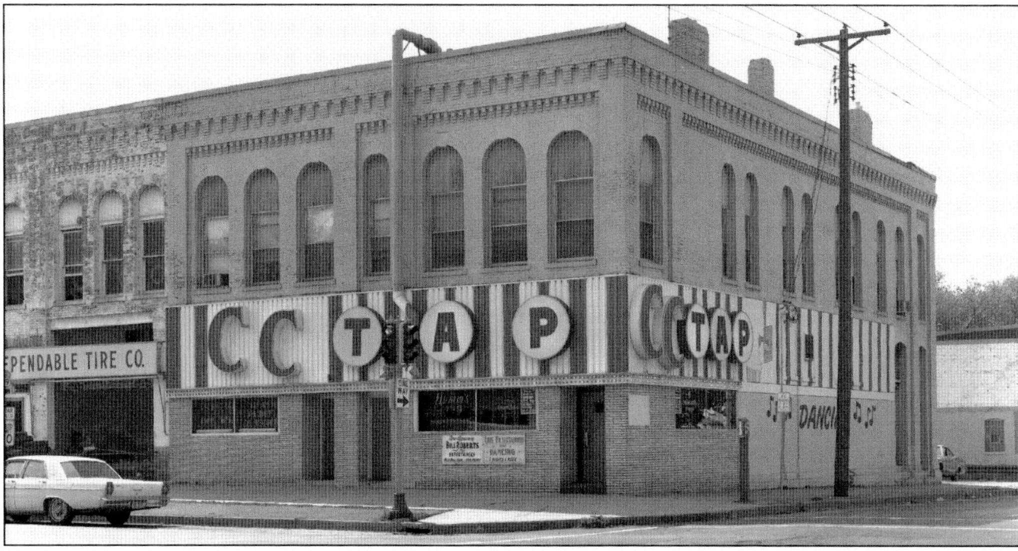

The CC Tap, now the CC Club, has stood on the corner of Twenty-sixth Street and Lyndale Avenue since 1934, when it first opened to serve thirsty Lyn-Lake residents eager to raise a glass to the end of Prohibition. It is shown here in 1967. Nearly two decades later, the bar was memorialized in The Replacements' song, "Here Comes a Regular." (Minnesota Historical Society; photograph by Norton and Peel.)

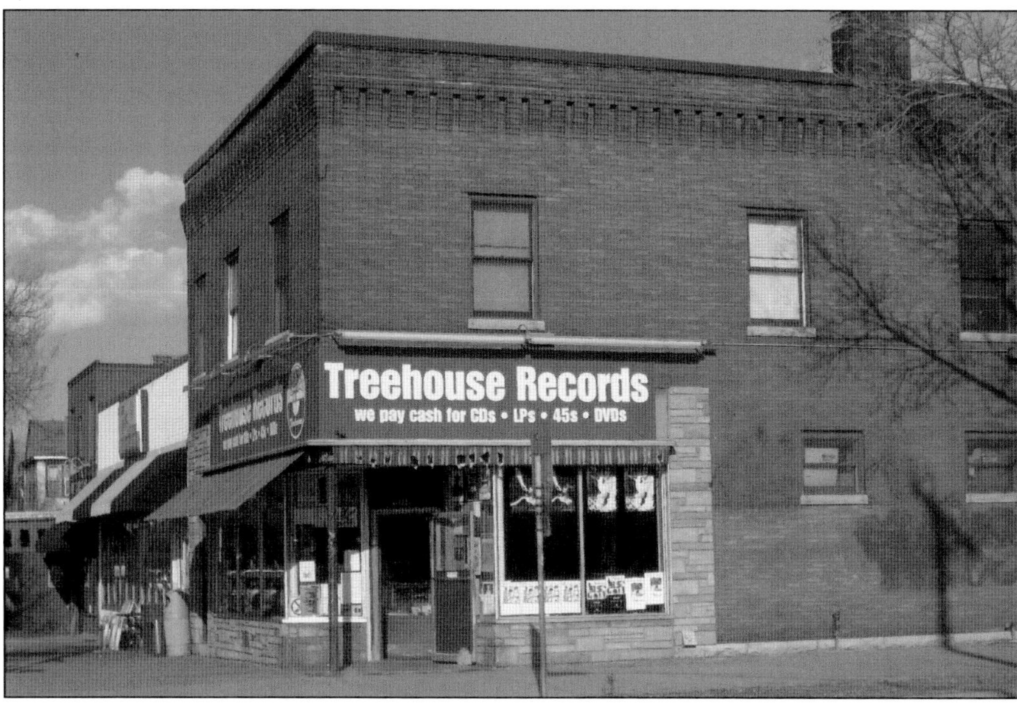

Minneapolis music aficionados will remember the iconic record store Oar Folkjokeopus at Lyndale Avenue and Twenty-sixth Street. During the 1980s, it was one of the centers of the Minneapolis punk rock scene; The Replacements, Hüsker Dü, and Soul Asylum were all regulars. Oar Folkjokeopus manager Mark Trehus bought the building and the business—but not the name—in 2001 and renamed it Treehouse Records. (Thatcher Imboden.)

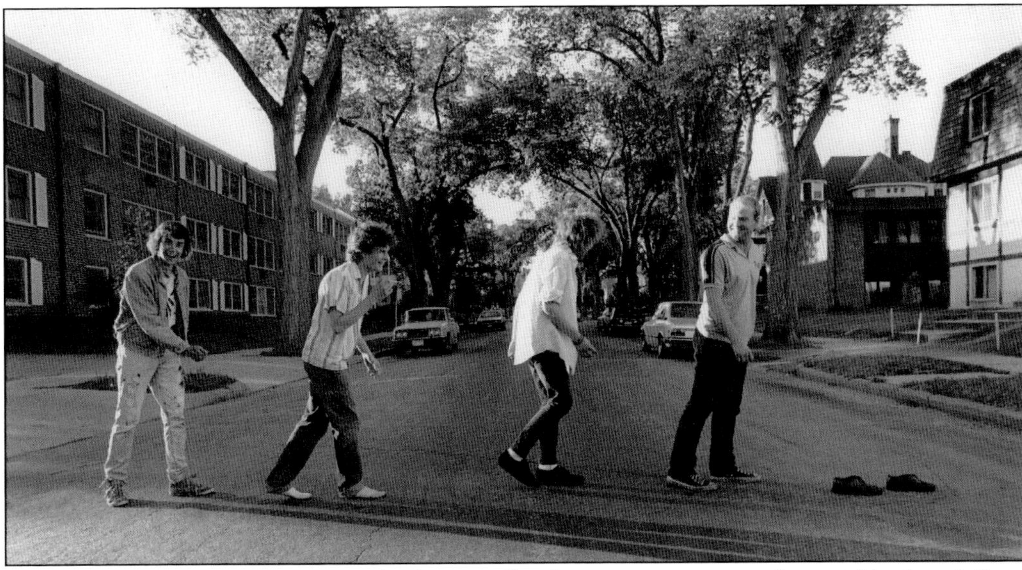

The Replacements, or "the Mats," had especially close connections to the neighborhood. Band members Tommy and Bob Stinson lived on the 2200 block of Bryant Avenue, and the band spent countless hours at the CC Club and Oar Folkjokeopus on Lyndale Avenue. Pictured are, from left to right, Chris Mars, Paul Westerberg, Tommy Stinson, and Bob Stinson on Bryant Avenue around 1983. (Hennepin History Museum; photograph by Greg Helgeson.)

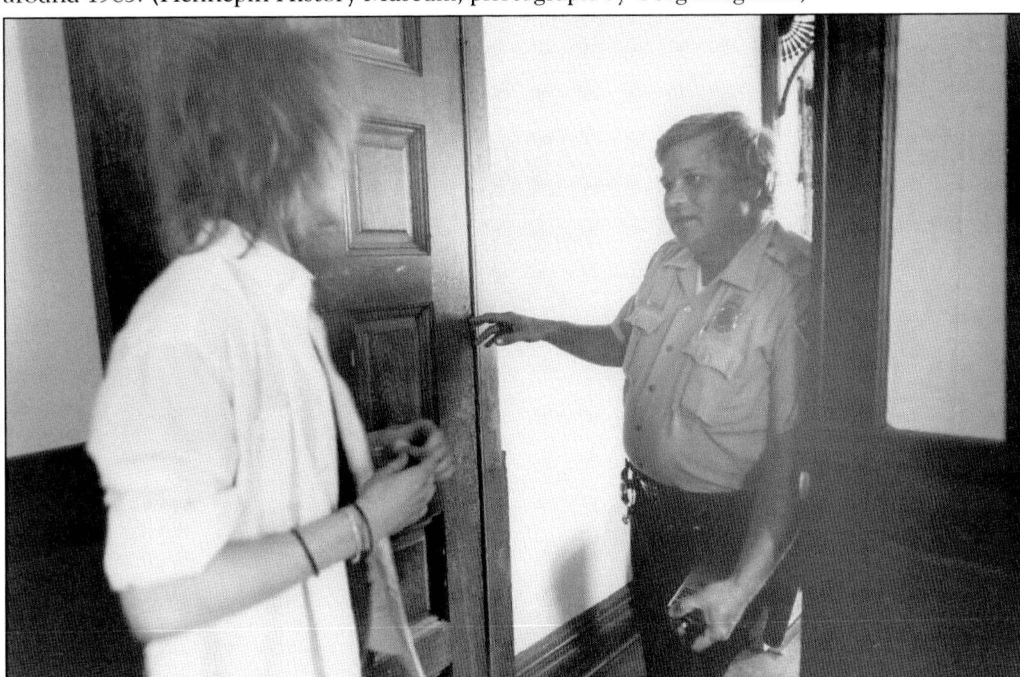

The Replacement's Tommy Stinson received an unexpected visit in 1983 from the police after a practice session at the Stinson's home on Bryant Avenue became too loud. Noisy practices had played a role in bringing the band together; Paul Westerberg first encountered Tommy and Bob Stinson and Chris Mars after walking past the Stinson home and hearing the music coming from within. (Hennepin History Museum; photograph by Greg Helgeson.)

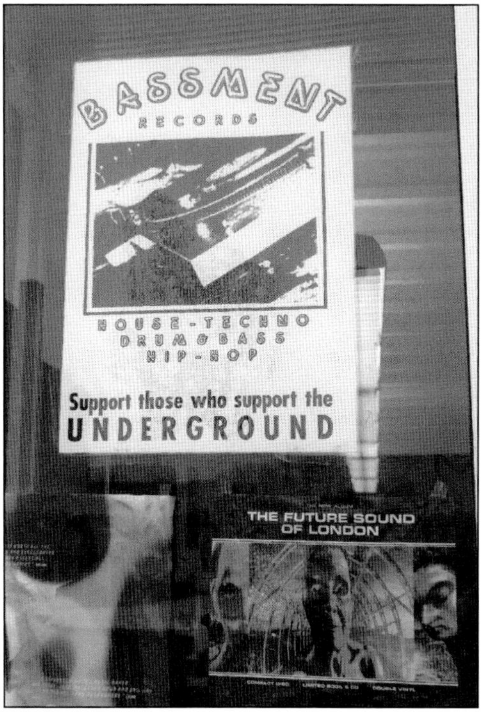

In 1996, David Drone opened up Bassment Records at 3017 Lyndale Avenue. It was the city's first all-vinyl record store and specialized in dance music. Drone, along with Bryan Gerrard, later created Celebrity Records in the shop. For more than six years, Drone manned the it by himself, but he eventually transitioned out of retail to focus more on his successful disc jockey career and the production side of things. (LNA.)

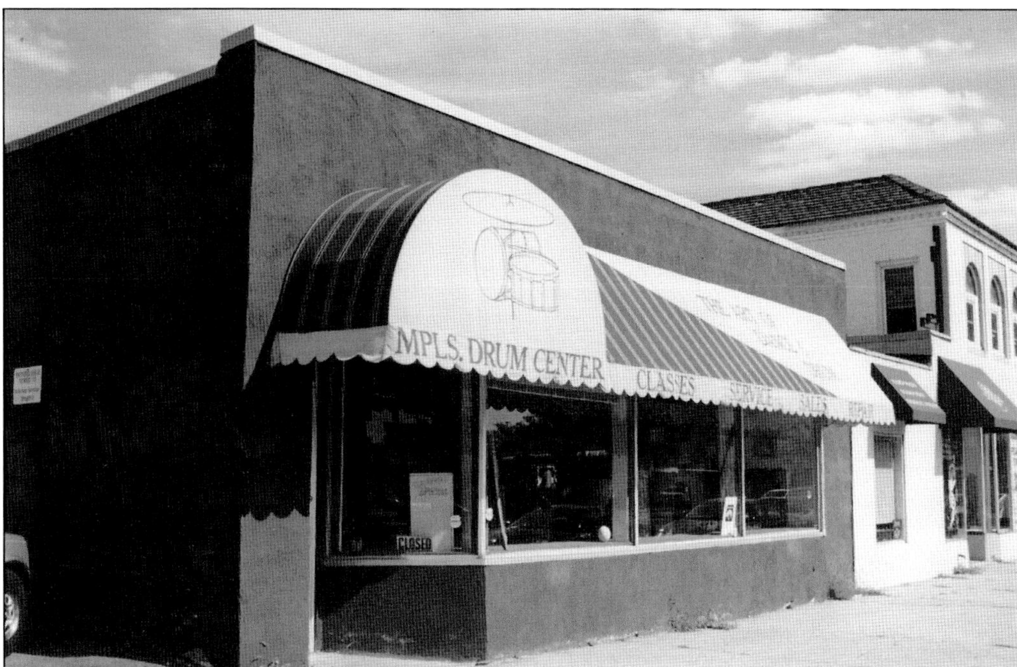

The Minneapolis DRUM Center moved into 3013 Lyndale Avenue in 1993. Founded by Andrea and Wallace Hill five years earlier, the center combined a storefront with classroom and performance space, all dedicated to African and African-inspired percussion and dance. They chose the location because it was an ethnic and cultural crossroads, as well as because Lyn-Lake was developing a reputation as being a good location for the arts. (LNA.)

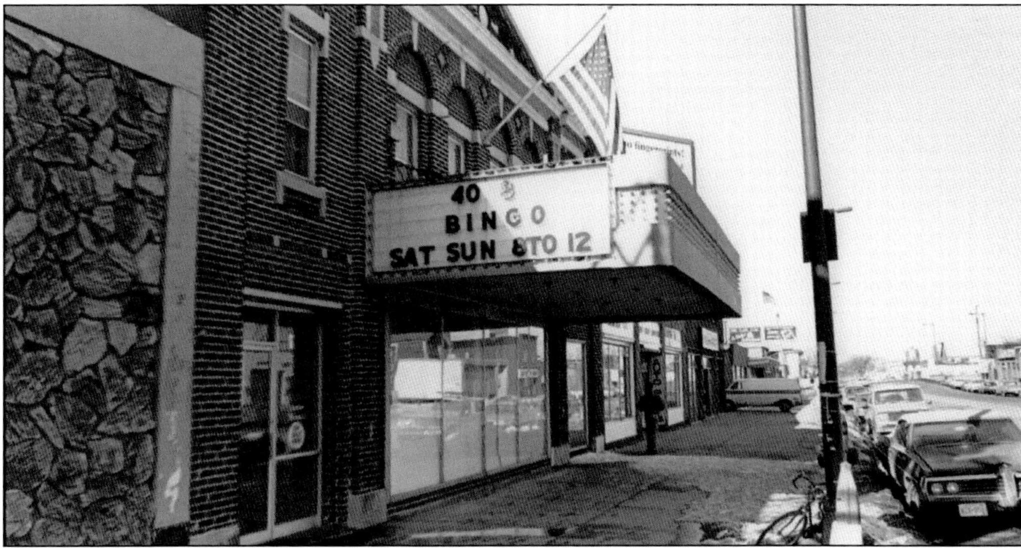

The New Lyndale Theater, at 2932 Lyndale Avenue, provided Lyn-Lakers with the latest films from 1915 to 1952. The 682-seat theater was "one of the most modern and completely equipped play houses in the Twin Cities," claimed the *Minneapolis Tribune* when it opened. By 1985, the year of this photograph, it was operating as a bingo parlor. (Hennepin County Library; photograph by Kurt Duerksen.)

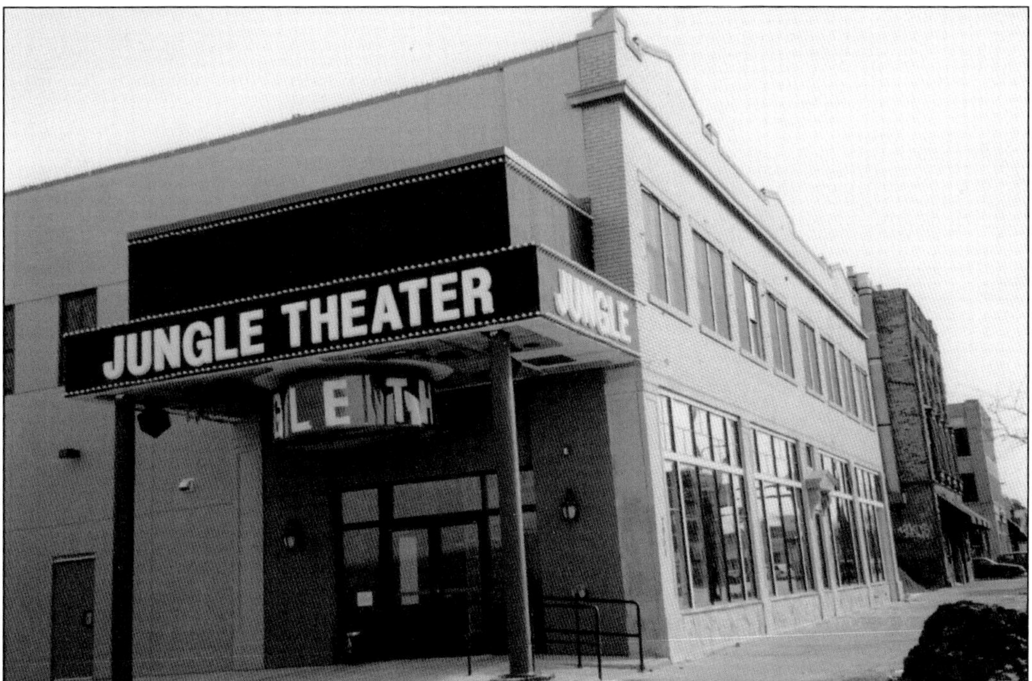

The Jungle Theater opened in Lyn-Lake in 1991. In 1999, it moved into this building, which became its permanent location. It is situated on the opposite quadrant of the Lyndale Avenue and Lake Street intersection from the previous storefront. The Jungle Theater, along with founder Bain Boehlke, has been credited with helping bring about Lyn-Lake's modern reputation as one of the city's centers for the arts. This photograph was taken in 1999. (LHENA.)

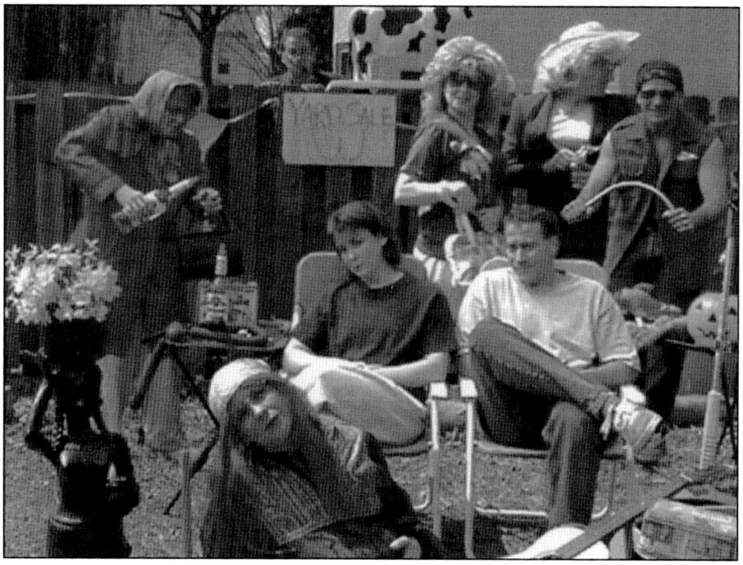

Bryant Lake Bowl's *Yard Sale 1999* proved to be so successful that it was followed up with a *Yard Sale 2000*, which is being promoted here. People were invited to bring in objects for the actors to incorporate into the play and to sit back, as the *Star Tribune* described, "In passive-aggressive bliss knowing it [the audience] helped create this work without ever having to get on stage." (LHENA.)

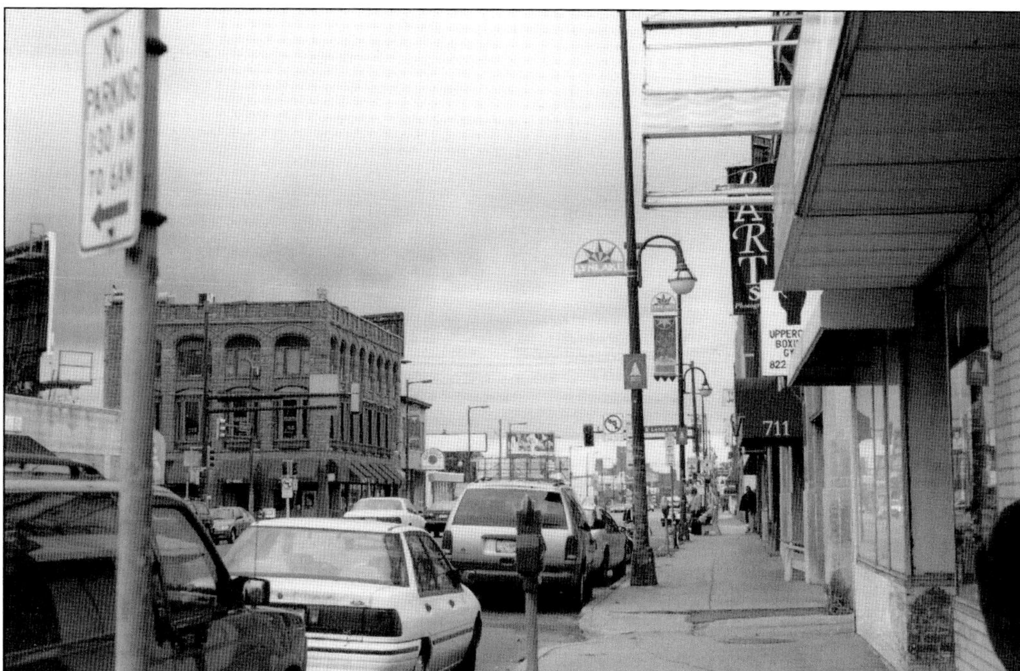

The local "arts pioneer" pARTs gallery, at 711 West Lake Street, is visible in this 1996 street scene. Artspace, an organization dedicated to providing affordable live-and-work space for working artists, had recently purchased the building and spent $1.1 million to renovate the 44,000 square feet. Artspace later sold the building, but Lyn-Lake remains a thriving center for artists and arts organizations. (LHENA.)

Intermedia Arts, at 2822 Lyndale Avenue, has frequently been at the center of neighborhood and city debates regarding graffiti art. The argument that takes place is whether or not graffiti should be considered as art. It has also been debated as to whether or not the organization's open spray-can art wall, shown here in 2002, was contributing to graffiti elsewhere in the Lyn-Lake area. A 1997 graffiti show at Intermedia Arts brought the issue to a boiling point, but the debate has raged for years. (LHENA.)

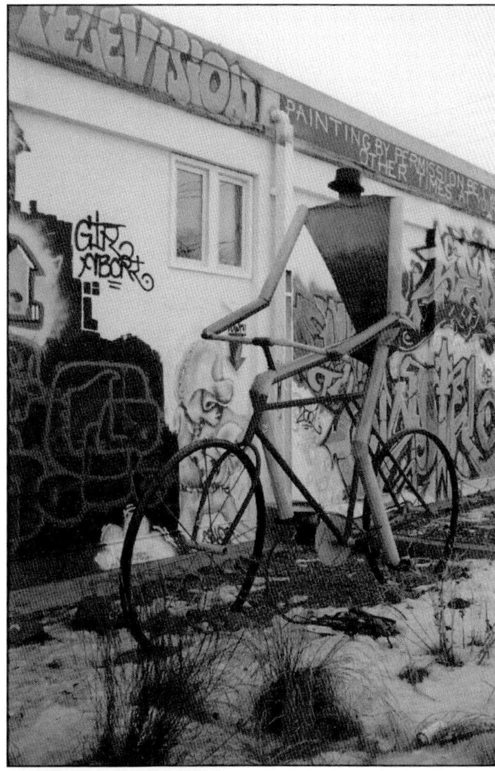

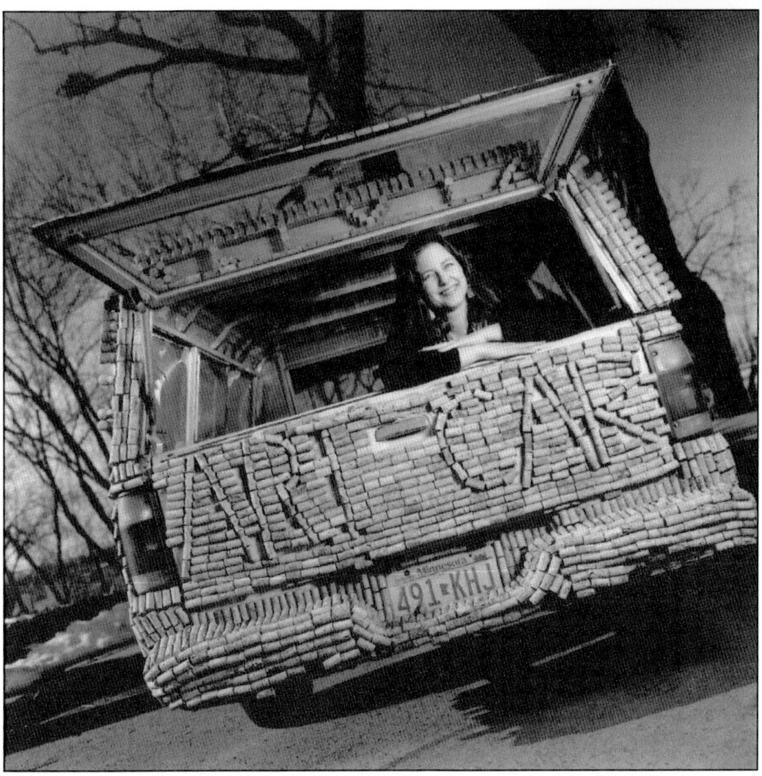

Intermedia Arts moved into the Bee-Line Automotive Building on Lyndale Avenue in 1994. It was fitting that the following summer it celebrated being in the new neighborhood and its converted garage space by sponsoring the first "Wheels as Art" exhibit, held during the annual Lyn-Lake Street Fair. Coordinator Jan Elftmann poses here with her cork-covered pickup truck. Art cars remain a common year-round sight in Lyn-Lake. (LHENA; photograph by Marc Norberg.)

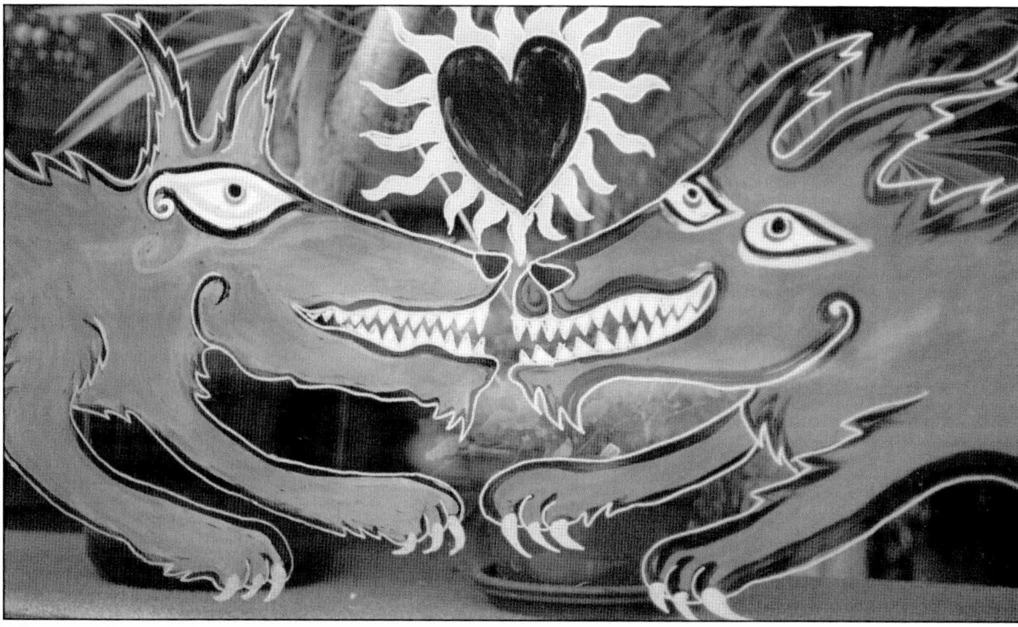

This window mural was photographed at the Luna-tik boutique, at 612 West Lake Street, in 1992 as part of the "Picturing Hennepin" exhibition for the Hennepin History Museum. "I photographed the lovesick dogs very cautiously and quietly," photographer Roger Sexter wrote in his artist statement. "They looked viscous and crazed. I feared they might notice me and attack without a provocation." (Hennepin History Museum; photograph by Roger Sexter.)

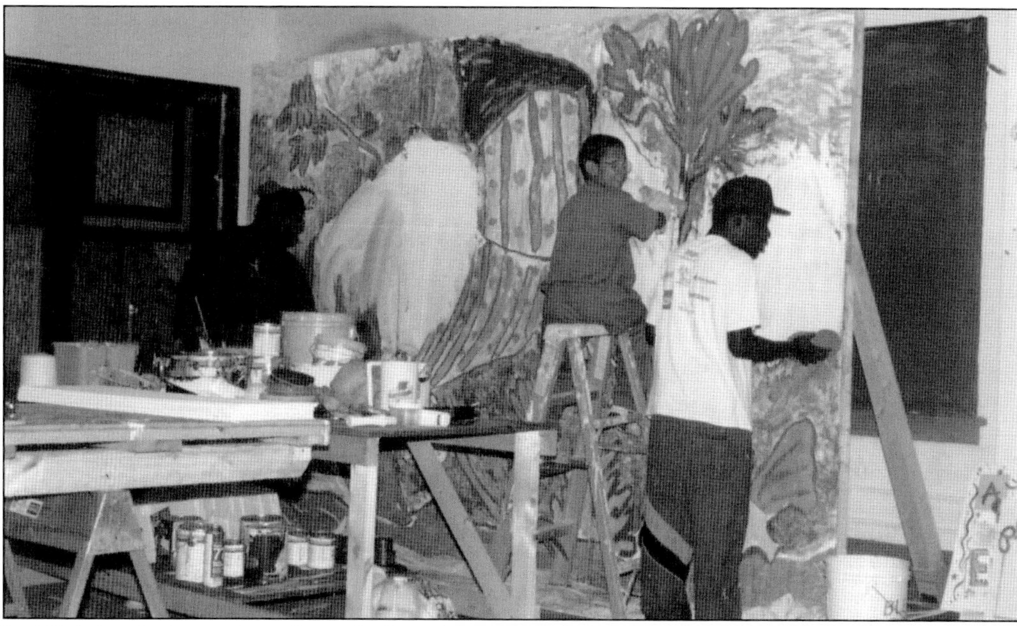

In 1995, Lyn-Lake residents Steve Lick and Leisa Luis led a movement to turn the Northern States Power substation on Garfield Avenue and Thirty-third Street into a giant aquarium. Neighborhood residents painted giant fish scenes on 10-foot-tall masonite panels that were ultimately fastened on the filled-in windows of the hulking substation. These artists, who were participants in the local Summer Youth Employment Program, helped create the underwater fantasy. (LNA.)

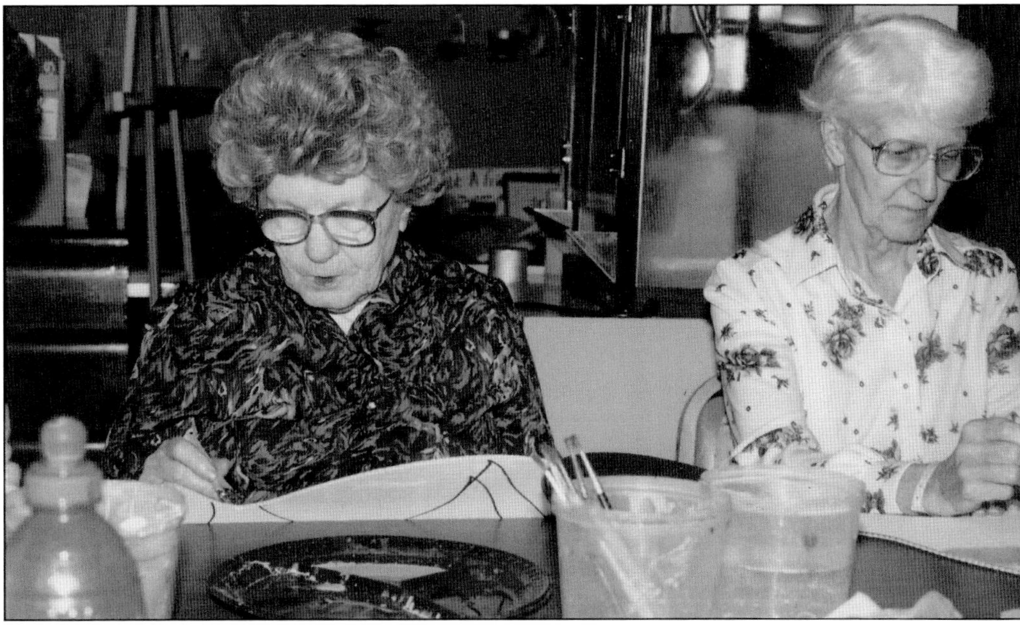

The creation of the Garfield Avenue substation mural was truly a community endeavor, with people of all ages and backgrounds participating in its design and execution. The concept of a large community-created mural was a perfect fit for the Lyndale neighborhood, which claims to be home to one of the highest number of artists in the nation. These women were residents of Redeemer Residence on Lyndale Avenue and Thirty-first Street. (LNA.)

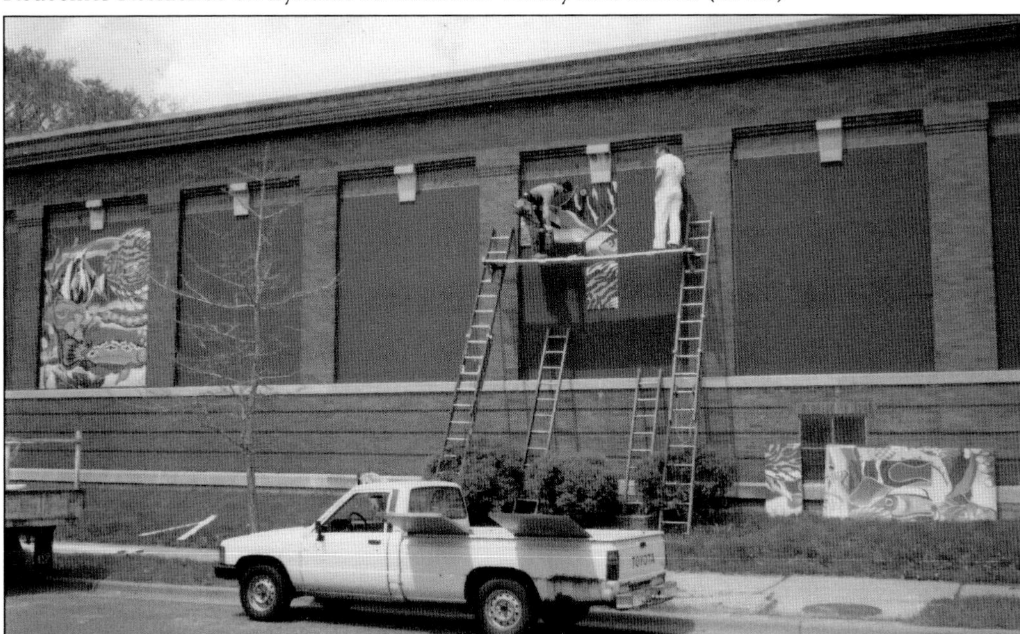

The volunteers here install 1 of 10 painted masonite panels onto the exterior of the Garfield Avenue NSP substation (now the Garfield Aquarium) in May 1996. Each panel is 10 feet tall and 8 feet wide and is painted with exterior latex gloss enamel. The community mural has spurred a new local tradition: the annual Fish Fest. (LNA.)

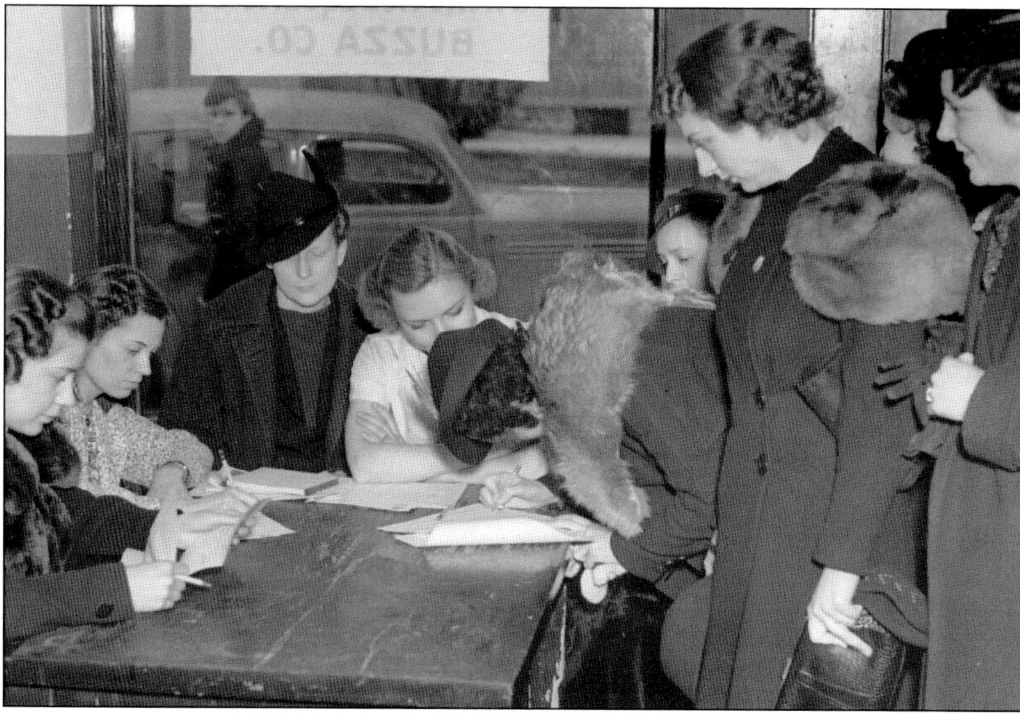

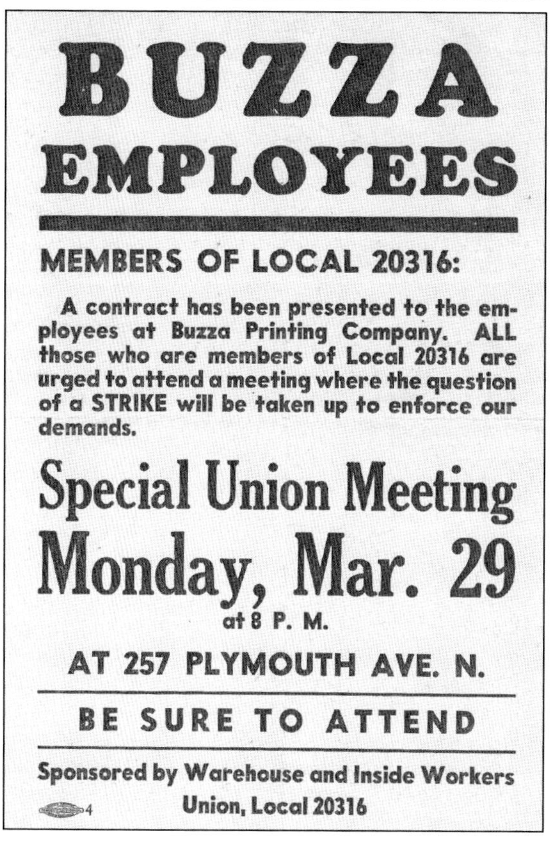

BUZZA EMPLOYEES

MEMBERS OF LOCAL 20316:

A contract has been presented to the employees at Buzza Printing Company. ALL those who are members of Local 20316 are urged to attend a meeting where the question of a STRIKE will be taken up to enforce our demands.

Special Union Meeting
Monday, Mar. 29
at 8 P. M.

AT 257 PLYMOUTH AVE. N.

BE SURE TO ATTEND

Sponsored by Warehouse and Inside Workers Union, Local 20316

Lyn-Lake's role as a haven for artists, both working and amateur, is not just a recent phenomenon. The Buzza Greeting Card Company, once the second-largest card company in the United States, was headquartered at 1006 West Lake Street, with all of its commercial art activities contained within its "Craftacres" campus. In 1937, disgruntled Buzza employees, shown here, went on strike to protest wages and demanded union recognition. (Hennepin County Library.)

Unlike many people working in arts-related jobs, the employees of the Buzza Card Company were eligible for union membership. Relations between employees and management were generally good, but a one-week strike kept nearly 400 employees away from work in 1937. Following successful negotiations, the Buzza staff gathered at the corner of Dupont Avenue and Lake Street and returned to work as a group. (Hennepin County Library.)

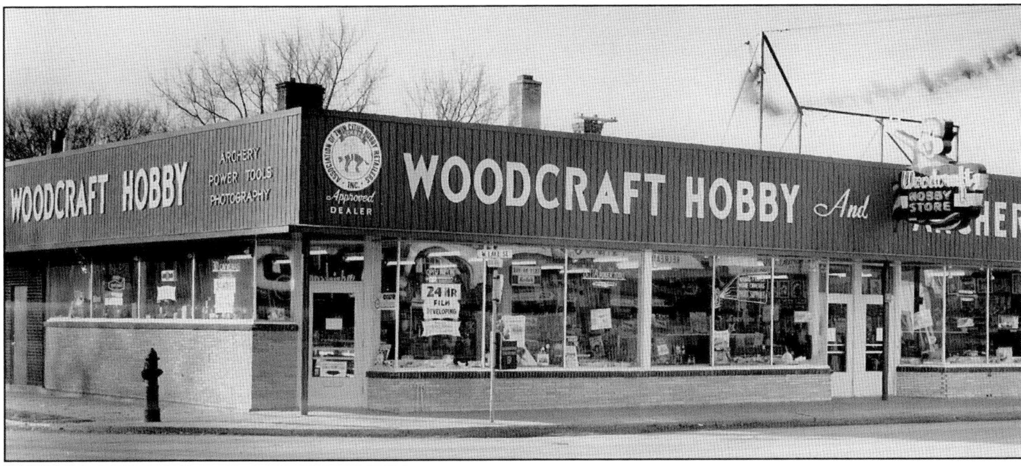

Claude Newman and his partner opened Woodcraft Hobby and Sport in the late 1930s at 903–905 West Lake Street, next to Doyle's Chicken Shack. The business sold wood products that it made, including shower shoes, children's furniture sets, miniature 60-foot bowling alleys and pins, and archery equipment. Woodcraft expanded into the entire building after Doyle's had a fire. (Paul Newman.)

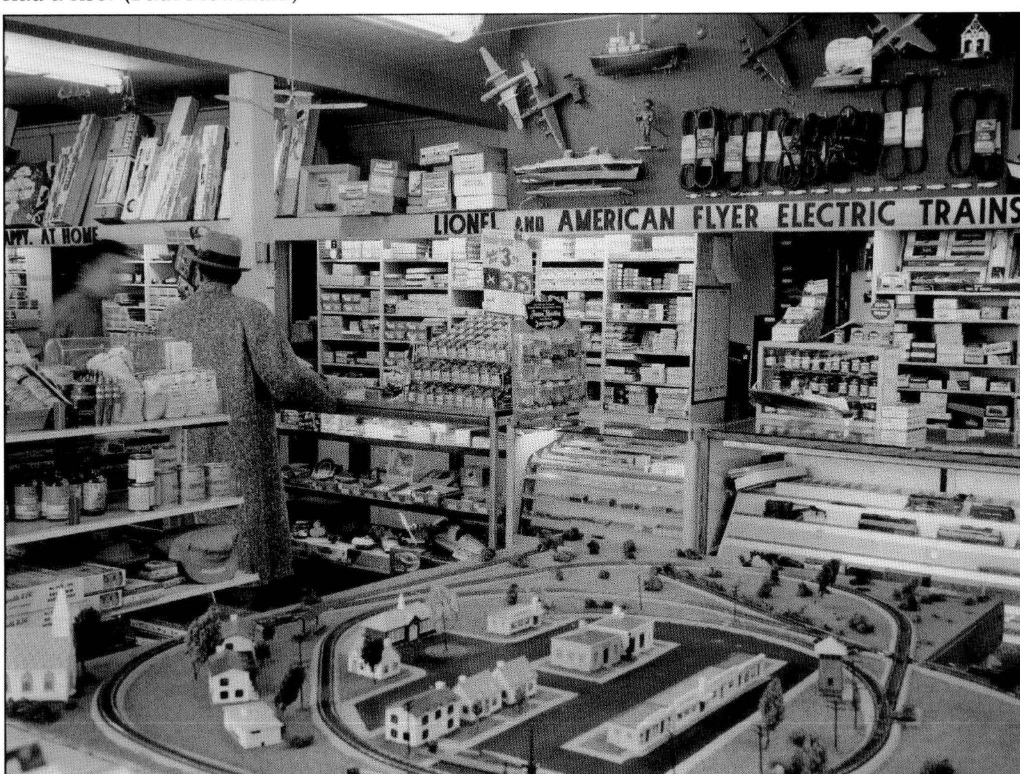

They selected the Bryant-Lake intersection for the Woodcraft store because of its prominent location near multiple streetcar lines, as Woodcraft was a destination and customers came in from as far away as Wayzata. After World War II, more materials were available, and Woodcraft began selling more hobby supplies and products. Newman and his partner split, with the partner opening a gun shop across the street. (Paul Newman.)

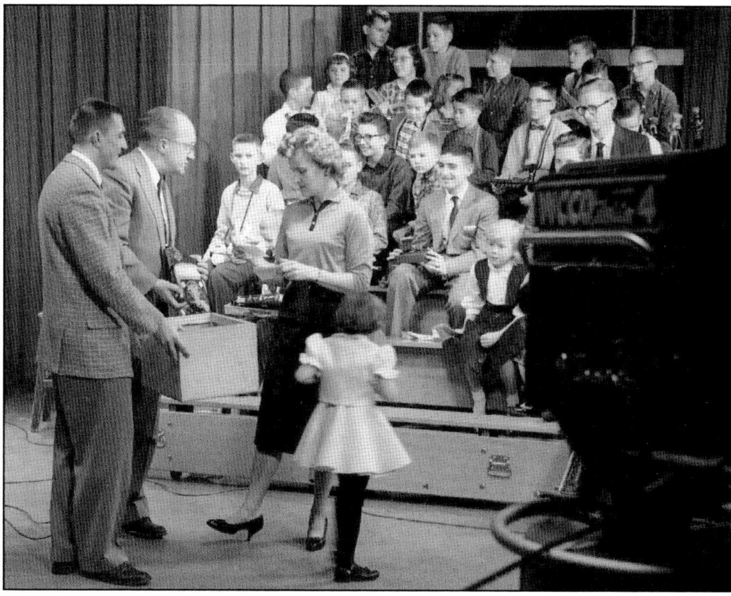

Many remember Claude Newman's Saturday television program *The Woodcraft Hobby Show*, which aired on WCCO and KARE for nearly 30 years. Newman was invited to do the show following an interview he gave at a Woodcraft-sponsored Minneapolis Aquatennial archery event. For much of the show's history, it was paired with *The World of Aviation* program. (Paul Newman.)

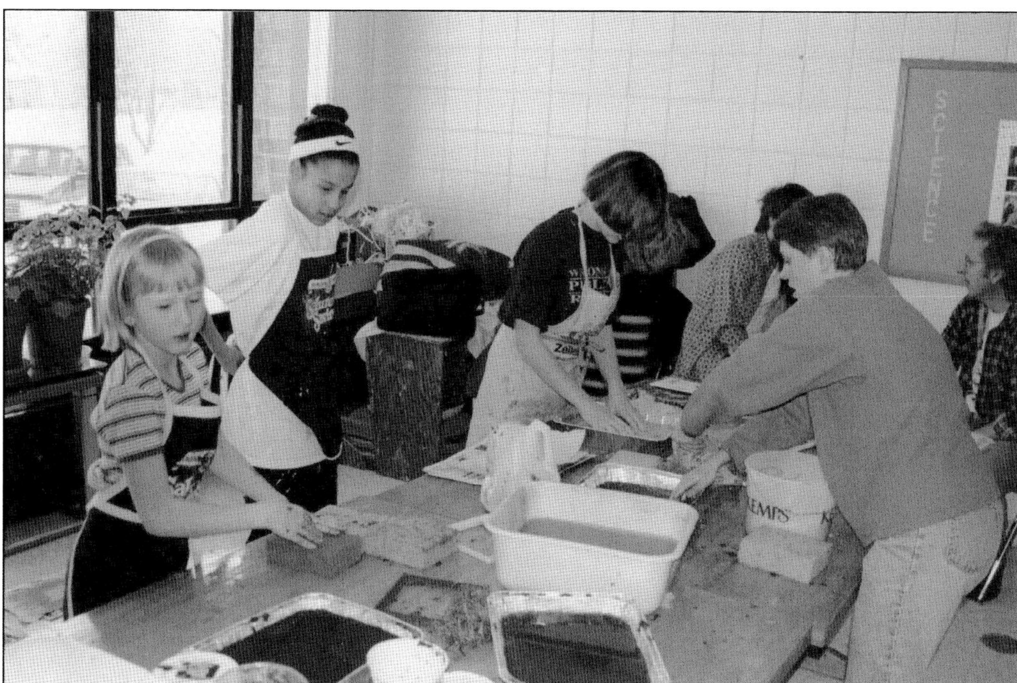

The Lyn-Lake art scene was not just for professional artists or even adults; programs in the neighborhood's multiple parks and other gathering places have long endeavored to make artistic expression and experiences available to neighborhood residents of all ages and backgrounds. These children are seen taking advantage of an art class held at Painter Park in the spring of 1997. (LNA.)

Six

HOME

Everyone knows the following old cliché: home is where the heart is. In the case of Lyn-Lake, it is the homes, and especially the great variety of homes, that give it much of its soul. Unlike neighborhoods where all the houses are from the same time period, of the same style, and for people of the same socioeconomic status, Lyn-Lake's housing varies widely.

Historically there were different types of residents within the neighborhood that included people ranging from executives to scullery maids, from teachers to blacksmiths, and from salesmen to artists, which meant there was a wide variety of housing types. There are both modest and deluxe single-family homes, duplexes, large sprawling apartment homes, and modern lofts—Lyn-Lake has it all.

The homes along the former 29th Street railroad trench once offered some of the most affordable housing options in the neighborhood. To live next to heavy industry wasn't desirable for those who could afford to live a few blocks away from the dirtiest industrial areas, but it was both affordable and convenient for many. In more recent years, the housing adjacent to the former railroad trench, now named the "Midtown Greenway," has transformed from industrial thoroughfare to landscaped bicycle and walking path. This conversion has made the area the most desirable, or at least the trendiest, housing in the neighborhood. New apartment buildings have sprung up on the sites of abandoned industrial sites. Meanwhile, neighborhood organizations have actively promoted home ownership and financially assist with the rehabilitation of its aging housing stock.

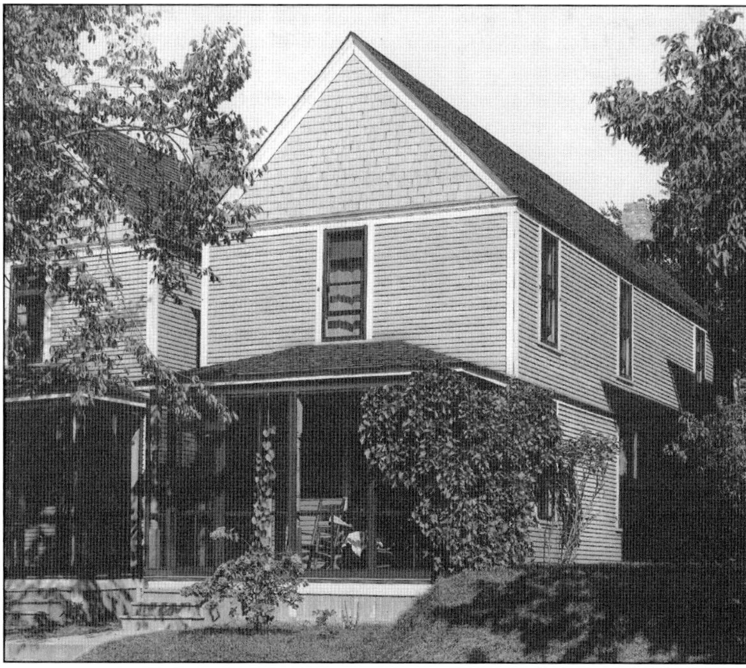

In December 1897, the newspaper printed that Frank Barrons was building two matching homes, at 2621 and 2623 Aldrich Avenue, each at a cost of $1,250. Over the years, these houses, each with 1,280 square feet of living space, provided affordable options for the many people who worked in the neighborhood, as well as for those who commuted to jobs downtown. (Hennepin History Museum; photograph by A. D. Roth.)

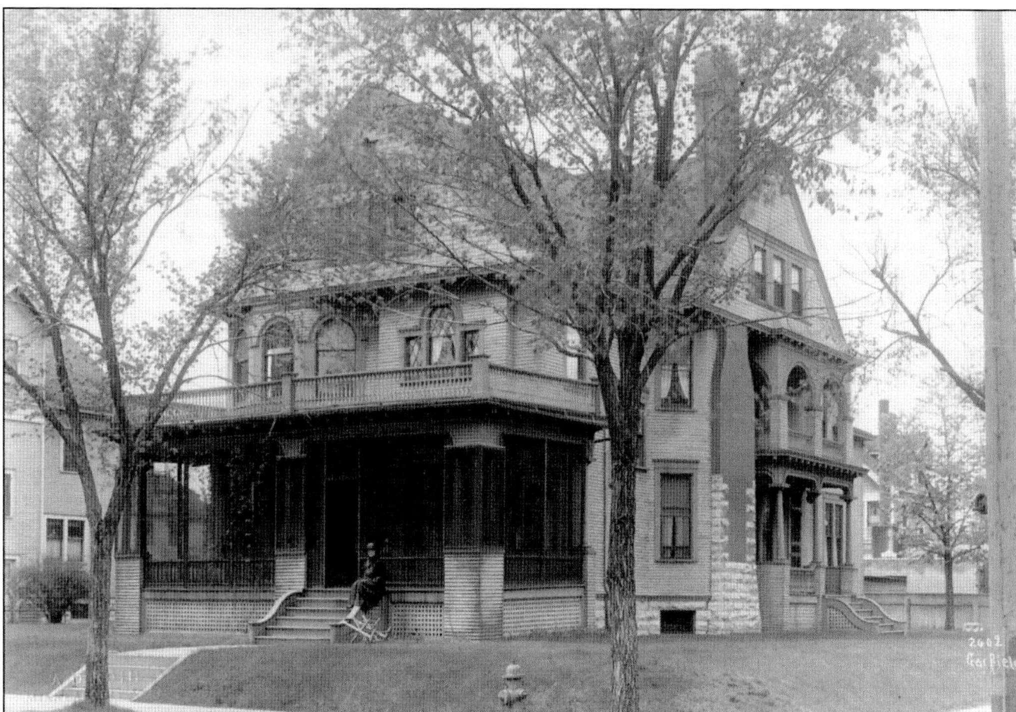

This duplex at 2602 Garfield Avenue is representative of the upscale late-19th-century homes built in the northern portion of the neighborhood for the city's middle-to-upper-class residents. This home was presumably one of many victims in the 1970s rush to build sprawling apartment buildings. The structure standing on the corner today was built in 1973. (Hennepin History Museum; photograph by A. D. Roth.)

June and early July in 1910 were hot and dusty months, and it was a welcome relief when rain finally came on July 10. The area around the intersection of Lyndale Avenue and Thirty-third Street (shown here) experienced some minor flooding, but it was presumably due to a drainage problem and not to excessive rain; the total rainfall in Minneapolis remained a measly .03 inches. (Hennepin History Museum.)

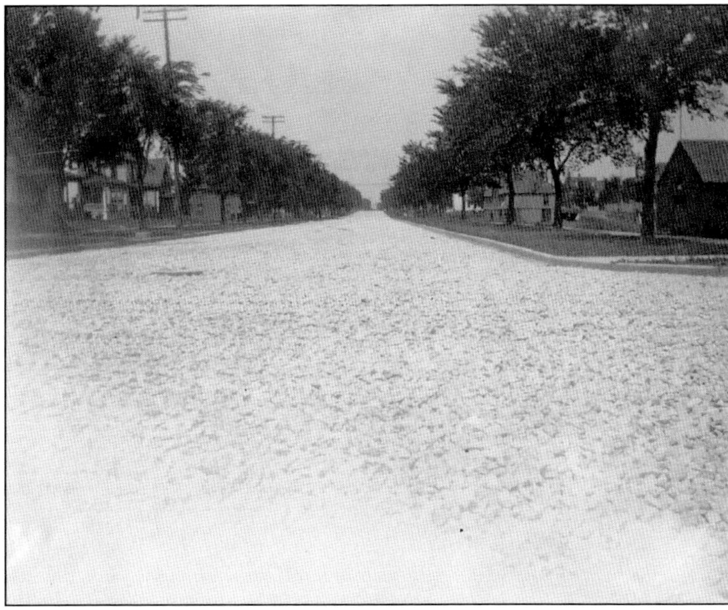

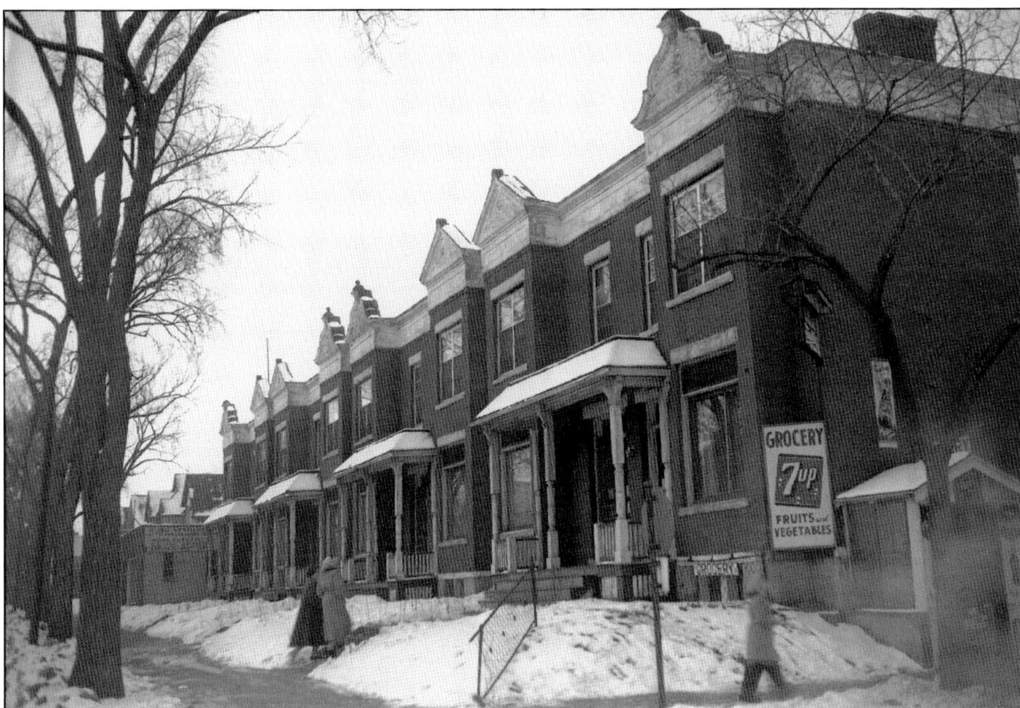

These row houses at 2500–2514 Lyndale Avenue were photographed on a snowy day in 1952. For much of the 20th century, small markets and other specialized shops dotted the neighborhood, ensuring that no resident was more than a short walk from being able to buy the basics for dinner. The residents of these homes were able to do some of their shopping at the basement grocery store located on the corner. The buildings—and the small attached exterior entranceway shed—still stand, although the store space is no longer used for commercial purposes. (Minnesota Historical Society.)

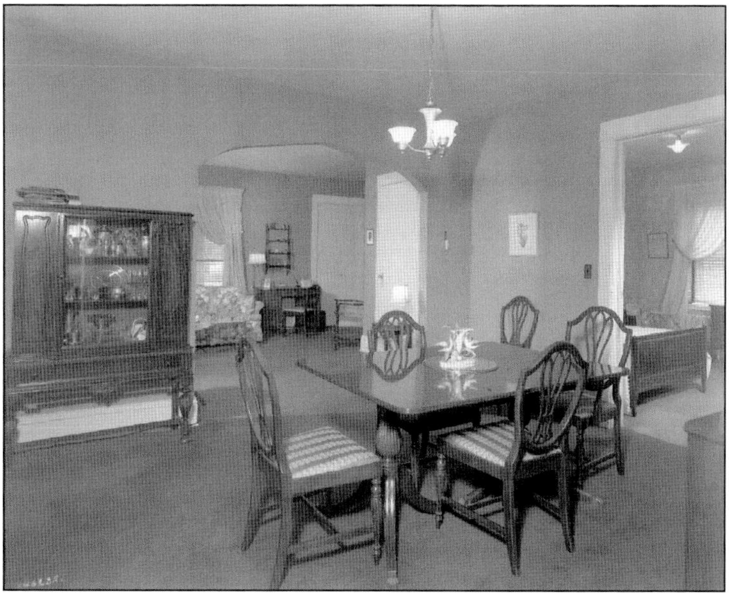

Local photographer J. H. Kammerdiener took this 1926 interior photograph for the Confer Realty Company. The house, at 2511 Garfield Avenue, was the former home of furrier W. Claude Stevenson and his wife, Olivia. By the 1930s, the Stevensons had sold the home (perhaps with this Confer listing) and migrated south to 4224 Garfield. (Hennepin History Museum; photograph by J. H. Kammerdiener.)

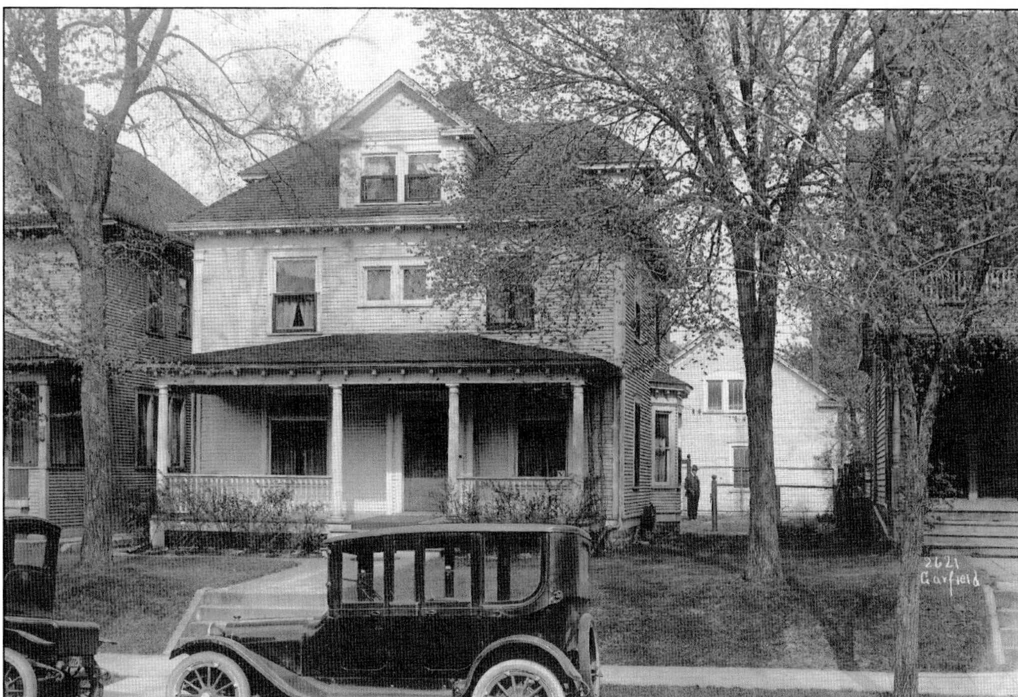

The dwelling at 2621 Garfield Avenue was for many years the home of Ingwer and Elizabeth Bruer of the Bruer Brothers Lumber Company. By the early 1930s, their son Franz, at that point vice president of the firm, was married and living in his own house at 4916 Aldrich Avenue, Ingwer was deceased, and Elizabeth had moved into a smaller apartment. The migration of families southward in the city was a common pattern. (Hennepin History Museum.)

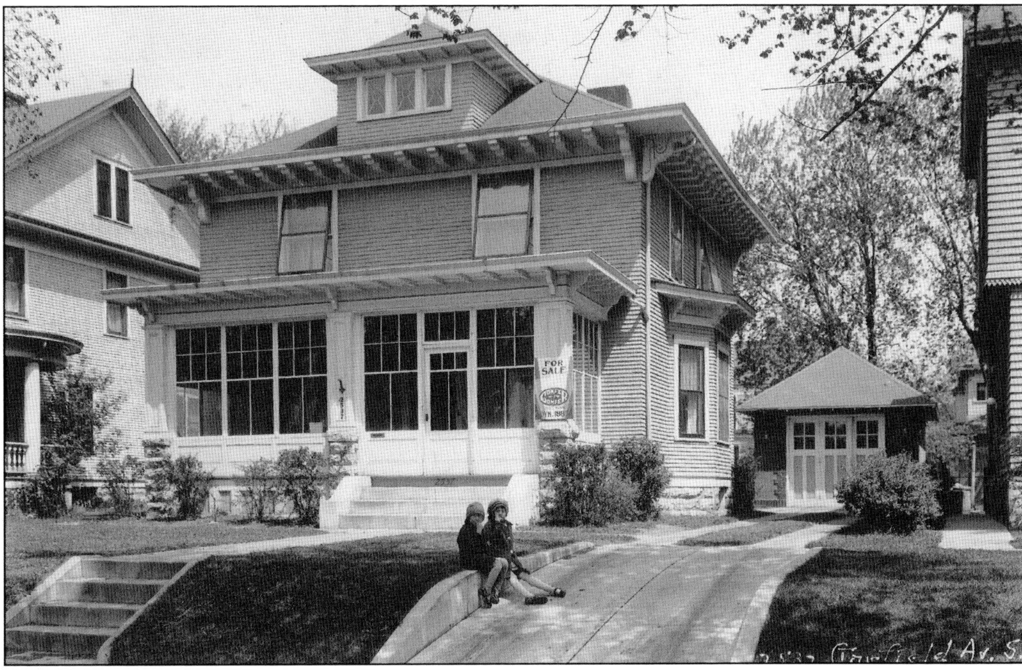

Two neighborhood children, bundled up for a slightly chilly May day in 1929, pose outside the 2537 Garfield Avenue home of Clarence Gunn, secretary of the Minneapolis Builders' Exchange; his wife, Hermine; and their adult daughter Gertrude. Note the open windows of the house; although seldom seen in Lyn-Lake in modern times, these awning windows were once seen frequently in both local houses and apartment buildings. (Hennepin History Museum.)

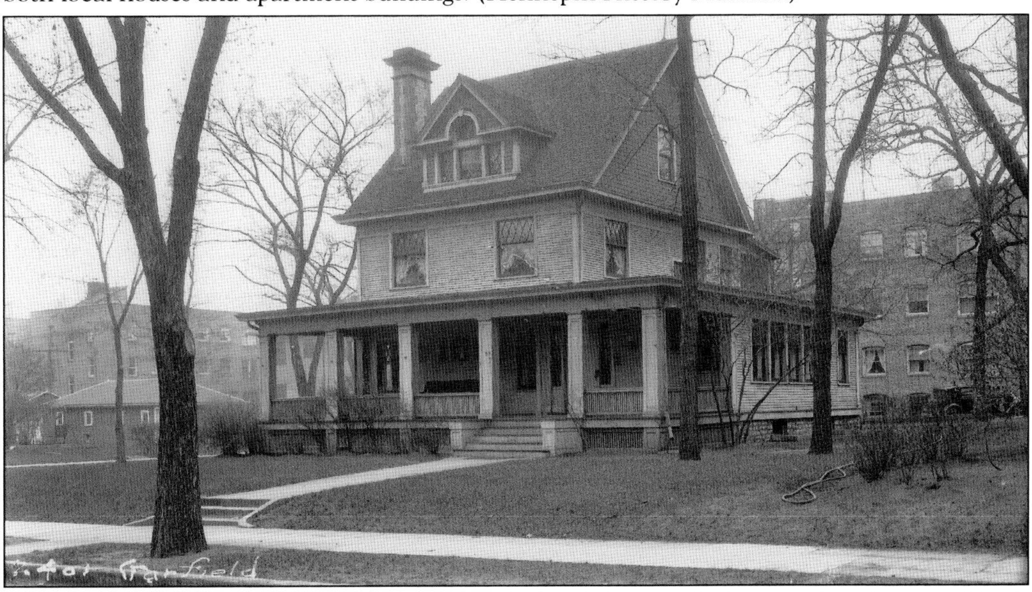

The Lyn-Lake area had a mixture of grand single-family homes, duplexes and triplexes, and both small and large apartment buildings. Over the course of the 20th century, the largest single-family homes were often subdivided into multiple units or, in some cases, demolished for new developments. During the 1920s, securities grain dealer Arthur McIntyre lived in this house at 2401 Garfield Avenue with his wife, Mary. (Hennepin History Museum.)

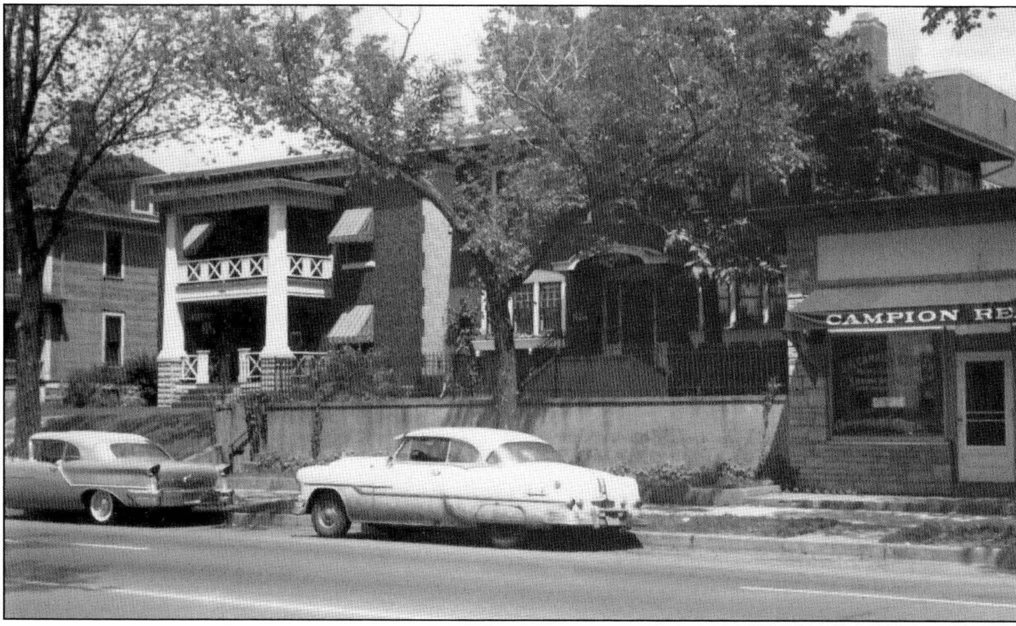

This 1960 street view of the east side of the 2600 block of Lyndale Avenue looks remarkably similar today and features the mix of small-scale retail, apartment buildings, and houses that are typical of the street. Many local residents purchased or sold their homes through the realty company on the far right. James P. Campion invited would-be sellers by saying, "Let Campion be your champion in quick sales." (City of Minneapolis.)

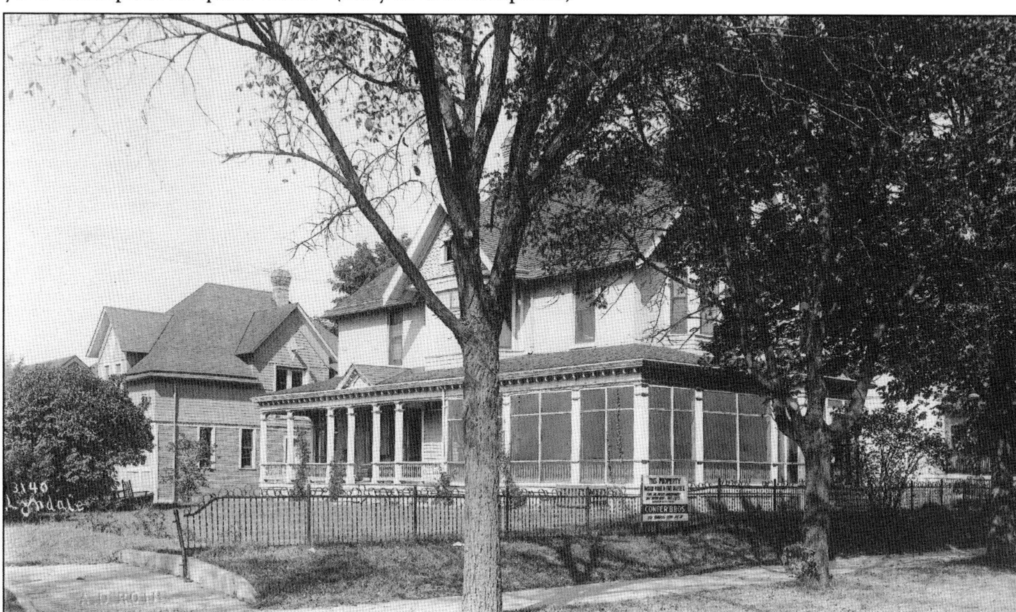

The longtime home of the socially active Gerber family was at 3140 Lyndale Avenue. The house was the site of many parties and events, most notably the Gerber's 15th wedding anniversary celebration, which included 150 of the couple's closest friends. Color-themed décor and refreshments, live orchestra music in the front hall, and plentiful amounts of ices, frappes, and other hot-weather treats delighted guests. (Hennepin History Museum; photograph by A. D. Roth.)

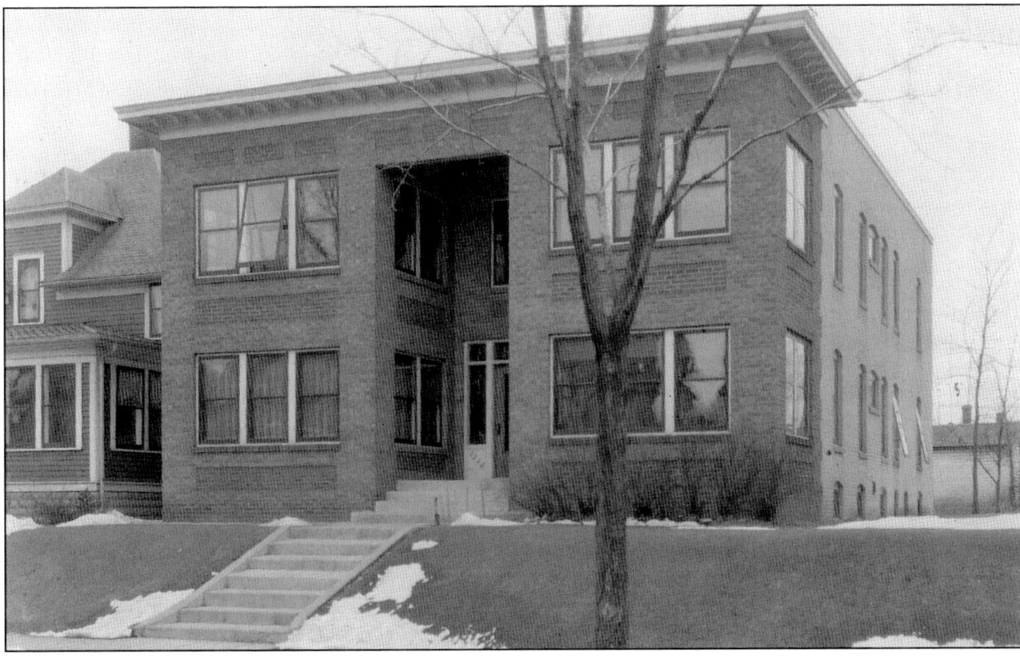

Small apartment buildings like this one at 3222 Aldrich Avenue are staples of the Lyn-Lake area. Confer Realty listed this building for sale for $6,850 in the mid- to late 1920s. Fred and Eva Streeter lived in one of the units, and their neighbors included the widowed Lillian Stevens and Acme Metal Company spinner Henry Dahl. (Hennepin History Museum.)

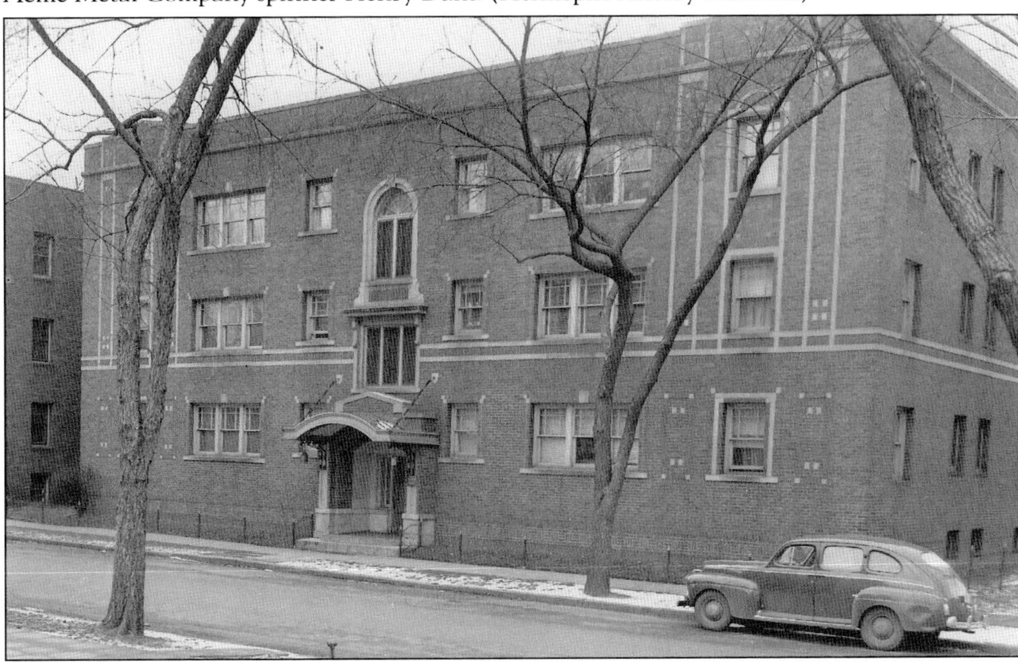

The three-story Coolidge Hall apartment, located at 2216 Garfield Avenue, contained 26 units. A look at some of the residents living there in 1946 shows a cross-section of the city. The building was home to a blend of young singles, couples, and retiree residents with jobs that included a private secretary, several salesmen, and a teacher at nearby Jefferson School. (City of Minneapolis.)

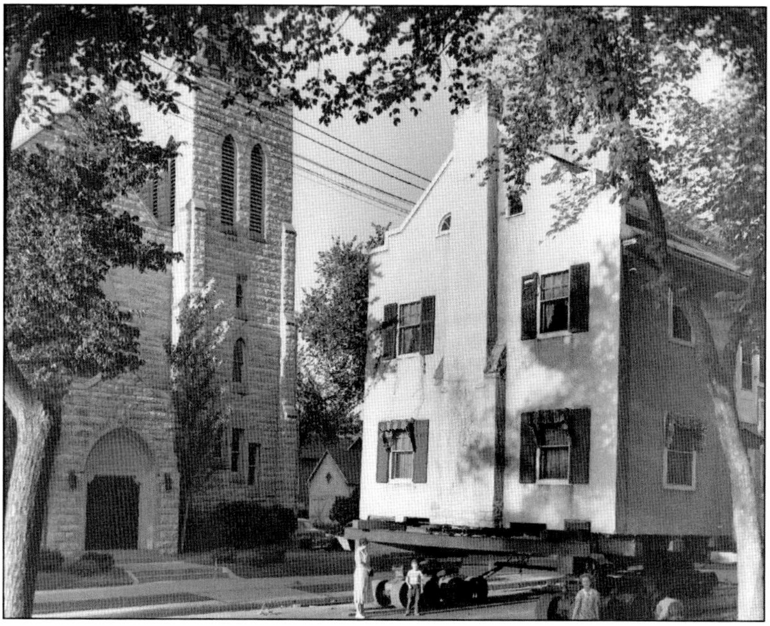

Most of the local churches all provided homes for their ministers, sometimes directly adjacent to the church itself but more typically several blocks away. In 1951, Salem English Lutheran placed its 1928 parsonage on a truck and relocated it to 2741 Pleasant Avenue. The movement of homes within the neighborhood was once far more common than it is now. (SELC.)

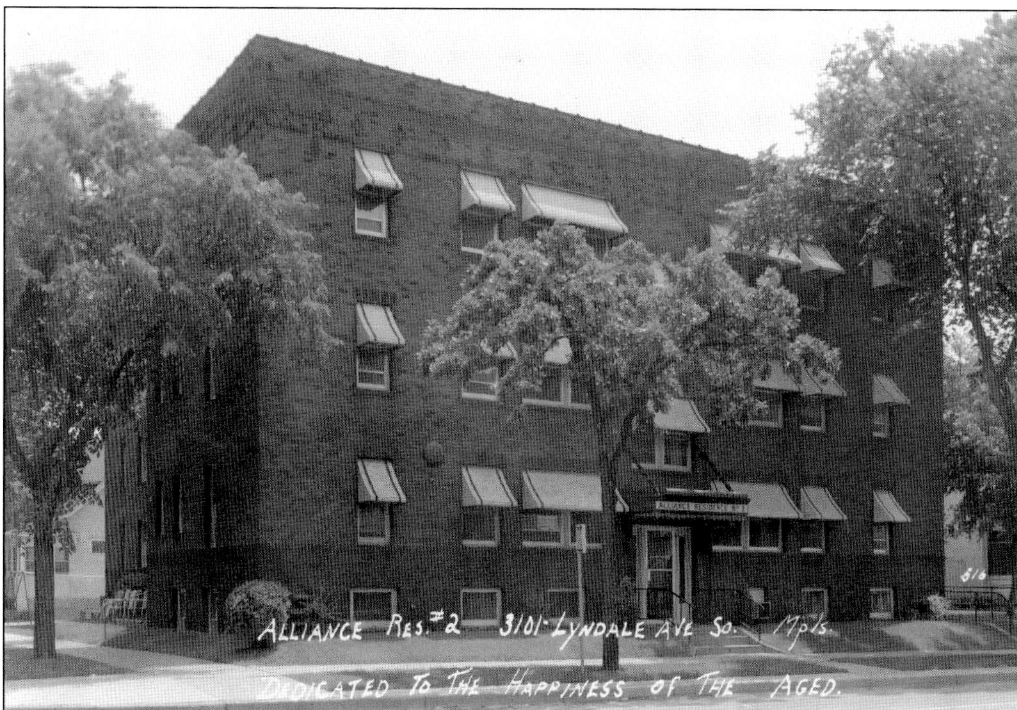

This is 3101 Lyndale Avenue, which has a history that encompasses both the oldest and the youngest members of society. The building was constructed in 1921 as "Fairyland," an apartment that catered exclusively to tenants with children. Amenities included a staffed basement playroom, an on-call nanny, and a well-stocked playground. In 1951, Alliance Church purchased it for use as a home for the aged. (Minnesota Historical Society.)

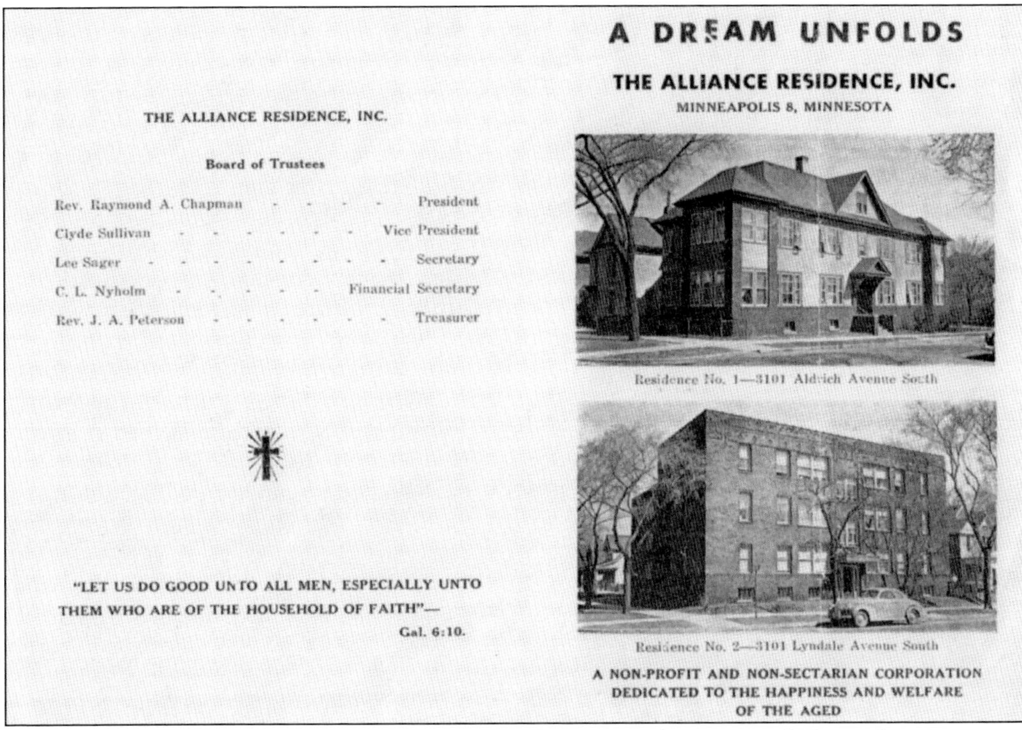

THE ALLIANCE RESIDENCE, INC.

Board of Trustees

Rev. Raymond A. Chapman	President
Clyde Sullivan	Vice President
Lee Sager	Secretary
C. L. Nyholm	Financial Secretary
Rev. J. A. Peterson	Treasurer

"LET US DO GOOD UNTO ALL MEN, ESPECIALLY UNTO THEM WHO ARE OF THE HOUSEHOLD OF FAITH"—
Gal. 6:10.

A DREAM UNFOLDS

THE ALLIANCE RESIDENCE, INC.

MINNEAPOLIS 8, MINNESOTA

Residence No. 1—3101 Aldrich Avenue South

Residence No. 2—3101 Lyndale Avenue South

A NON-PROFIT AND NON-SECTARIAN CORPORATION DEDICATED TO THE HAPPINESS AND WELFARE OF THE AGED

The first Alliance residence was located one block away on the corner of Thirty-first Street and Aldrich Avenue. In 1946, Raymond Chapman, minister of the nearby Grand Avenue Alliance Church, purchased a building at Thirty-first and Aldrich as a home for the elderly women in his congregation. The demand was so great that it was soon filled to capacity, and a second home was purchased in 1951. (Redeemer Residence.)

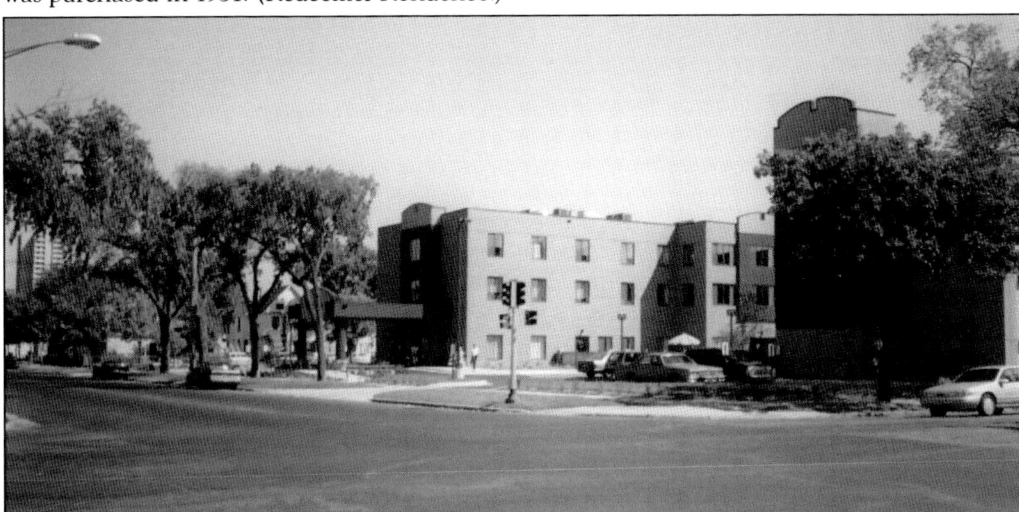

The Redeemer Residence at Thirty-first Street and Lyndale Avenue continued to be expanded during the 1960s and 1970s. By 1995, it had outgrown the expanded space and decided to embark on another addition. This photograph was taken in the mid-1990s and shows the new building with its entrance on Thirty-first Street. Today Redeemer Residence also offers rehabilitative care. It is now affiliated with Elim Care Incorporated and the Evangelical Free Church. (LNA.)

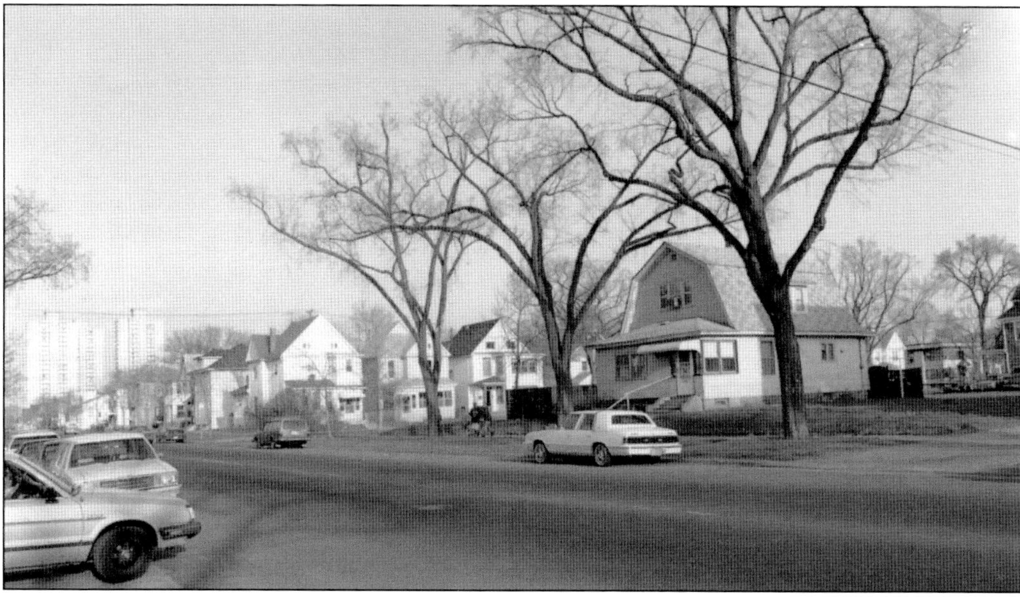

This photograph, taken in the mid-1990s, looks east along Thirty-first Street from Lyndale Avenue. During the 1990s, the Lyndale Neighborhood joined forces with other nonprofit groups to purchase and rehabilitate or demolish problem properties in the neighborhood, with much of that money going toward locations along Thirty-first Street. By 1997, more than $30 million had been poured into improving this street alone, much of it housing related. (LNA.)

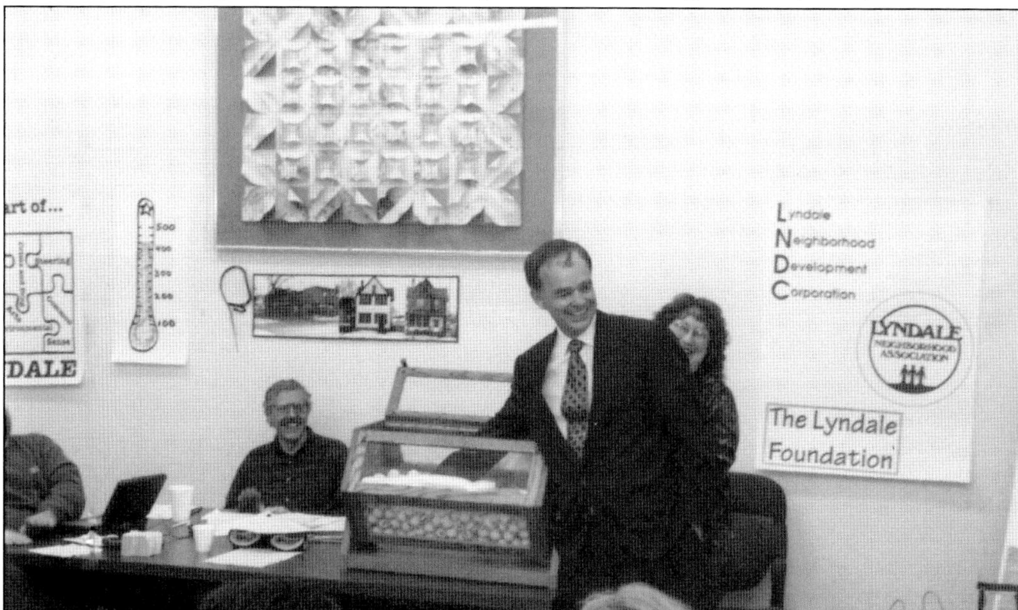

In 1990, the Lyndale Neighborhood Association identified improving the housing stock and encouraging home ownership as its top priorities and eventually created the Lyndale Neighborhood Development Corporation to manage housing-related initiatives. Annual lotteries helped disperse grants for the rehabilitation of existing housing. Ed Janezich, Norma Pietz, and Glen Taylor are seen helping the housing lottery and distributing funds during this January 1997 LNA meeting. (LNA.)

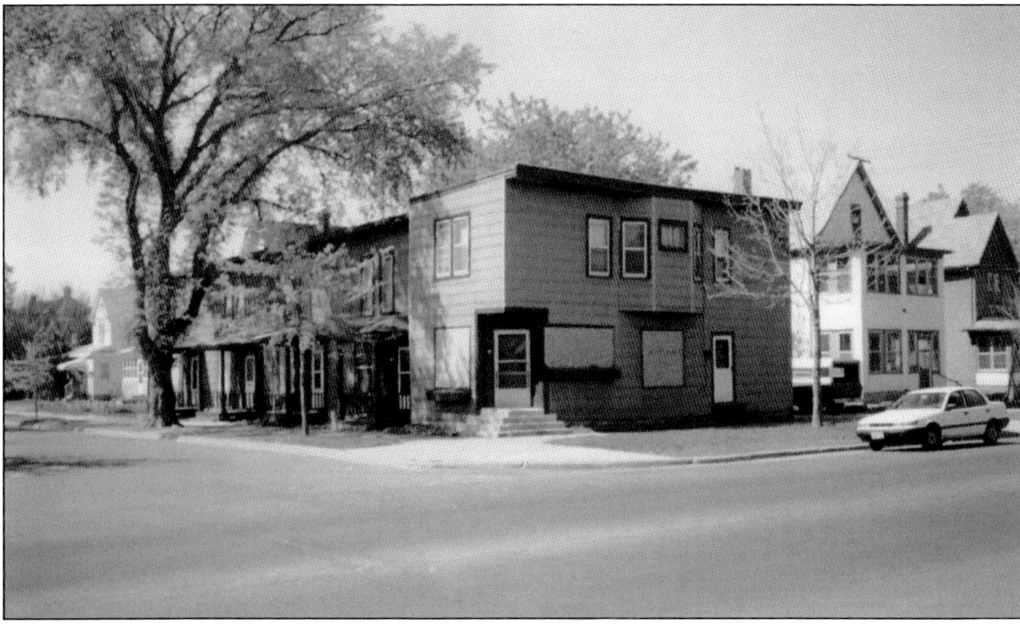

This building at 3100 Harriet Avenue, shown here in the mid-1990s, consisted of a set of five row-house units known locally as the "Green Snake." Following a disagreement with the city over the costs associated with acquiring the property, LNA's development arm demolished the dilapidated property to make room for the new Agape Dos group home for adults with HIV or AIDS. (LNA.)

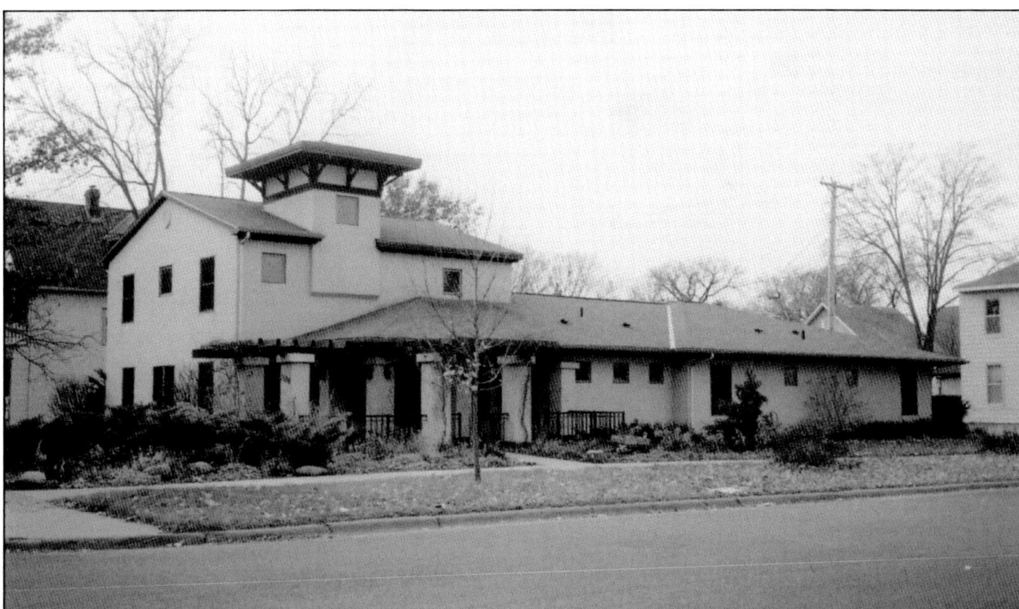

Agape Dos, a residential home for adults with HIV or AIDS, opened at 3100 Harriet Avenue in late 1999. The home was initially intended specifically for Hispanic residents, and the design, described as having a "Mexican/Caribbean feel," reflected that. More than 38 residents have lived in the home since its founding. In 2002, the project won a Committee on Urban Environment (CUE) award from the city. (LNA.)

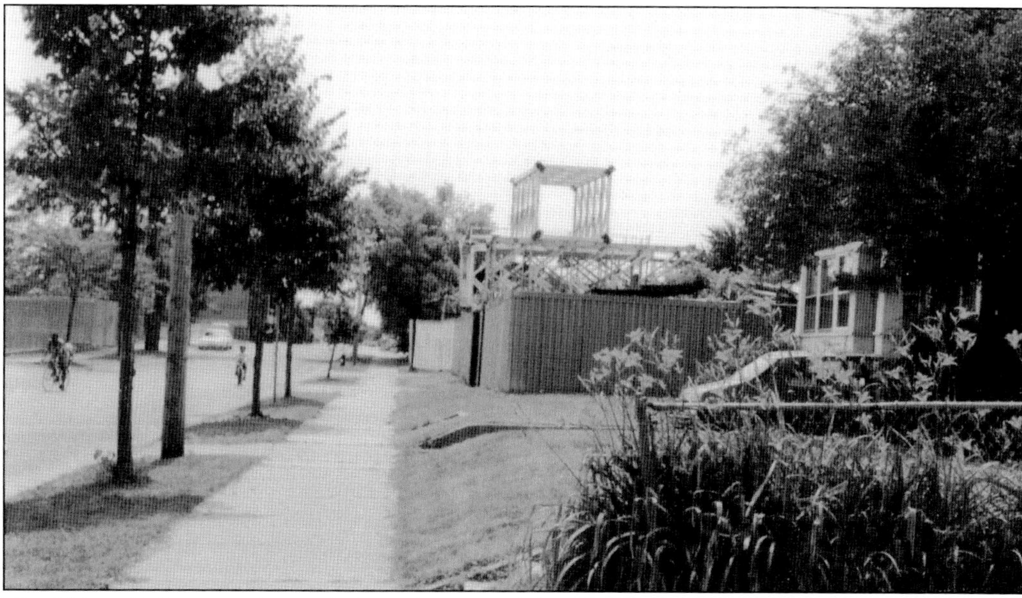

The Urban Village site, located along the new Midtown Greenway and the Twenty-ninth Street Corridor between Aldrich and Dupont Avenues, was envisioned to help transition this portion of Lyn-Lake's industrial landscape into a New Urbanist–inspired housing development. The plan required the relocation of several existing businesses and was not without its share of detractors. Some feel "Lyn-Lake's high-end development is subtle promotion of an elitist agenda," reported the *Lyn-Lake News* in 2001. (LHENA.)

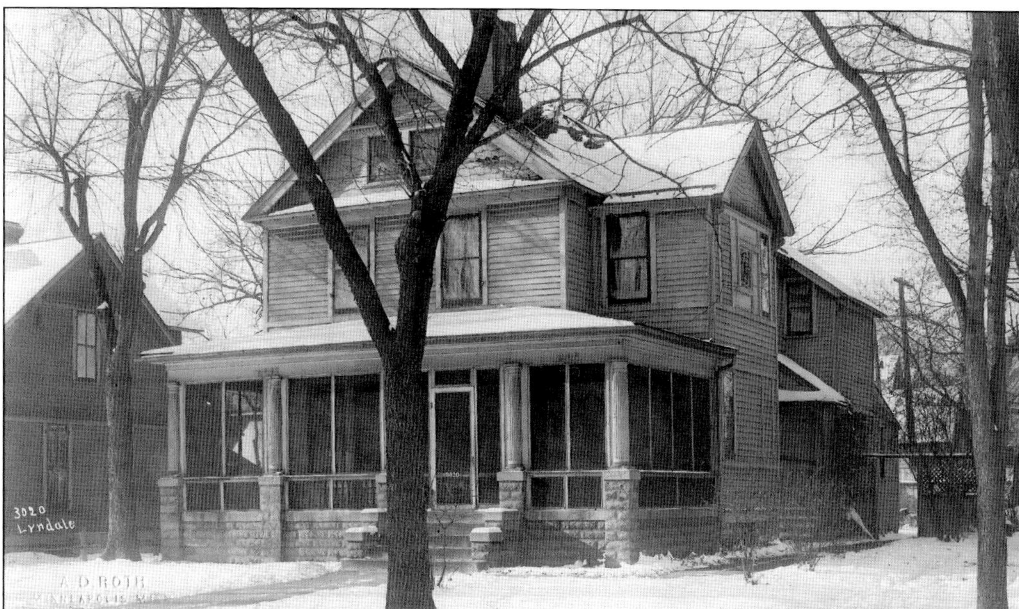

This house at 3020 Lyndale Avenue, the former home of osteopathic physician Fred Woodard, still stands—but perhaps not for long. The home is just south of Lake Street and is surrounded by commercial development. Already stripped of most of its historic exterior charm, it is perhaps only a matter of time before it falls to the wrecking ball in the name of progress. (Hennepin History Museum; photograph by A. D. Roth.)

Seven

SCHOOLS

For most of Lyn-Lake's history, schools have played an integral part in the creation of a sense of community. In an era before busing and magnet schools, children walked to their neighborhood elementary school. Lyn-Lake students attended the following three public elementary schools: Lyndale School, located at Thirty-fourth Street and Lyndale Avenue for much of its history; Whittier School, situated at Twenty-sixth Street and Blaisdell Avenue for much of its history; and Douglas School, near Franklin and Hennepin Avenues. While only one of these schools falls within the parameters of the Lyn-Lake area today, which is Lyndale School, this book includes the history of Whittier and Lyndale Elementary Schools, as they all played essential roles in the Lyn-Lake community and served the majority of its children.

During the 1970s, busing and attempts at desegregation scattered many of the neighborhood's children to schools across the city. In more recent years, there has been an attempt to return to community schools, although debate about school boundaries, racial integration, and access to specific programs or opportunities continues. Lyndale and Whittier Schools continue to serve a diverse blend of students, including large numbers of recent immigrants. While 100 years ago those immigrant children were likely to hail from Sweden or Norway, today's immigrant students are more likely to come from Somalia or Mexico. While the faces of Lyn-Lake's schools, and even their facades, have changed, they continue to pursue their mission to educate the neighborhood's youth.

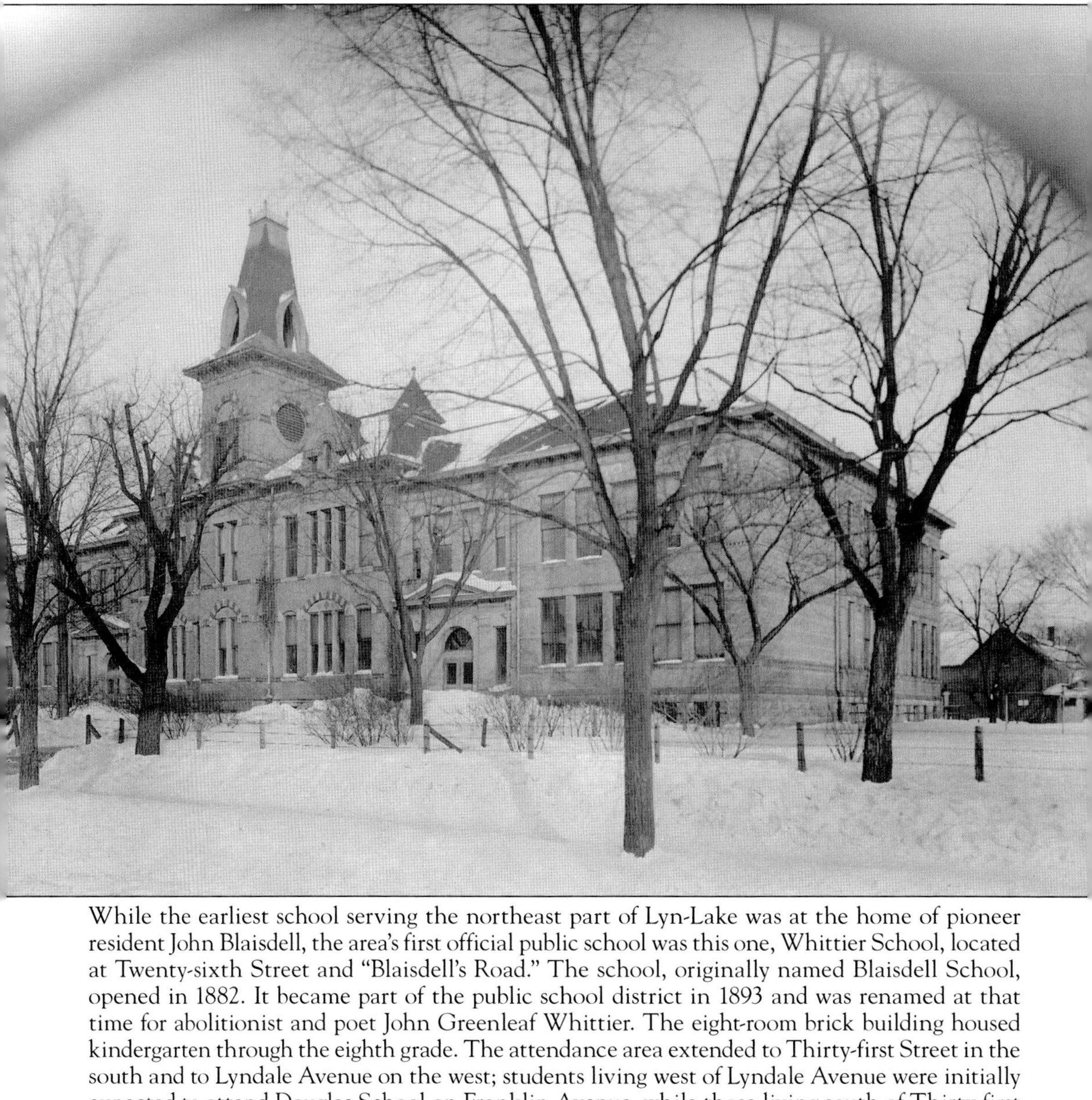

While the earliest school serving the northeast part of Lyn-Lake was at the home of pioneer resident John Blaisdell, the area's first official public school was this one, Whittier School, located at Twenty-sixth Street and "Blaisdell's Road." The school, originally named Blaisdell School, opened in 1882. It became part of the public school district in 1893 and was renamed at that time for abolitionist and poet John Greenleaf Whittier. The eight-room brick building housed kindergarten through the eighth grade. The attendance area extended to Thirty-first Street in the south and to Lyndale Avenue on the west; students living west of Lyndale Avenue were initially expected to attend Douglas School on Franklin Avenue, while those living south of Thirty-first Street attended Lyndale School. The school was soon expanded to meet the growing needs of the neighborhood; there had already been one expansion, as well as the addition of indoor plumbing by the time this photograph was taken in 1895. More additions and renovations came in 1903, 1910, and 1923. The school at this location was closed in 1975. (MPS.)

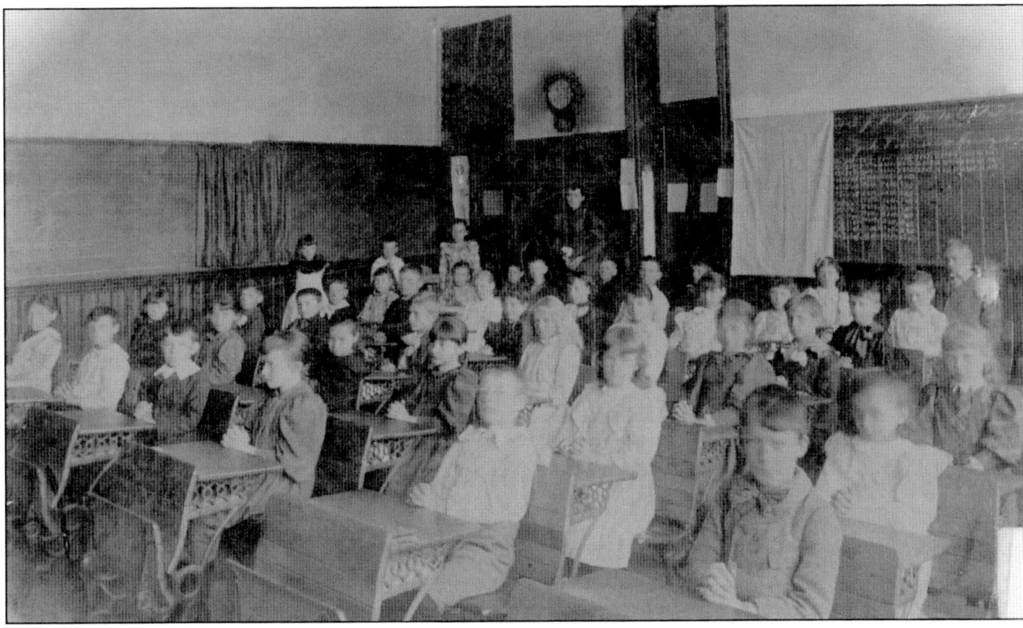

These students attended Whittier in the early 1890s. Anstice Abbott was one of the students in this classroom; she spent nine years at Whittier and graduated from the school's eighth grade in 1902. She recalled one December holiday season when a classroom's Christmas tree caught on fire from the lit candles. The fire was promptly put out, but not before firemen from the station at Twenty-eighth Street were called. (MPS.)

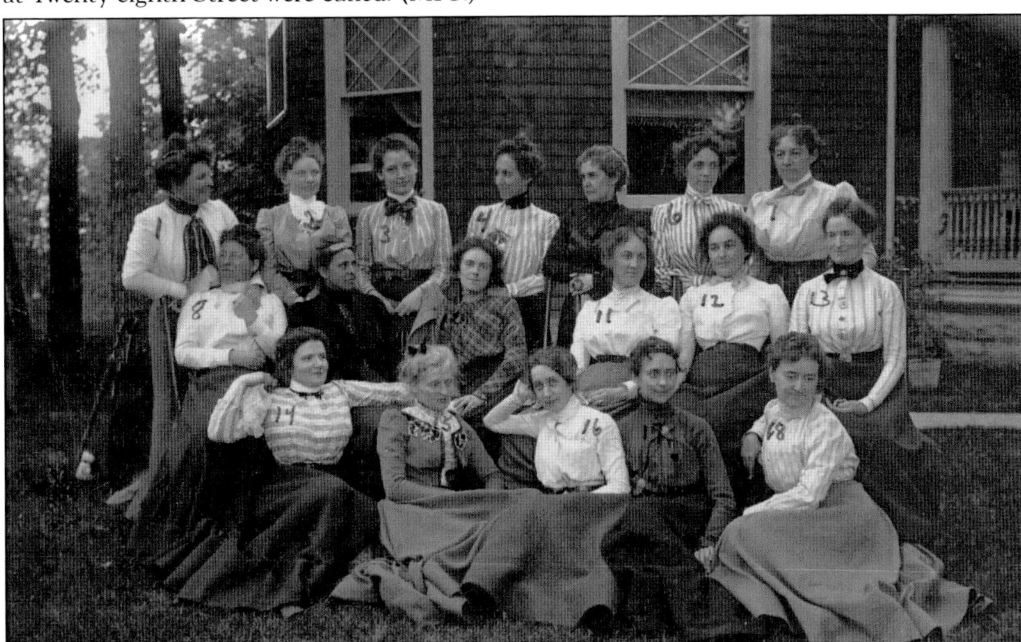

These Whittier teachers were photographed sometime around 1900 at the Fremont Avenue home of Jessie Bryant, one of the teachers. The image was given to Hennepin History Museum by 1902 graduate Anstice Abbott during a special program held at the time of Whittier's closing in 1975 prior to its revival in the 1990s. (Hennepin History Museum.)

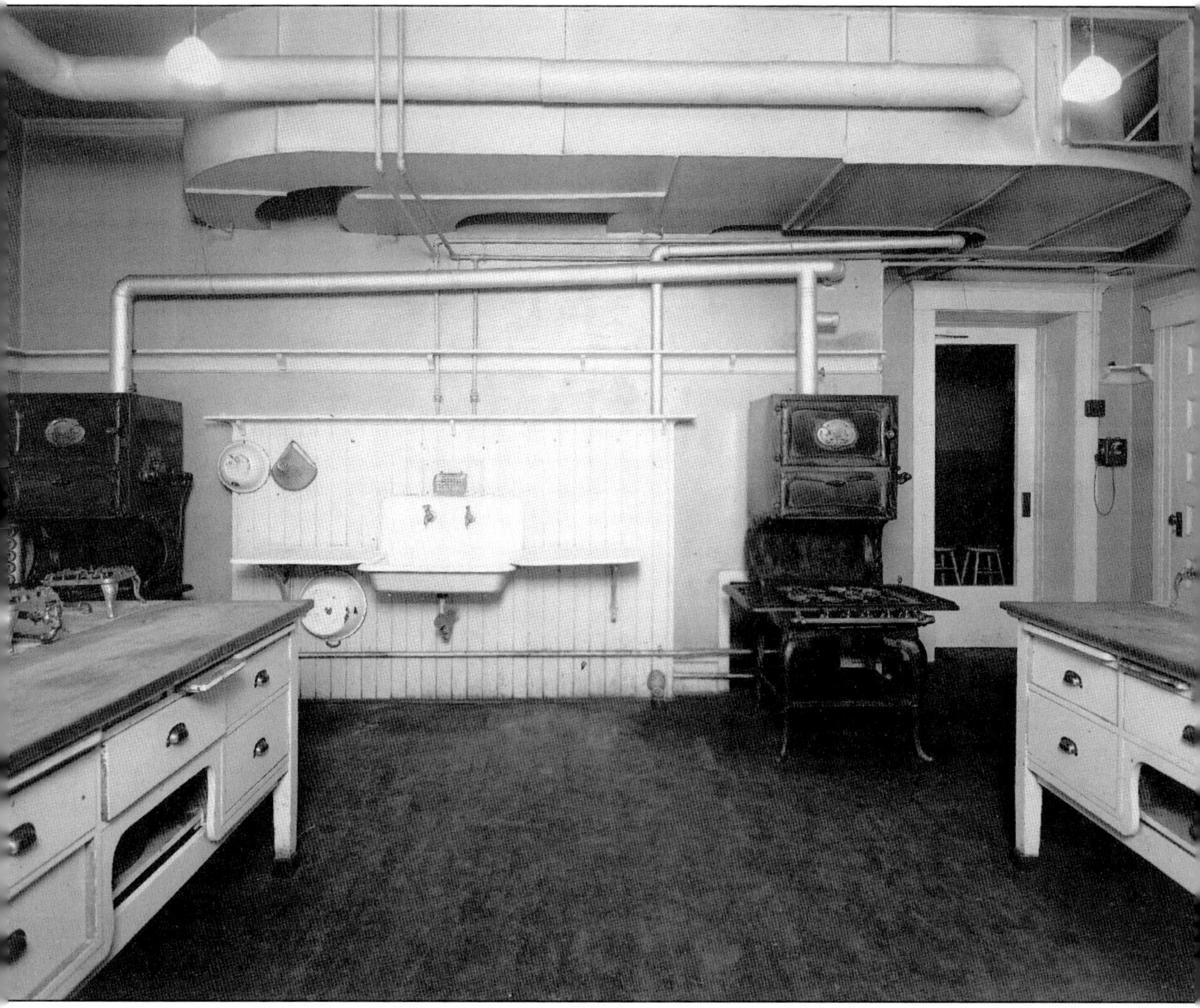

Whittier's kitchens received a great deal of use by students, staff, and the community. In 1911, domestic science expert Emma Barrows enjoyed a meal prepared by eighth-grade girls from Lyndale and Whittier Schools. Impressed by the results, she praised the students, as well as the kitchens themselves, when she told the *Minneapolis Tribune*, "I have not seen anything superior in any city." Two years later, Minneapolis Woman's Club members, society ladies who rarely, if ever, did any cooking themselves, visited the school's kitchens on Saturday mornings, where they followed the same curriculum used by students and pronounced it both enjoyable and educational. On the other end of the socioeconomic spectrum, a 1921 study of the district found one quarter of all students to be underweight. In response, nutrition clinics were set up in five schools, including Whittier. The district's efforts to provide nutrition for all of Whittier's students were further enhanced with the addition of a hot lunch meal program, the first school in the Minneapolis area to offer them. (MPS.)

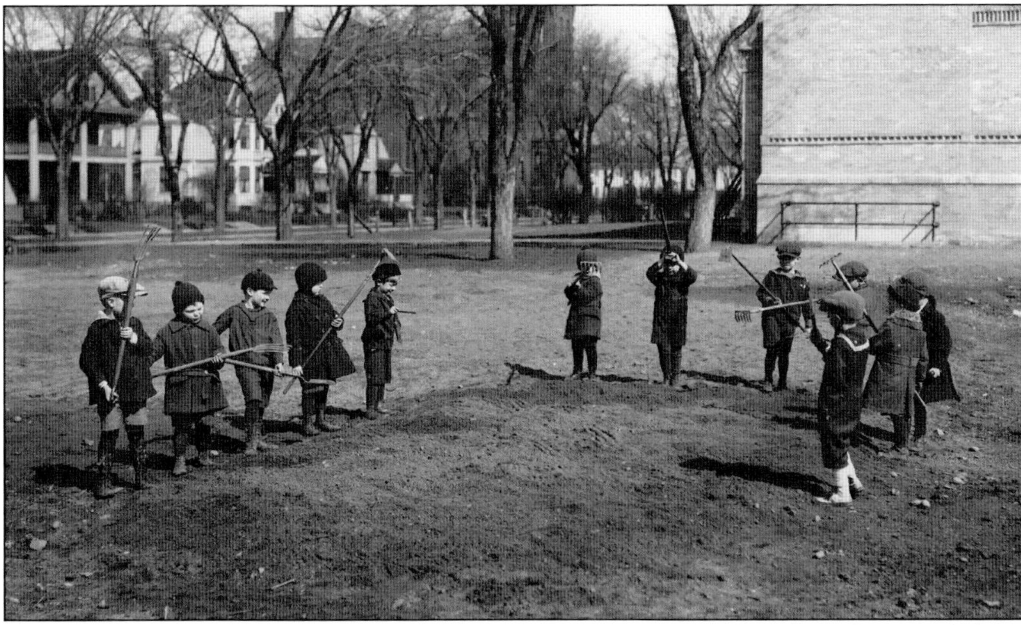

This undated photograph of young Whittier School students working outside is symbolic of Whittier's broader belief in the value of fresh air to aid in the health of students. In 1913, the school installed "fresh air rooms" inside some of its classrooms; the open windows (covered with cheesecloth in winter to prevent drafts) were part of a Red Cross seal–funded project to combat tuberculosis and other illnesses and to promote healthy weight gain. (MPS.)

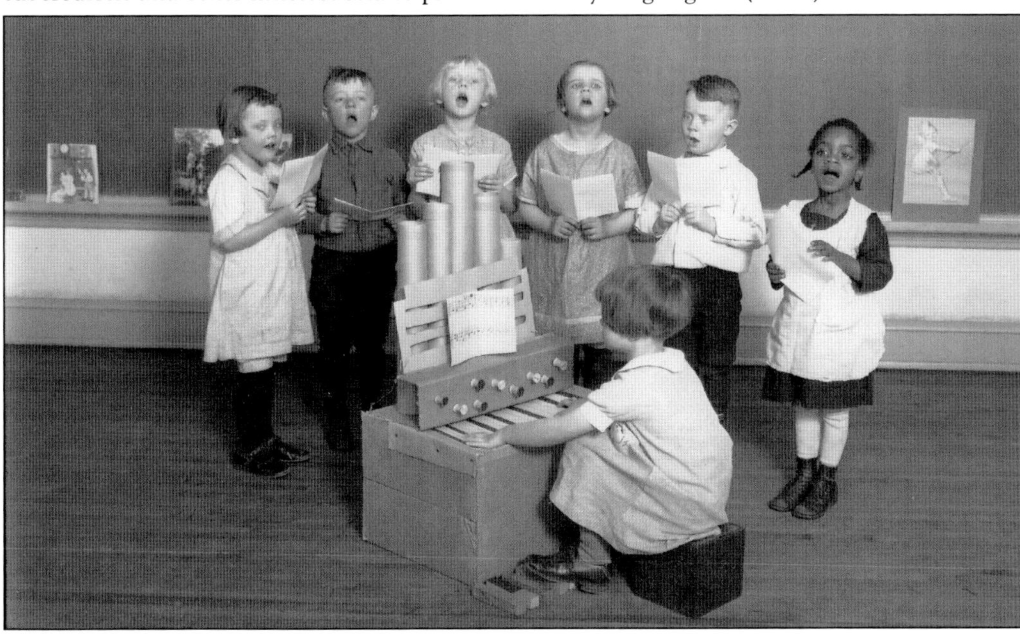

Whittier School's tradition of using a cardboard piano for "recitals" at school began in 1918, when Wilma Anderson Gilman used one to lead her group of children in a demonstration to show parents and teachers how the district was using pretend pianos as a way to provide a musical education to every child in the district. These Whittier children put on their performance in the late 1920s. (MHS.)

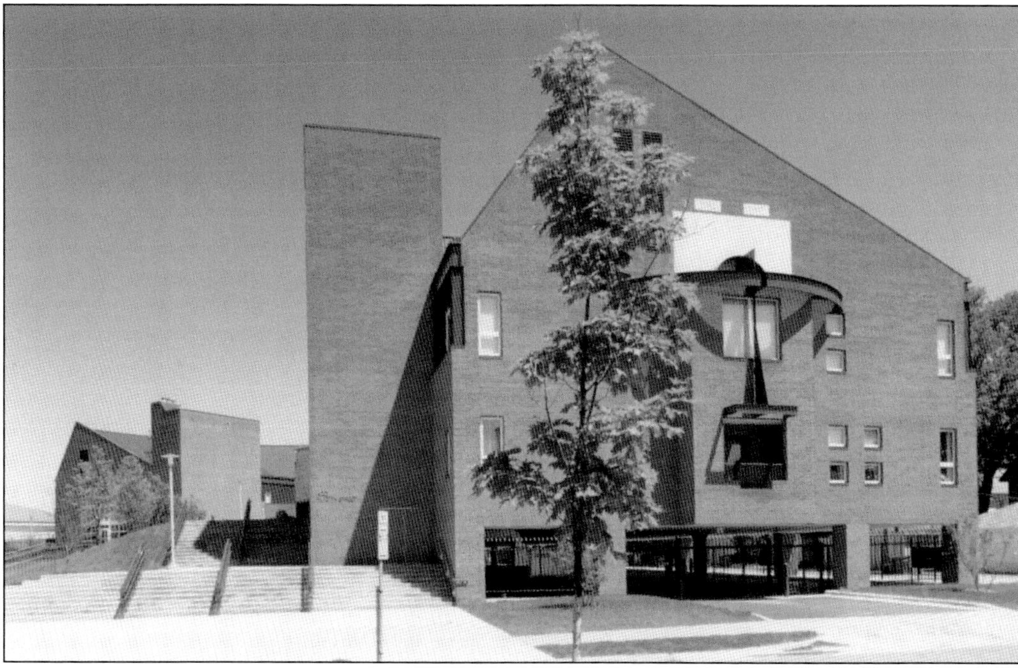

In 1997, work on a new Whittier School was completed. This new school, located at 315 West Twenty-sixth Street, shares space with Whittier Park and its community center, further enabling it to become a truly integrated central gathering place for the neighborhood. The school's updated name, Whittier International Elementary School, reflects both the diversity of its community as well as the international scope of its current academic programs. (MPS.)

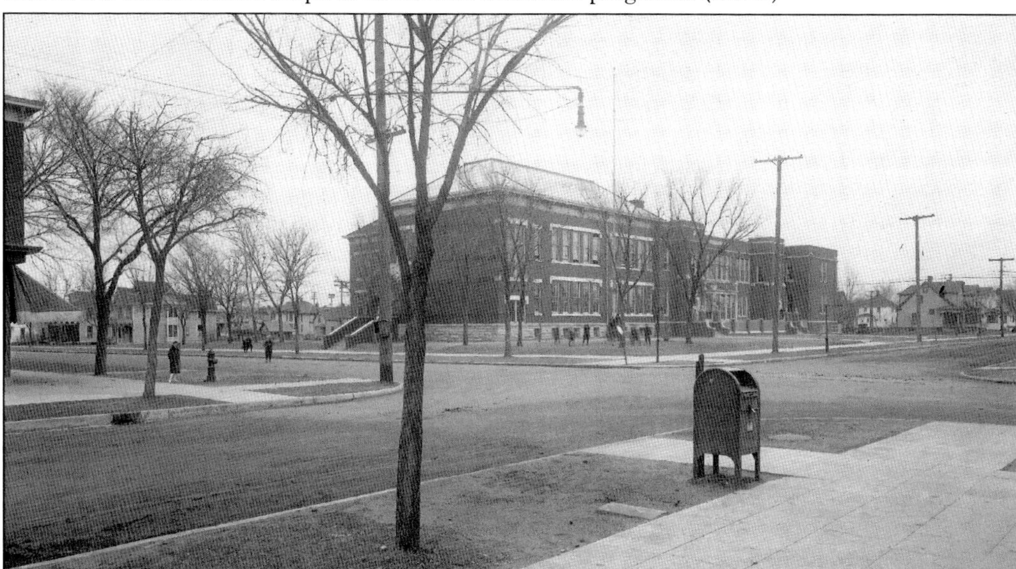

In 1884, parents in the growing Eighth Ward asked the school board for a new school to be constructed near their homes. The result was Lyndale School, located on the corner of Lyndale Avenue and Thirty-fourth Street. In 1902, the school board was able to buy six additional lots adjacent to the school. It was a good purchase; as this photograph shows, homes soon surrounded the school's expanded property. (MPS.)

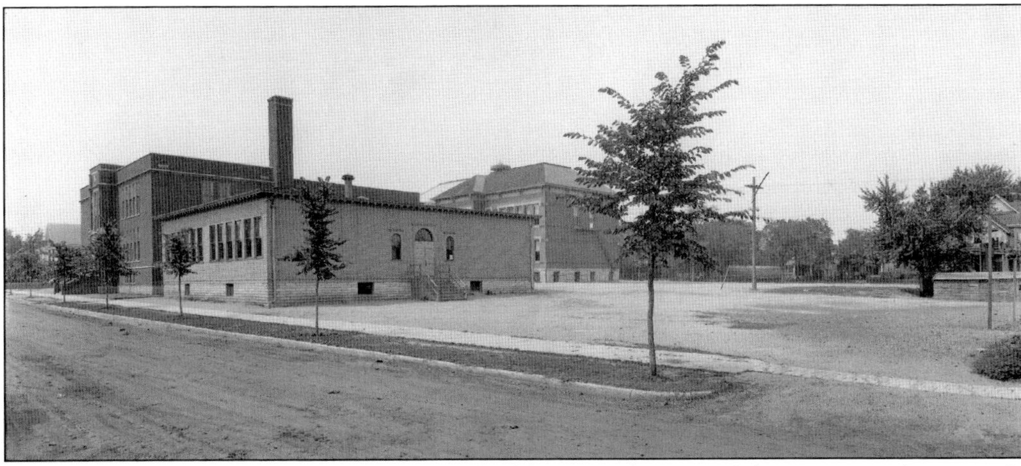

The earliest portion of the Lyndale School building was the part of the structure closest to the intersection of Lyndale Avenue and Thirty-fourth Street. More additions, some of them visible in this 1922 view of the school and its grounds, were built in 1899, 1915, and 1927. The lower-slung building in the foreground was the school's fireproof gymnasium and auditorium. (MPS.)

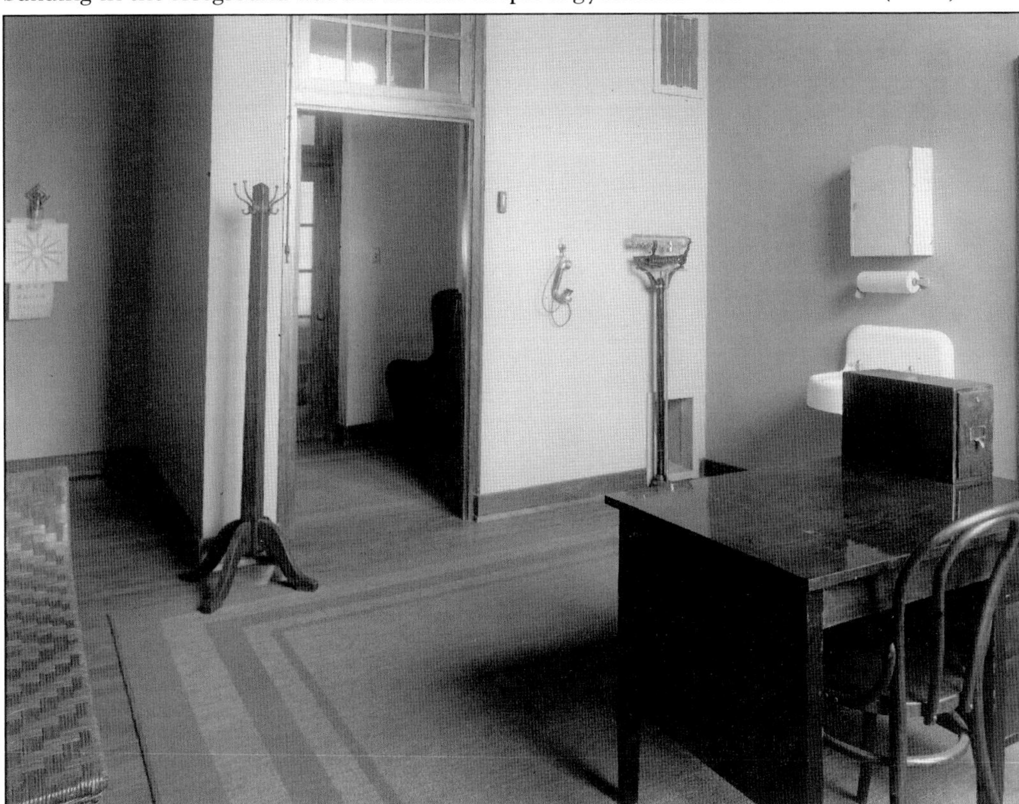

This photograph shows the old Lyndale School nurse's office before the start of school. Outbreaks of disease occasionally plagued the school, especially in the era before vaccinations. In 1904, it suffered an outbreak of typhoid and diphtheria. Parents pulled their children from the school and demanded an investigation into the its sanitary conditions, asking whether there was something wrong with the building's plumbing, ventilation, or water supply. (MPS.)

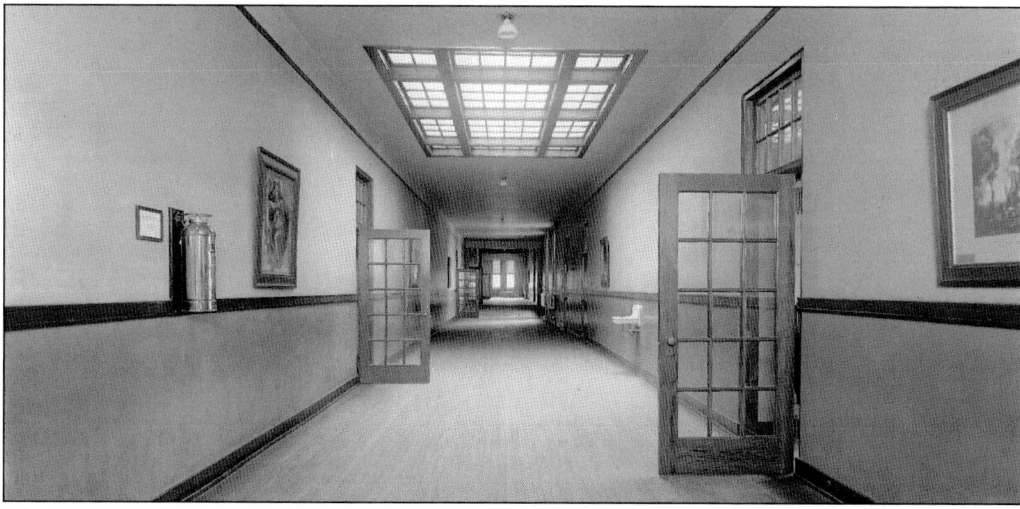

This formal hallway scene from the old Lyndale School might look familiar to some readers if not for one conspicuous absence—children. From its earliest days onward, Lyndale School suffered chronic issues of overcrowding, which was the result of a steadily growing neighborhood and its growing population of children. By 1963, shortly before the school's closure, Lyndale School had 666 students, which was more than 146 over its optimal capacity. (MPS.)

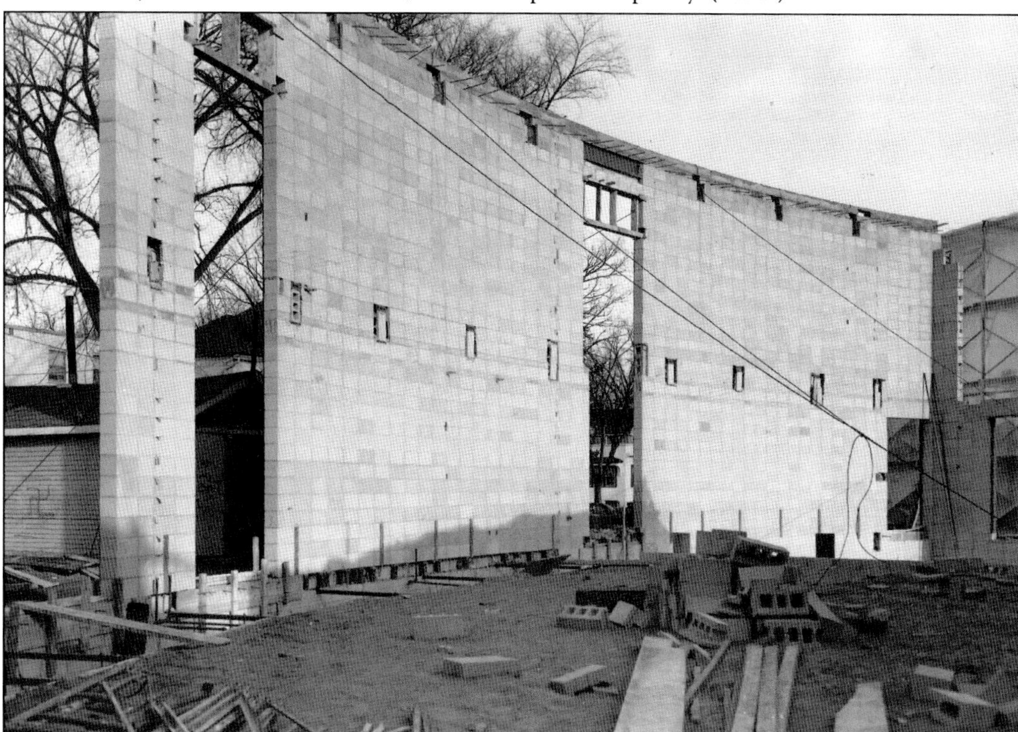

By the early 1960s, Lyndale School was overcrowded and in need of repairs and extensive renovations to ensure that it met modern building requirements. The city and district debated their options and decided to relocate the school to a site several blocks east of the original school. The new, two-story brick building with a distinctive curving exterior wall is shown under construction in 1967. (MPS.)

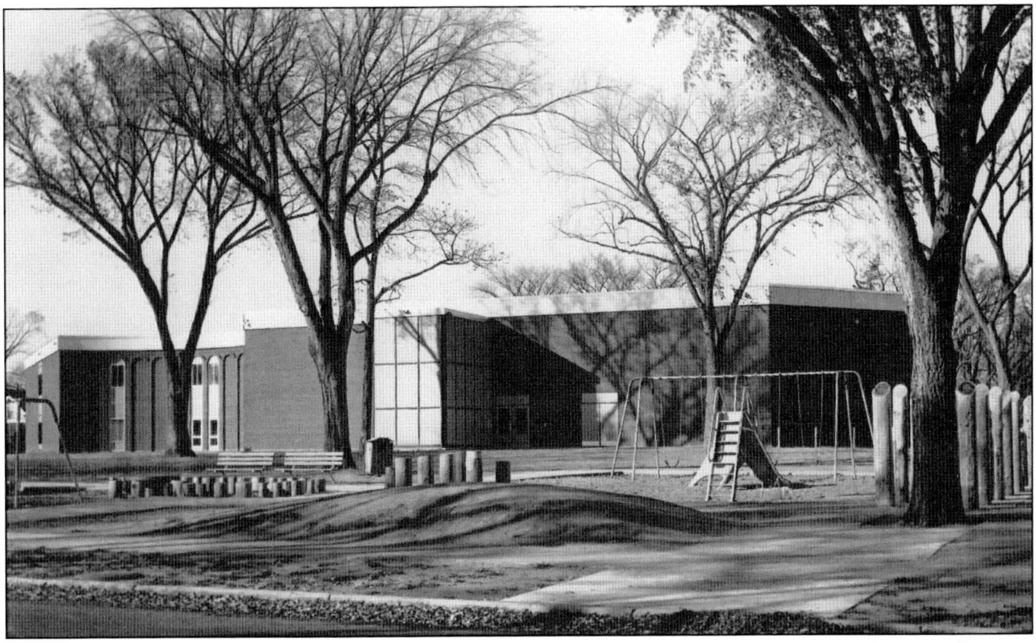

By 1969, the new Lyndale School's playground and exterior landscaping was in place, and a new era in both the school's and the neighborhood's history was underway. The former school at Thirty-fourth Street and Lyndale Avenue was ultimately demolished to make room for the public Painter Park; the park's recreation center stands approximately on the site of Lyndale School's original building. (MPS.)

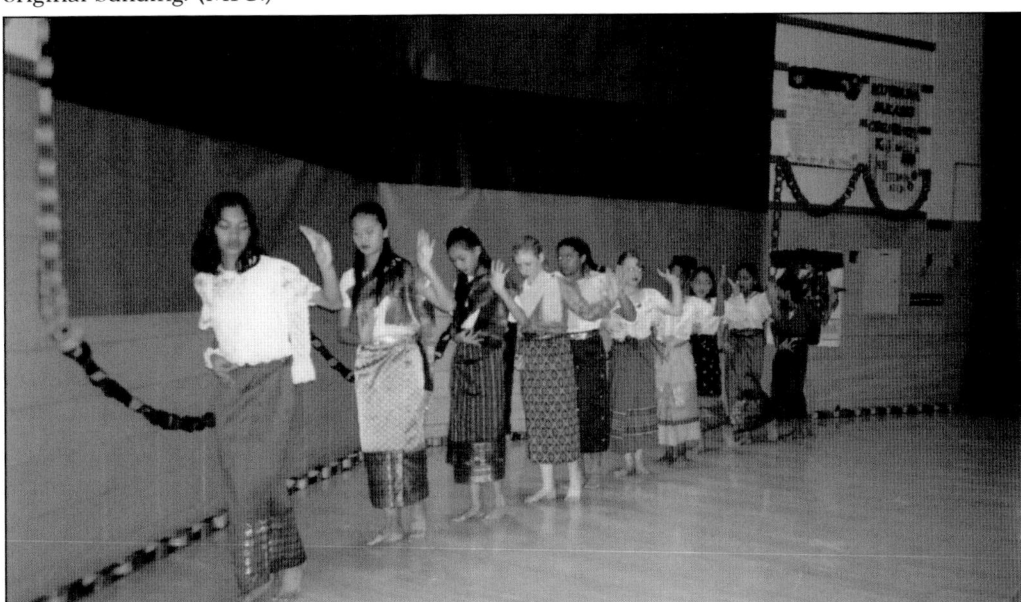

After 14 years as a school for fourth through sixth graders, Lyndale Community School opened its doors to kindergarten through fifth graders beginning in the 1996–1997 academic year. Here students perform a dance as part of the school's fifth-annual Kwanzaa celebration in December 1996. The program featured music, dancing, and songs from a diverse range of cultures, reflecting the diversity found within its student body. (MPS.)

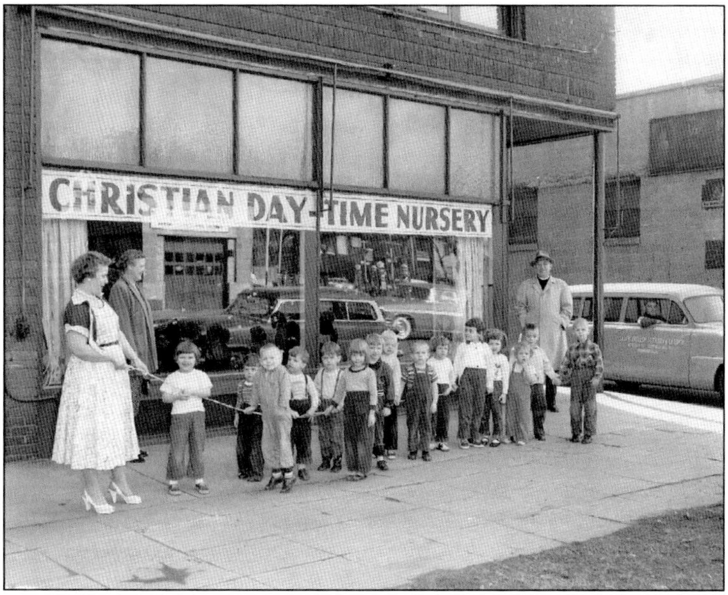

Salem English Lutheran Church opened the Christian Day-time Nursery in September 1954. Its opening was in recognition that many working families were in desperate need of quality day care. The school also functioned as a preschool and could accommodate up to 36 children each day. The name was later changed to Sugar Plum Tree Nursery. It was located in the church-owned Hanson Building at 2741 Lyndale Avenue. (SELC.)

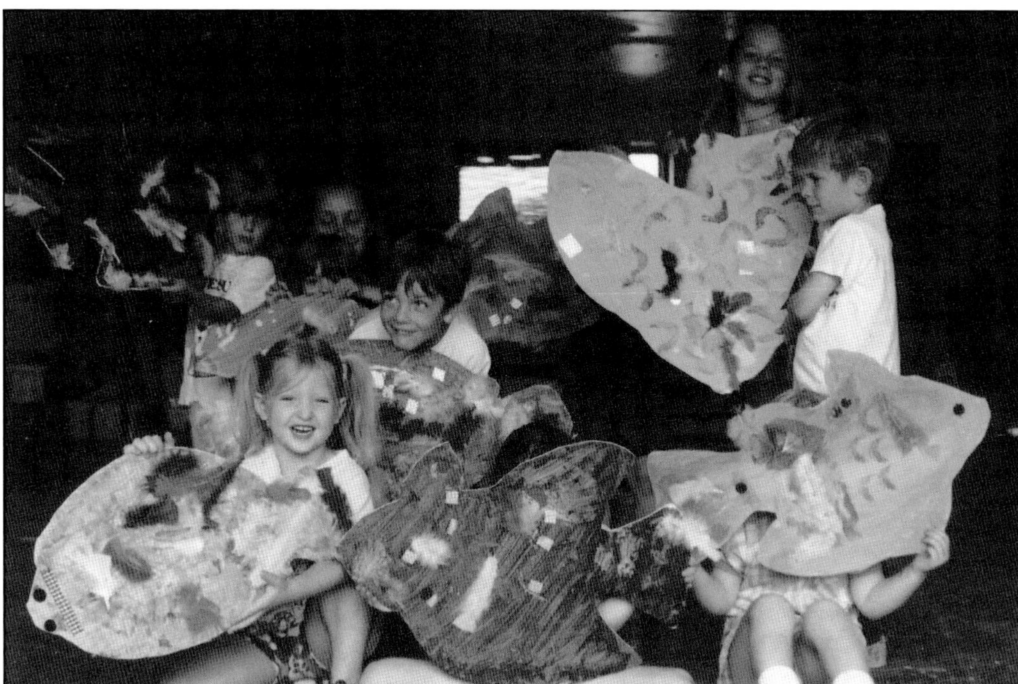

Minneapolis has long recognized that a quality preschool experience can be beneficial for children's development. In addition to state-funded Early Childhood Family Education (ECFE) classes offered through the school district since 1974, Minneapolis also has experimented with preschools offered through the park district. These preschoolers in the 1995–1996 Painter Park preschool program are assisting with the Garfield substation fish mural project. (LNA.)

Eight

Religion

While Lyn-Lake had some Jewish residents, who lived within walking distance of Uptown synagogues such as Adath Jeshurun and Temple Israel, the dominant religion in Lyn-Lake was Christianity. A large number of churches have called the area home over the years, from both the small to the large.

These churches have often taken a leading role in engaging the outside community, and they have also historically drawn many of their members from within walking distance of the church. During the 1940s and 1950s, Lyn-Lake churches also offered some of the largest vacation Bible schools in the country, drawing in both children from their own congregations as well as from around the city.

In more recent years, many of Lyn-Lake's churches have developed local and even national reputations known for their liberal stances, and sometimes groundbreaking actions, on nationally controversial topics such as the ordination of women and same-sex marriage.

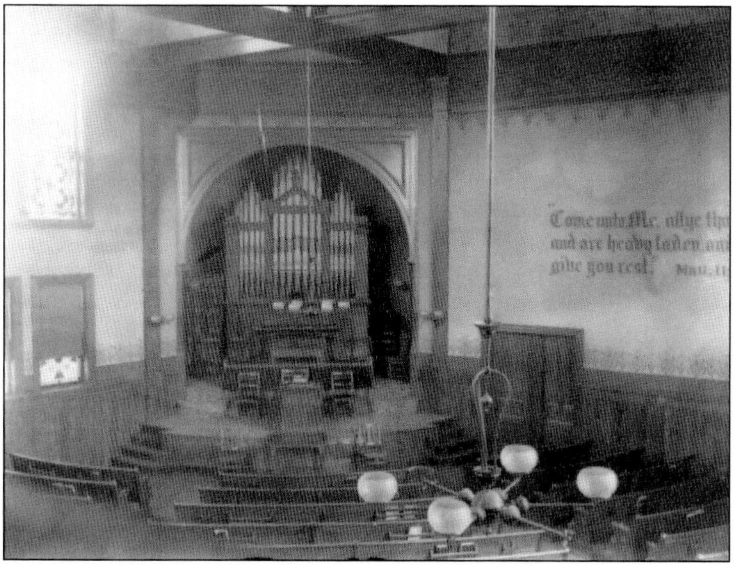

Lyndale Congregational Church, now Lyndale United Church of Christ, got its start in a portable chapel on the northeast corner of Lyndale Avenue and Lake Street in 1884. The members built a permanent church in 1887, shown here, on the corner of Lake Street and Aldrich Avenue. Most members lived in the neighborhood, and the church was a center of both spiritual and social activity. (LUCC.)

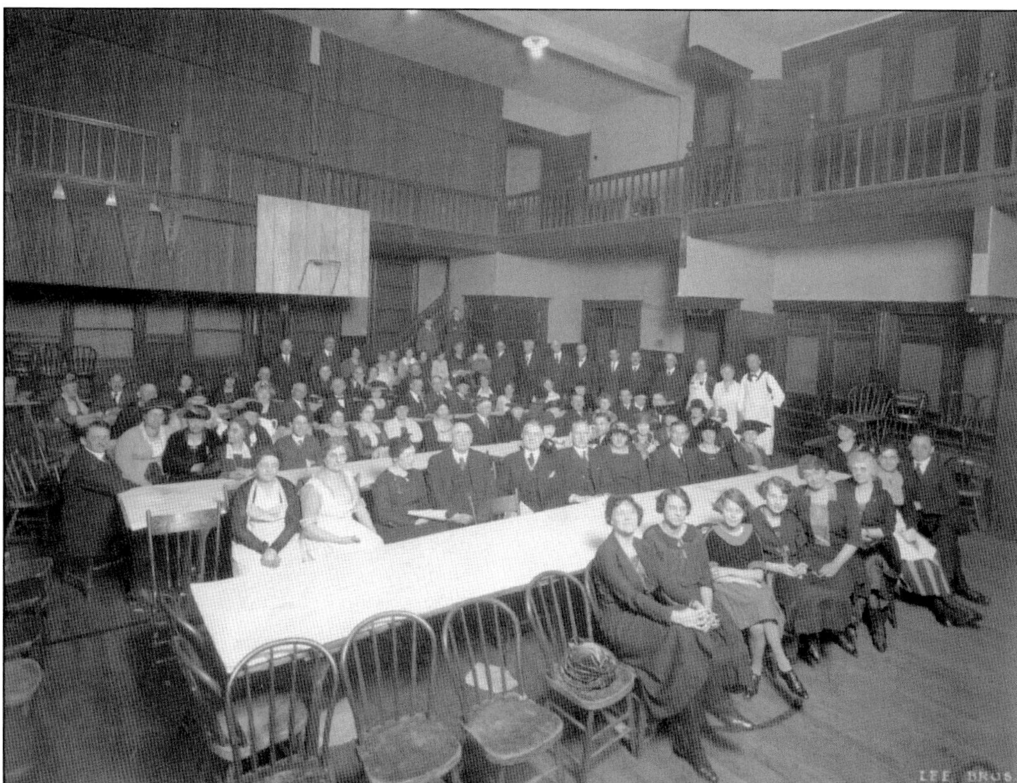

Prior to the 1924 opening of the new church building on Aldrich Avenue and Thirty-first Street, most large Lyndale Congregational Church events (like this annual meeting) took place in the original church's gymnasium. The 1902 gymnasium was used by both church members and non-members alike and offered exercise and sports for men, women, and children. The pennants hanging on the back wall honor the church's basketball teams. (LUCC.)

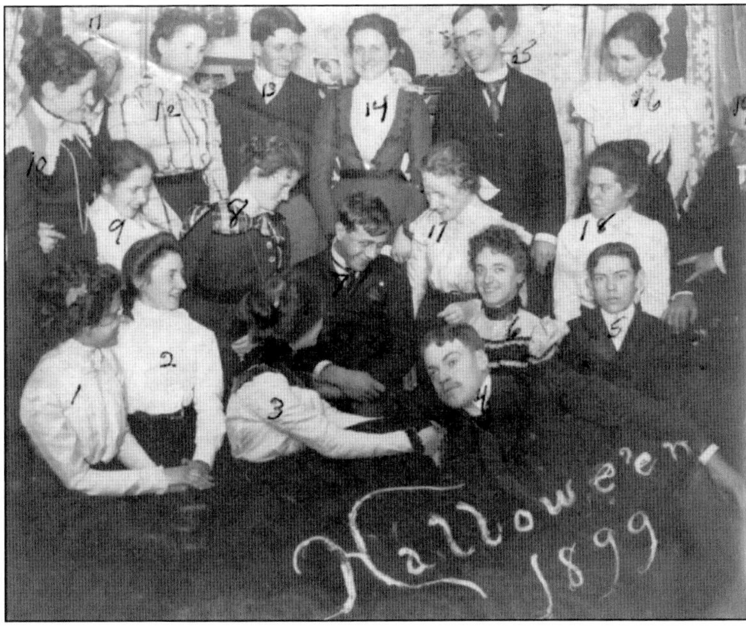

This group of young Lyndale Congregational Church members has gathered for a 1899 Halloween party. Churches provided a social network for many people in the neighborhood and hosted gatherings and outings for both members and non-members of all ages. Other options in 1899 included a wide variety of themed socials, a hayride to Edina, and a thimble bee among other activities. (LUCC.)

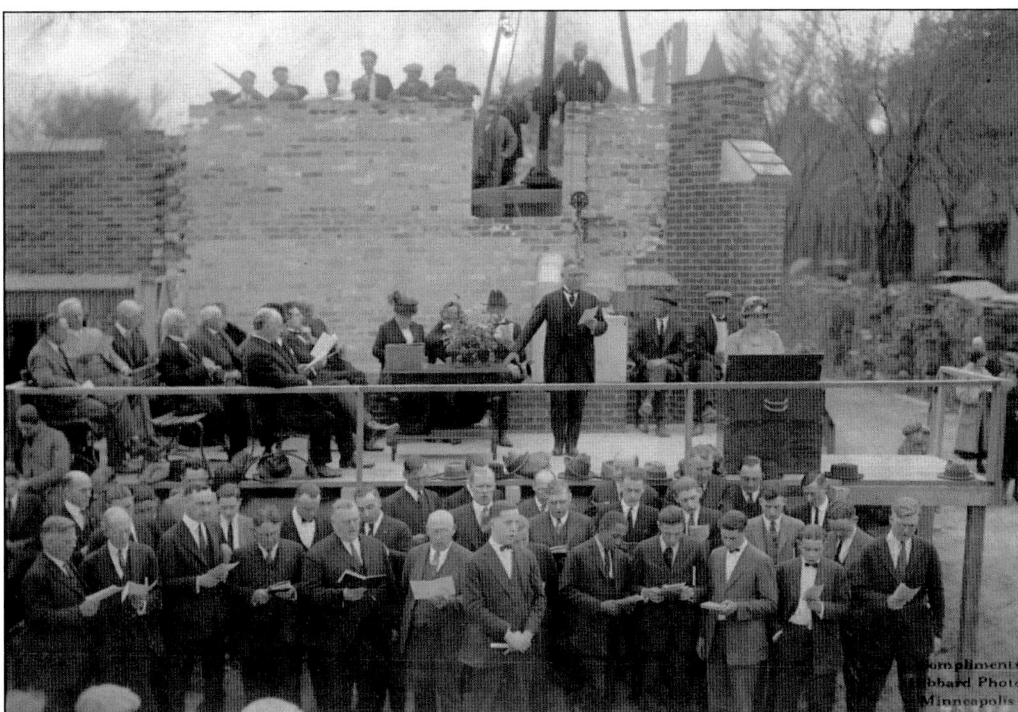

Members of the Lyndale Congregational Church have gathered on May 6, 1923, to celebrate the official dedication and the placing of the cornerstone for its new, bigger church at the corner of Aldrich Avenue and Thirty-first Street. "Rapid development of Lake Street commercially," coupled with the needs of a quickly growing congregation, led to the decision to move to the larger site. (LUCC; photograph by C. J. Hibbard.)

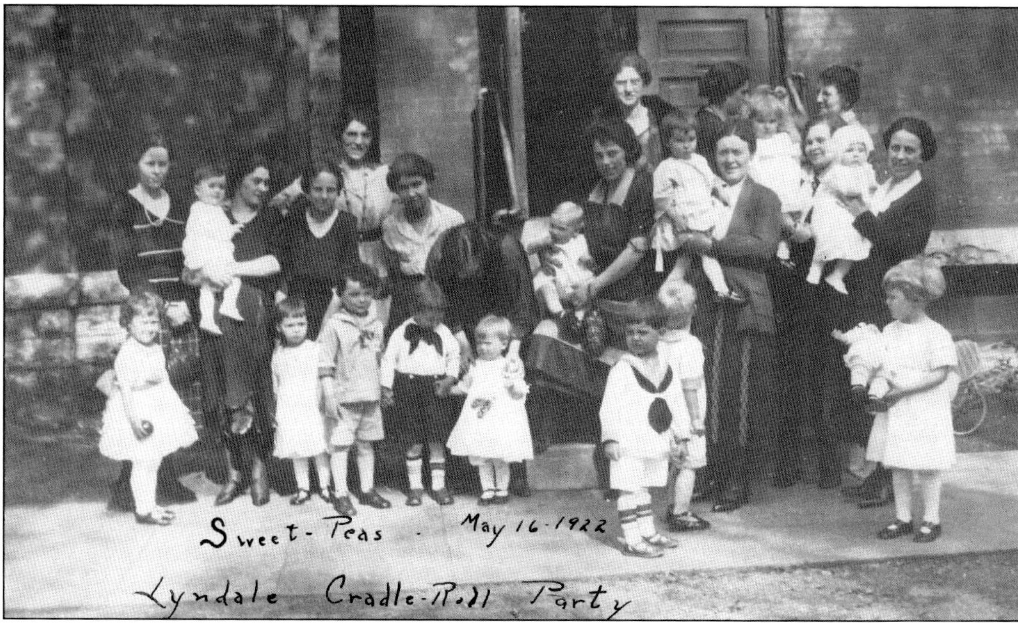

The needs of Lyndale Congregational Church's youngest members (and their parents) were not overlooked. The toddlers and infants, or "Sweet Peas," shown here were enjoying a May 1922 Cradle Roll party. Cradle Rolls were a popular activity for local mothers; while some formal entertainment was usually provided, the greater purpose was to let the mothers of young children relax and enjoy socializing with other women while their children played. (LUCC.)

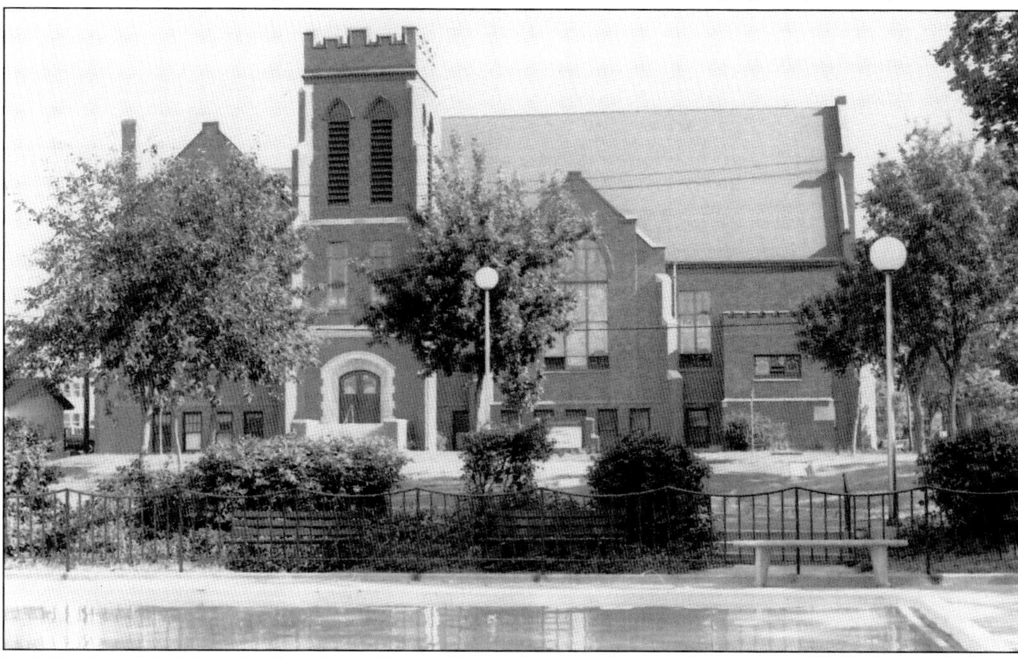

In 2010, Lyndale United Church of Christ (formerly Lyndale Congregational Church) moved from this 1924 building into temporary quarters shared with Salem English Lutheran Church. The building, too large for Lyndale's current needs, was sold to the New Wine Church. New Wine is a non-denominational church with a "church with the heart for the city." (LUCC.)

For decades, Aldrich Avenue Presbyterian Church, located at Thirty-fifth Street and Aldrich Avenue, has attended to the spiritual needs of its congregation and the larger community. During the mid-20th century, its vacation Bible school was one of the best attended in the area, with scores of children from the immediate neighborhood participating. The church continues to sponsor lectures, arts programs, and other activities, both religious and secular. (Hennepin History Museum.)

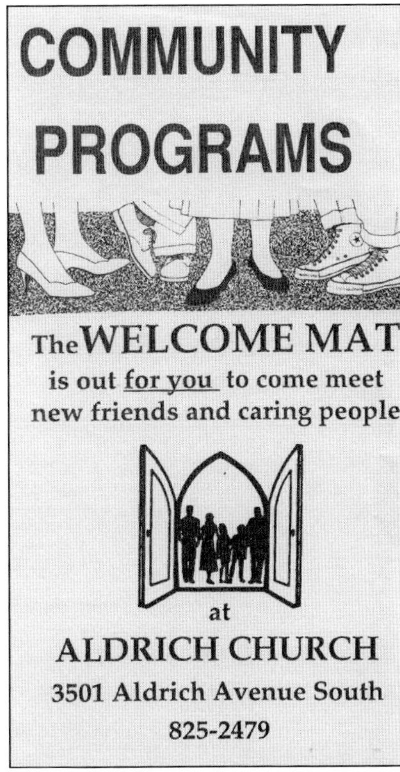

When Salem English Church at Twenty-eighth Street and Garfield Avenue was founded in 1889, it first built a small wooden structure. By 1890, it had 16 charter members. By 1904, the congregation decided to build a much larger stone church. By 1928, the approximate year of this photograph, the congregation numbered 432 and the church had just erected a parsonage. (SELC.)

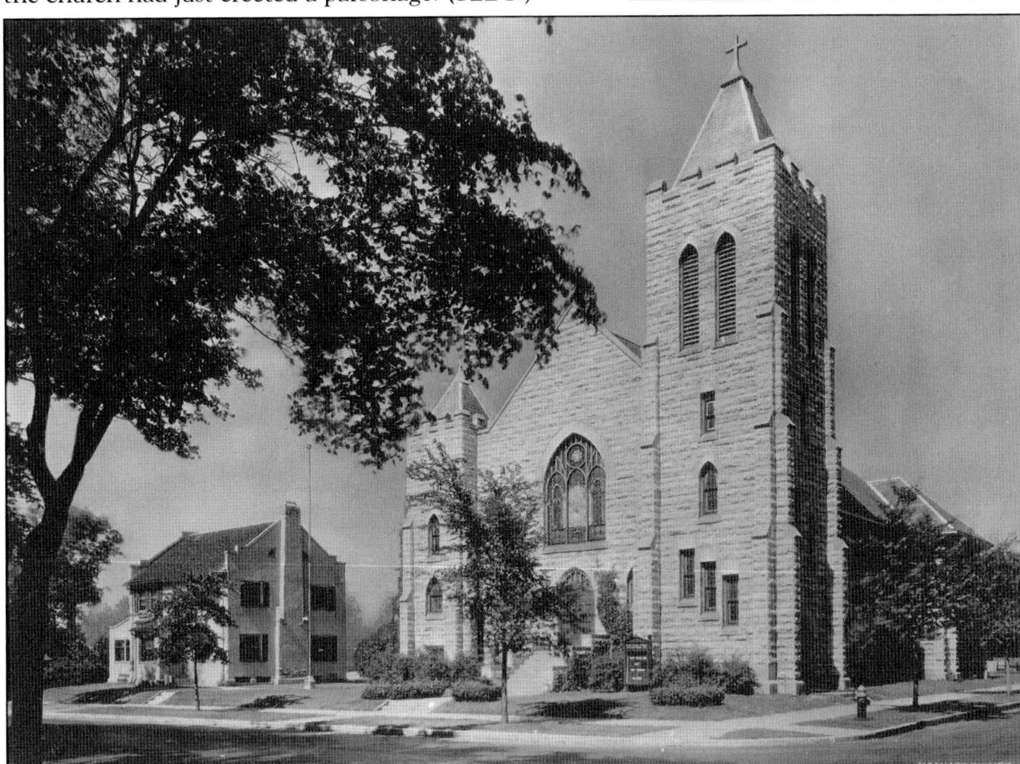

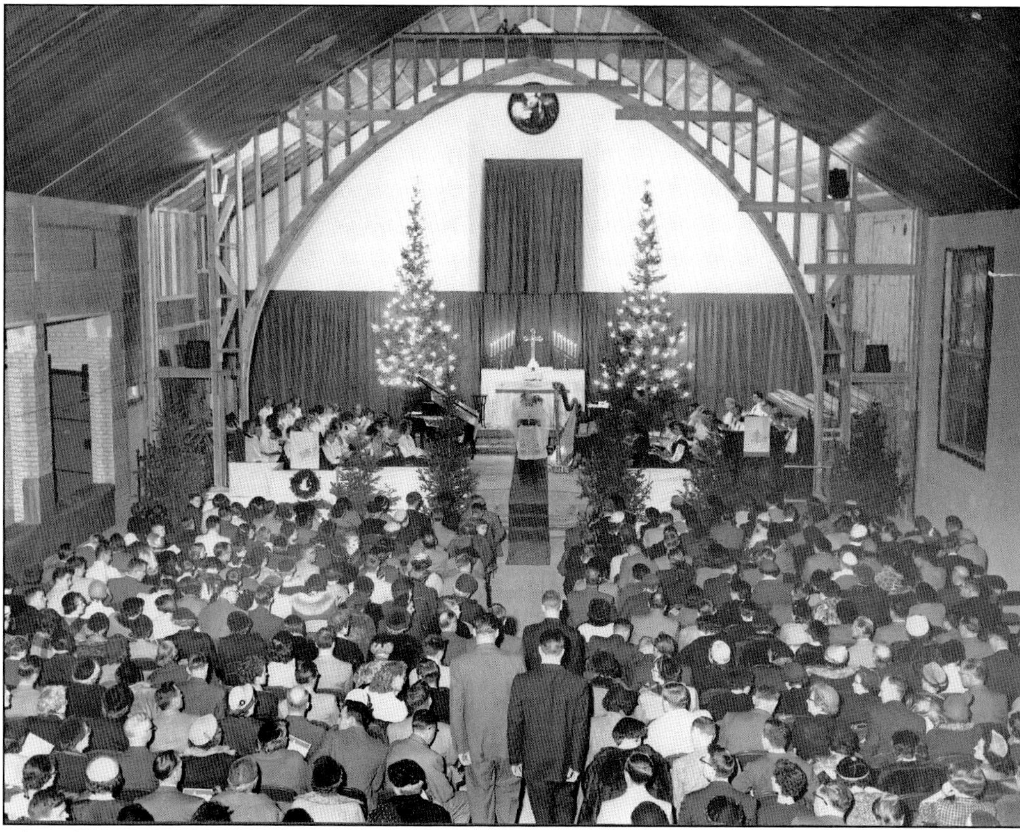

The Christmas Eve 1953 Salem English Lutheran Church service was conducted in English. When first founded, Lutheran churches in Minneapolis conducted their services in the languages of their immigrant members. When Salem English Lutheran Church chose to work in English, the "language of the children," they became the second Lutheran church west of Chicago to do so. (SELC.)

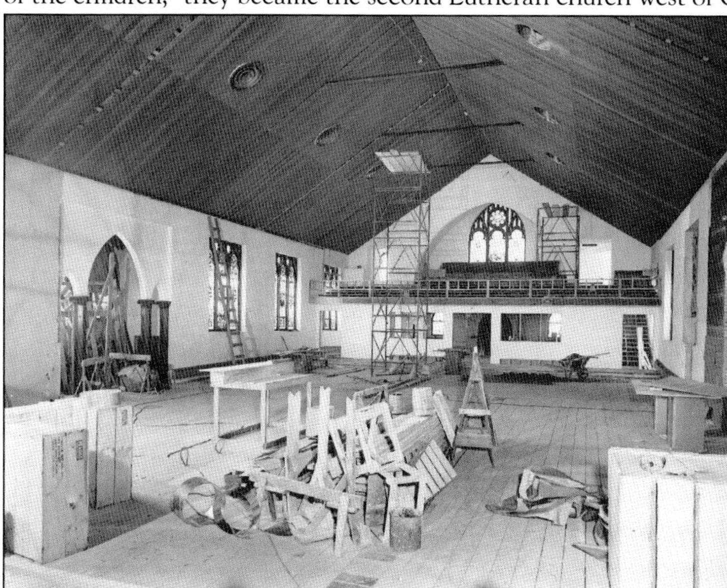

During the post-war baby-boom period, Salem English Lutheran Church's membership exploded, and its space filled to capacity. In 1952, ground broke for a new, larger sanctuary. During the construction period (shown here), services were held at the nearby Jefferson Elementary School. The new church was dedicated in September 1954. (SELC.)

In 1950, Salem English Lutheran Church purchased the Hanson's Store Building and lot at 2741 Lyndale Avenue. For 10 years, the building was used for various educational functions, but in 1962 a decision was made to demolish and clear the site and to build a new Twenty-eighth Street wing that was large enough to handle the growing congregation. Here the newly completed building is being dedicated in November 1964. (SELC.)

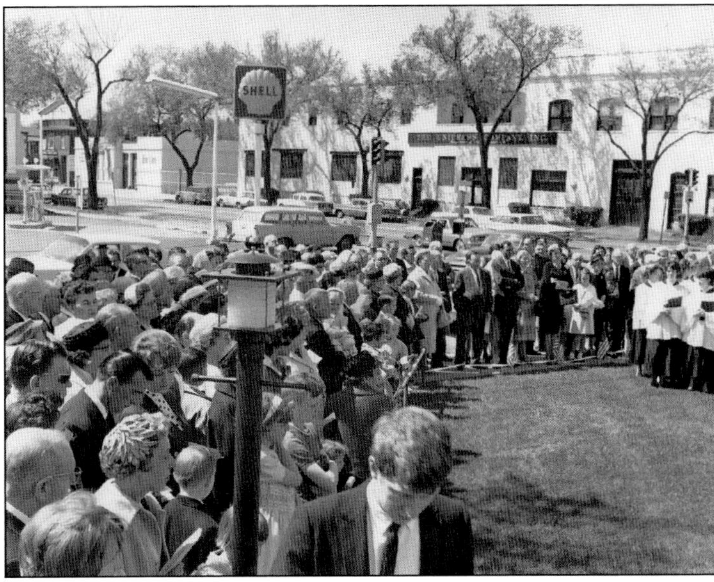

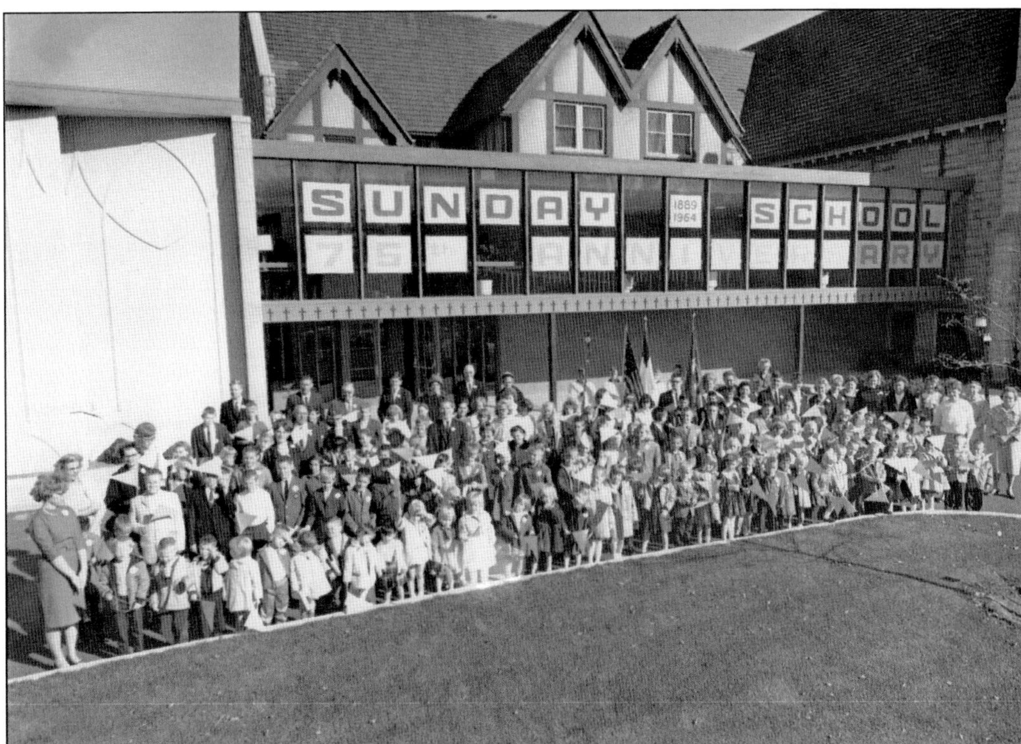

In 1964, Salem English Lutheran Church's families and youth gathered to celebrate its new Sunday school space and to commemorate its 75th anniversary. In addition to classrooms, the extension also included a chapel, nurseries, and a lounge. At one point, the church had hosted the largest daily vacation Bible school in the United Lutheran Church in America. The new building could more easily handle such large undertakings. (SELC.)

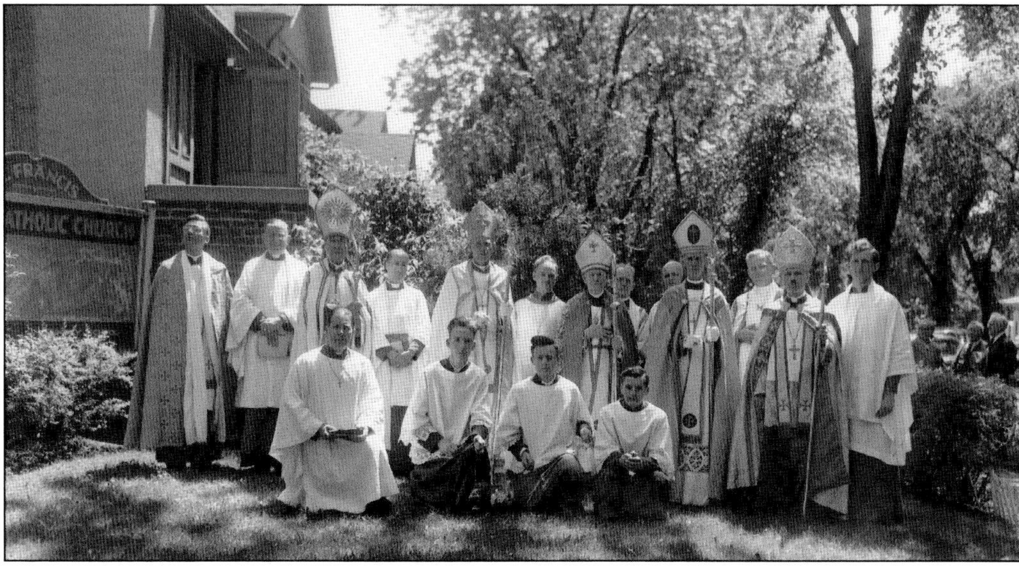

St. Francis Liberal Catholic Church, at 3201 Pleasant Avenue, has been in the neighborhood since it was founded by a theosophist in 1927. The building originally opened onto Pleasant Avenue, as shown in this early photograph, but later moved the main entrance to face Thirty-second Street. As evident in these images, some aspects of the church are similar to those found in the Roman Catholic Church, while other elements are dramatically different. (SFLCC.)

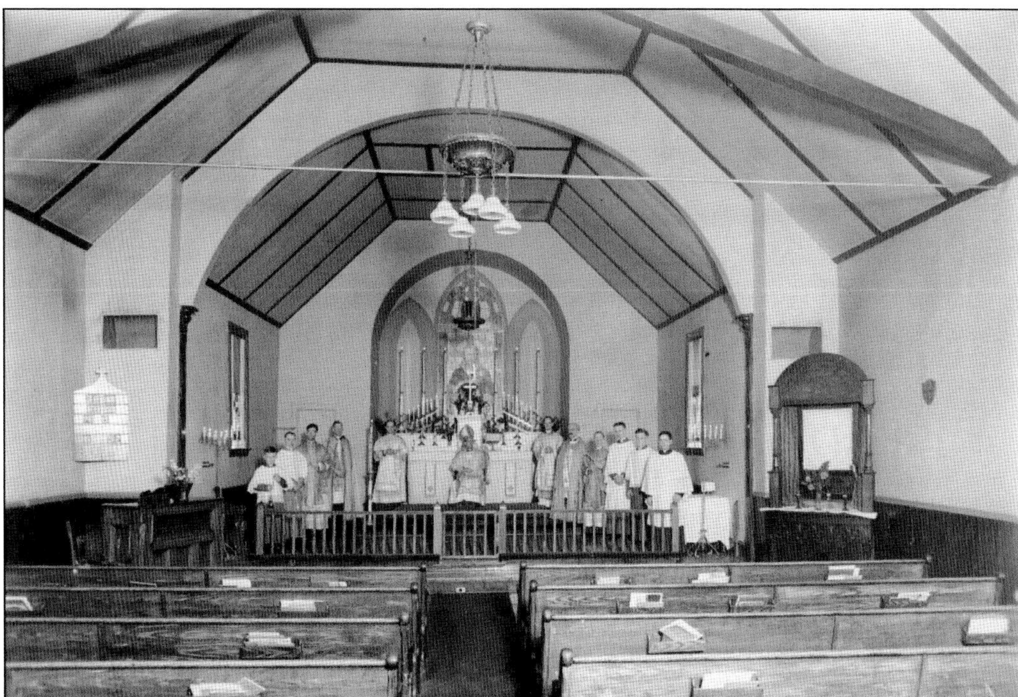

This interior view of the St. Francis Liberal Catholic Church on Pleasant Avenue was likely taken to commemorate its opening. The small congregation purchased the building from a Lutheran church in 1926 and has been there ever since. In 1984, the church suffered a major fire; while much of the interior was damaged and the steeple destroyed, the altar was unharmed. (SFLCC.)

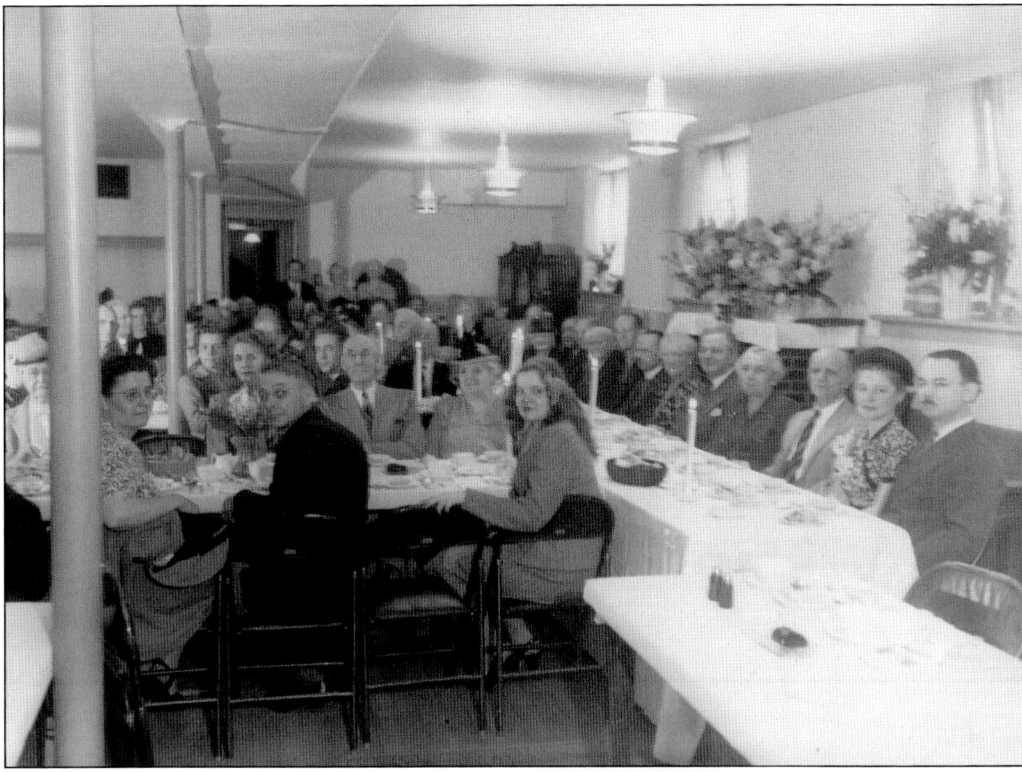

The members of St. Francis Liberal Catholic Church have gathered here in this undated photograph for a special dinner in the church's basement. The congregation, made largely of theosophists, was small and drew its members from beyond just the neighborhood's boundaries. The church's philosophy is one of inclusion—all are welcome, and none are denied sacraments. (SFLCC.)

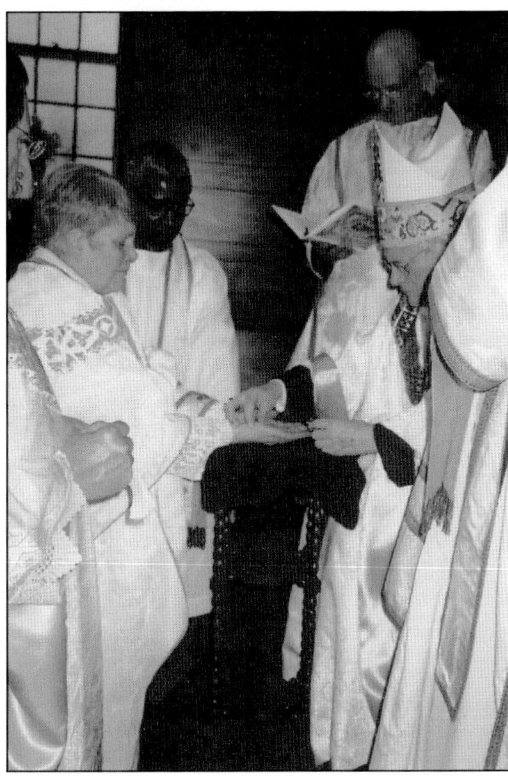

In 2003, St. Francis Liberal Catholic Church chose to break away from the main church and align with a branch that ordains women. In April 2009, Judie Cilcain (left) became the first Minnesotan woman to be ordained as a Liberal Catholic Church priest. From left to right, Rev. Lee Dunn, Rev. Wallace Zick, and Bishop James Zinzow participate in the ordination ceremony. (SFLCC.)

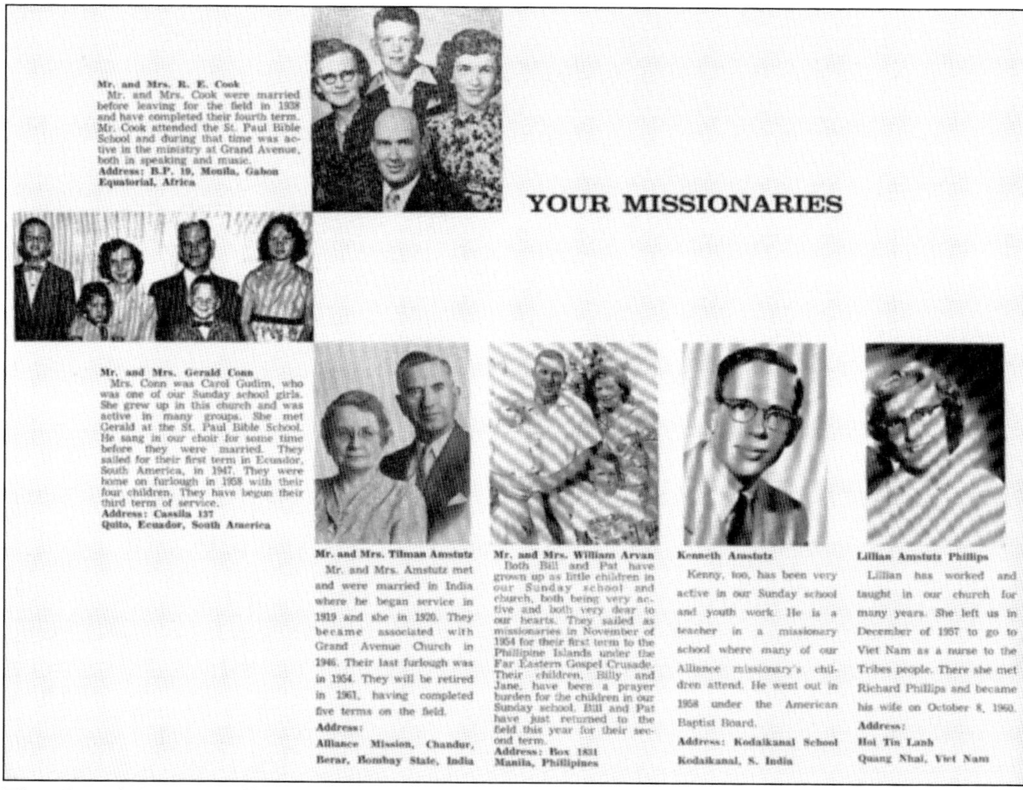

YOUR MISSIONARIES

Mr. and Mrs. R. E. Cook
Mr. and Mrs. Cook were married before leaving for the field in 1938 and have completed their fourth term. Mr. Cook attended the St. Paul Bible School and during that time was active in the ministry at Grand Avenue, both in speaking and music.
Address: B.P. 19, Mouila, Gabon Equatorial, Africa

Mr. and Mrs. Gerald Conn
Mrs. Conn was Carol Gudim, who was one of our Sunday school girls. She grew up in this church and was active in many groups. She met Gerald at the St. Paul Bible School. He sang in our choir for some time before they were married. They sailed for their first term in Ecuador, South America, in 1947. They were home on furlough in 1958 with their four children. They have begun their third term of service.
Address: Cassilla 137 Quito, Ecuador, South America

Mr. and Mrs. Tilman Amstutz
Mr. and Mrs. Amstutz met and were married in India where he began service in 1919 and she in 1920. They became associated with Grand Avenue Church in 1946. Their last furlough was in 1954. They will be retired in 1961, having completed five terms on the field.
Address:
Alliance Mission, Chandur, Berar, Bombay State, India

Mr. and Mrs. William Arvan
Both Bill and Pat have grown up as little children in our Sunday school and church, both being very active and both very dear to our hearts. They sailed as missionaries in November of 1954 for their first term to the Phillipine Islands under the Far Eastern Gospel Crusade. Their children, Billy and Jane, have been a prayer burden for the children in our Sunday school. Bill and Pat have just returned to the field this year for their second term.
Address: Box 1831 Manila, Phillipines

Kenneth Amstutz
Kenny, too, has been very active in our Sunday school and youth work. He is a teacher in a missionary school where many of our Alliance missionary's children attend. He went out in 1958 under the American Baptist Board.
Address: Kodaikanal School Kodaikanal, S. India

Lillian Amstutz Phillips
Lillian has worked and taught in our church for many years. She left us in December of 1957 to go to Viet Nam as a nurse to the Tribes people. There she met Richard Phillips and became his wife on October 8, 1960.
Address:
Hoi Tin Lanh Quang Nhai, Viet Nam

The Grand Avenue Alliance Church, located at 3100 Grand Avenue, had placed an emphasis on evangelical and missionary activities ever since its founding. The Grand Avenue missionaries, shown here, were living and working abroad in 1960, having taken to heart the church's invitation "to meet the spiritual needs of this neighborhood and to accept the challenges of the regions beyond." "Beyond" in 1960 included, among other destinations, Gabon, the Philippines, and Ecuador. (Hennepin County Library.)

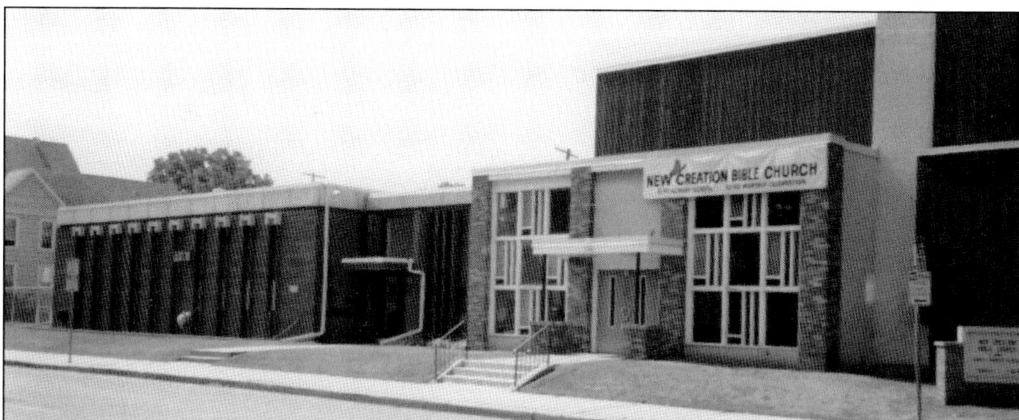

The church at 3100 Grand Avenue was at one point the home of New Creation Bible Church, which has since moved to 115 West Thirty-first Street. It church building is now home to the Vietnamese Alliance Church. The structure was built in 1960 for the Grand Avenue Alliance Church. Construction of the educational annex, which is visible here, a modernized sanctuary, and a new entryway were intended to send a message of welcome to all, visitors and members alike. (LNA.)

Nine

Transportation

Transportation of all types has had a starring role in the evolution of the Lyn-Lake neighborhood. For much of the 20th century, the railroad trench along Twenty-ninth Street shaped the neighborhood; it provided the neighborhood's many manufacturing or industrial businesses easy access to the region and country, as well as a physical landmark that functioned much in the same way as would an industrialized river or canal. When the trench was converted to a bicycle path in the late 1990s, it ushered in yet another era in Lyn-Lake's history. Although instead of industry, this modern transportation development has spurred new housing and retail.

Another major transportation-related issue in Lyn-Lake over the years has been parking. As early as the 1920s, businesses were concerned about the problem of finding convenient parking access for their customers. In the 1990s, the problem escalated as the neighborhood increasingly gained a trendy reputation. In a highly controversial move, the city forcibly relocated several long-standing local businesses to build parking lots. For much of the beginning of the 21st century, debate raged over whether a light rail line should be built through Lyn-Lake, and an alternate route was finally chosen, so the battle for the coming years will likely revolve around the potential for streetcars, bike lanes, and, as always, parking.

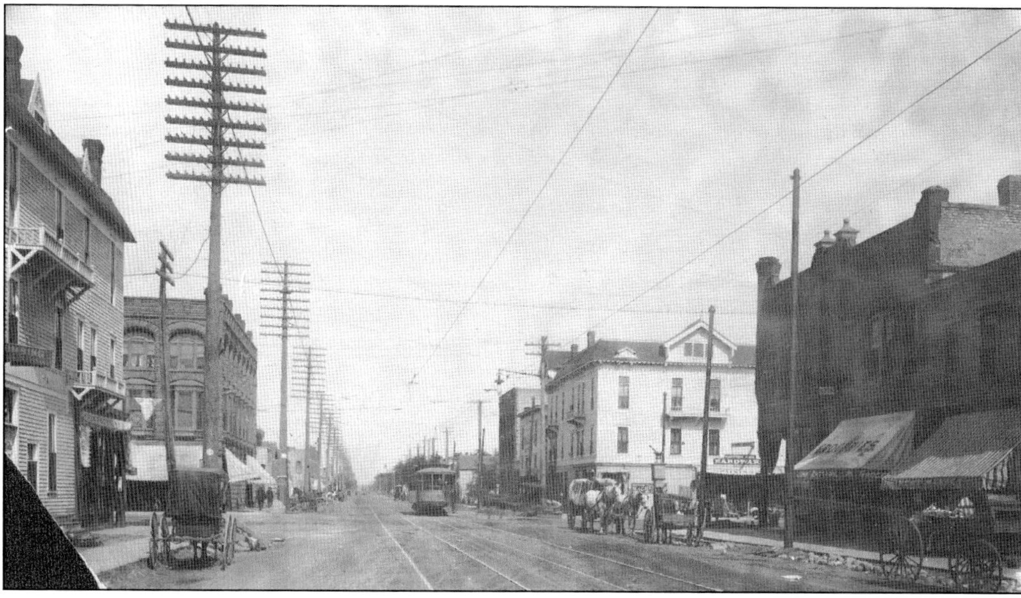

The intersection of Lake Street and Lyndale Avenue had been firmly established as an important south Minneapolis commercial node by the end of the 19th century. Its growth owed much to the proximity of two streetcar lines, the busy Lake Street line (pictured) and another line on nearby Bryant Avenue. This photograph was taken in 1906; some of the buildings still stand. (Minnesota Historical Society.)

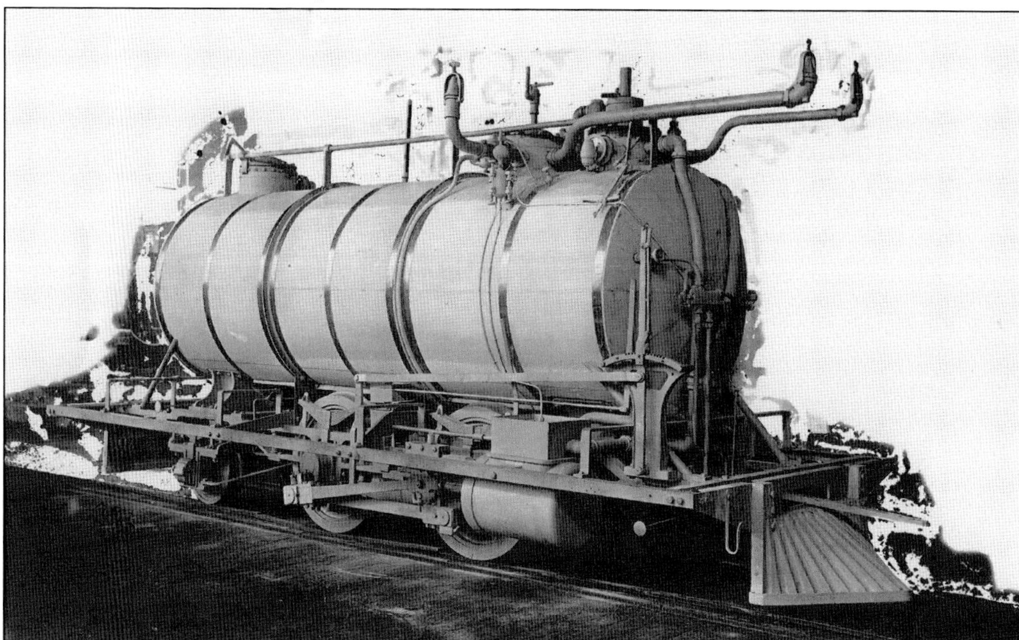

The Minneapolis, Lyndale, and Minnetonka Railroad provided transportation options from downtown to Lyn-Lake and southwest Minneapolis. This 1886 photograph shows one of four soda motors especially developed for the line in Philadelphia. They did not work well, so it was only a matter of months before all four were rebuilt to be used as regular coal-operated locomotives. (Hennepin County Library.)

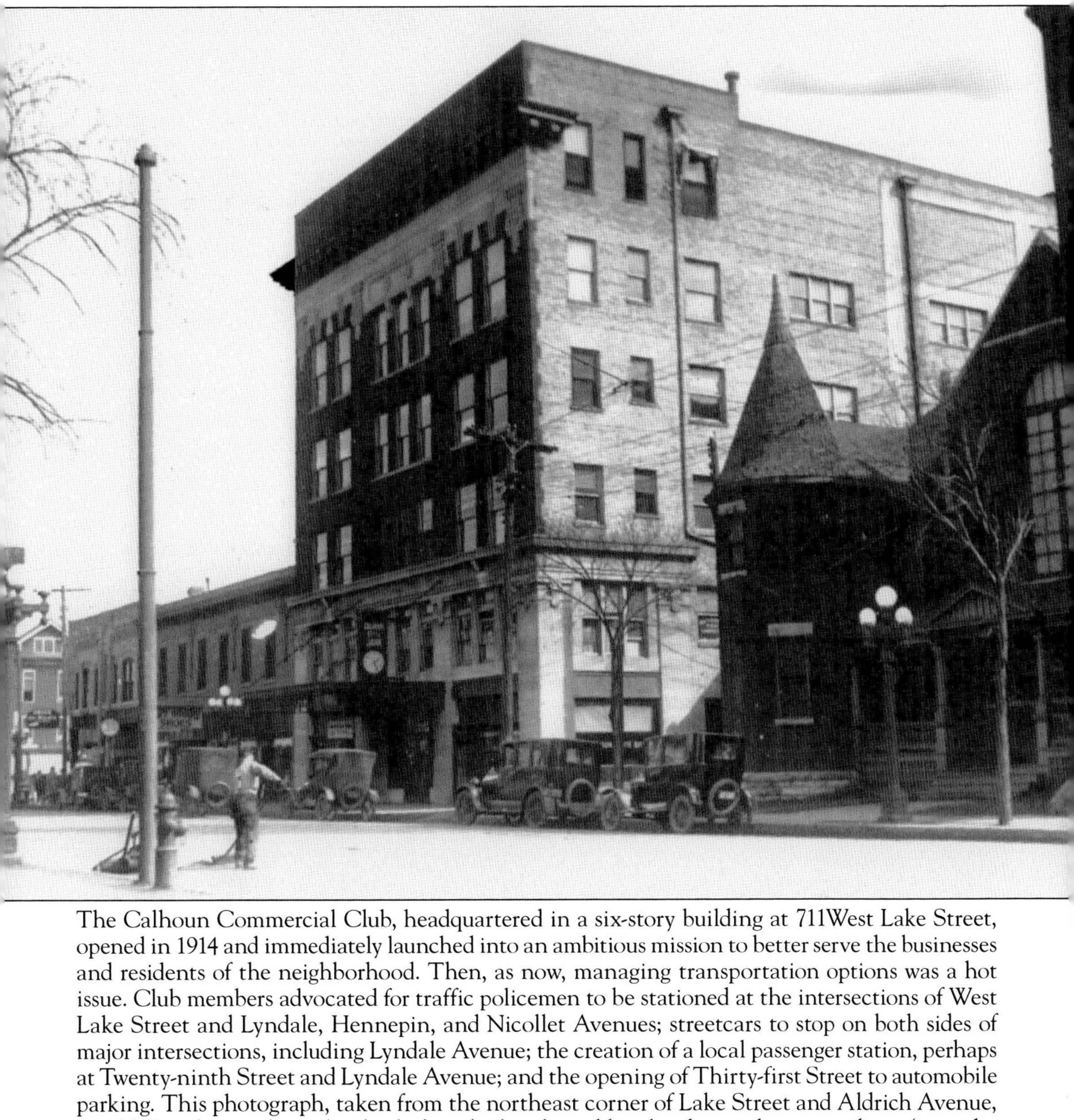

The Calhoun Commercial Club, headquartered in a six-story building at 711West Lake Street, opened in 1914 and immediately launched into an ambitious mission to better serve the businesses and residents of the neighborhood. Then, as now, managing transportation options was a hot issue. Club members advocated for traffic policemen to be stationed at the intersections of West Lake Street and Lyndale, Hennepin, and Nicollet Avenues; streetcars to stop on both sides of major intersections, including Lyndale Avenue; the creation of a local passenger station, perhaps at Twenty-ninth Street and Lyndale Avenue; and the opening of Thirty-first Street to automobile parking. This photograph, taken from the northeast corner of Lake Street and Aldrich Avenue, was likely taken early in the day before the hustle and bustle of several streetcar lines (note the wires), increasing levels of automobile traffic, as well as many pedestrians and bikes thronged the streets of the Lyndale Avenue and Lake Street intersection. Today the streetcars are long gone, but bus routes still traverse Lake Street and Lyndale Avenue. (LUCC.)

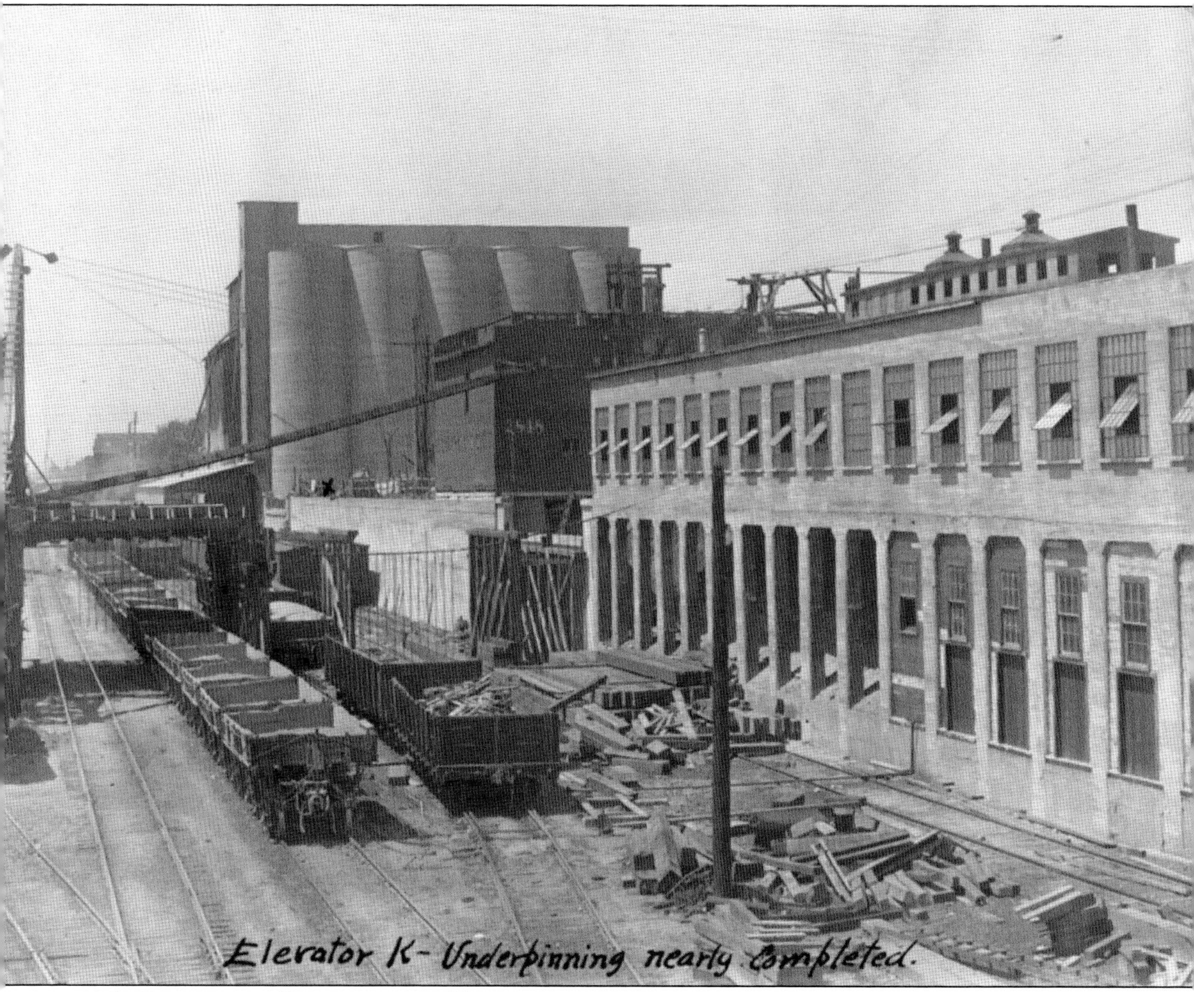

The Benton Cutoff was constructed between 1879 and 1881, providing better train tracks connecting southwestern Minnesota and the southern Dakota Territory to Minneapolis via Twenty-ninth Street on the southern edge of Minneapolis. Industry soon followed the new track, and as more people settled south of the tracks concern grew over dangerous crossings. Debate raged about whether to elevate, depress, or remove the track, resulting in a 1910 Minneapolis ordinance ordering the Chicago Milwaukee and St. Paul (Milwaukee Road) to depress the track. Subsequent legal challenges failed, which allowed construction of the 2.8-mile-long depressed rail corridor to begin in 1912. The project was completed in 1916. The 22-foot-deep trench required the construction of 37 reinforced-concrete street bridges. This photograph, taken sometime between 1912 and 1916, shows construction of the Grand Avenue Bridge over the tracks and the industry that had adapted to its newly urbanizing surroundings. All of the bridges over the depressed tracks shared a nearly identical design. (Minnesota Historical Society.)

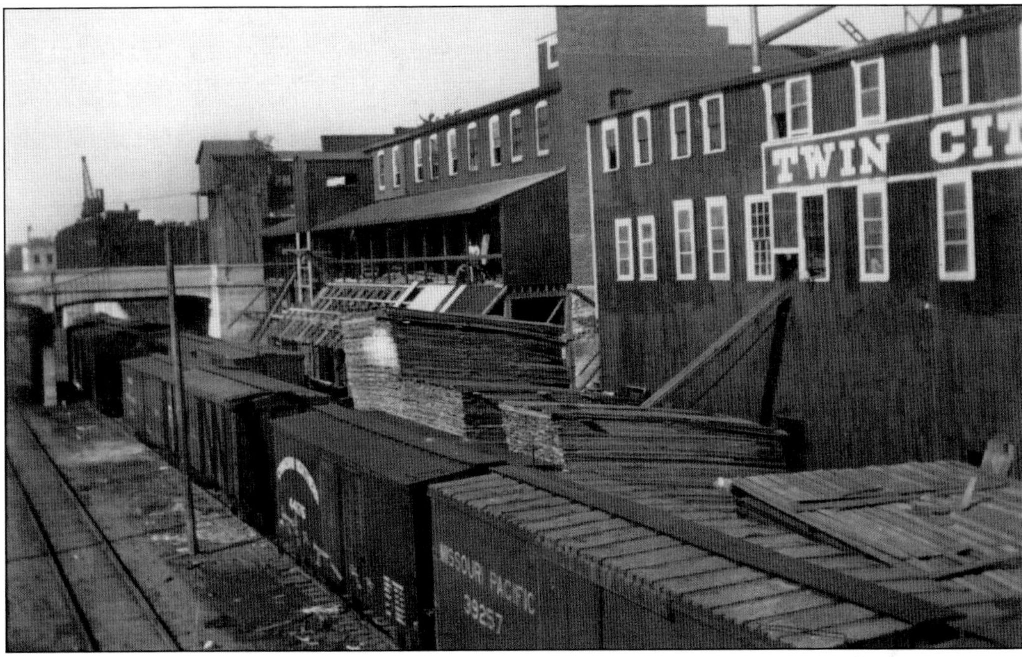

Local businesses worried that the track change would harm both business and property. Many buildings had no basements and would require significant changes to load the cars. The Twin City Separator Company fought a losing court battle against the depression; it chose to stay and build a new train-accessible basement accompanied by an intensive piling system to reduce damage from settling. This photograph dates to around 1915. (Hennepin County Library.)

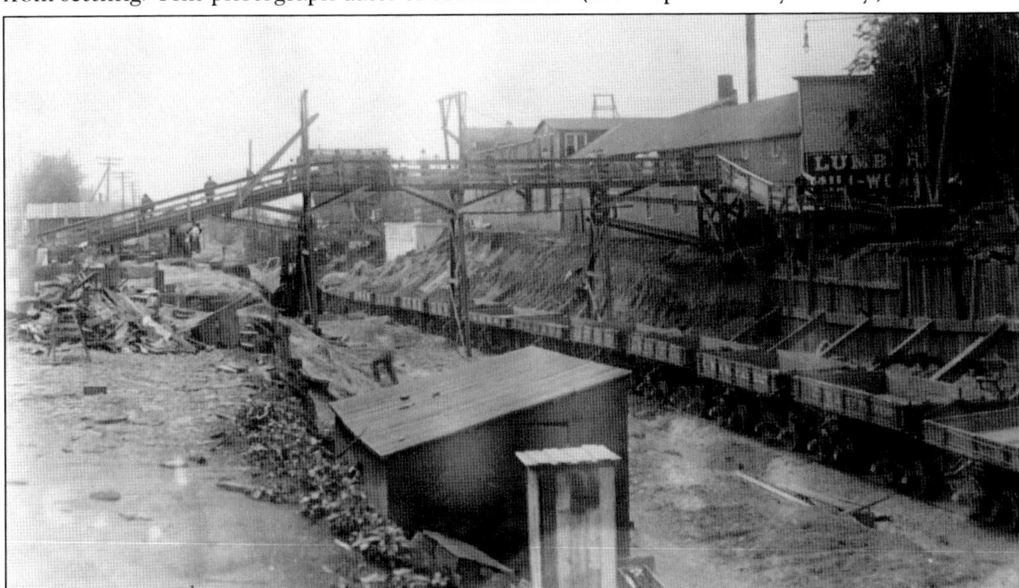

Streetcar service on Lyndale Avenue at Twenty-ninth Street was altered during the 1912 Milwaukee Road track depression construction period, with streetcars rerouted to temporary tracks. A footbridge was constructed over the depression for the benefit of pedestrians. The construction's impact was significant for local residents and commuters, but many thought the end result—a railroad in a trench, below traffic and homes—to be worth it. (Minnesota Historical Society.)

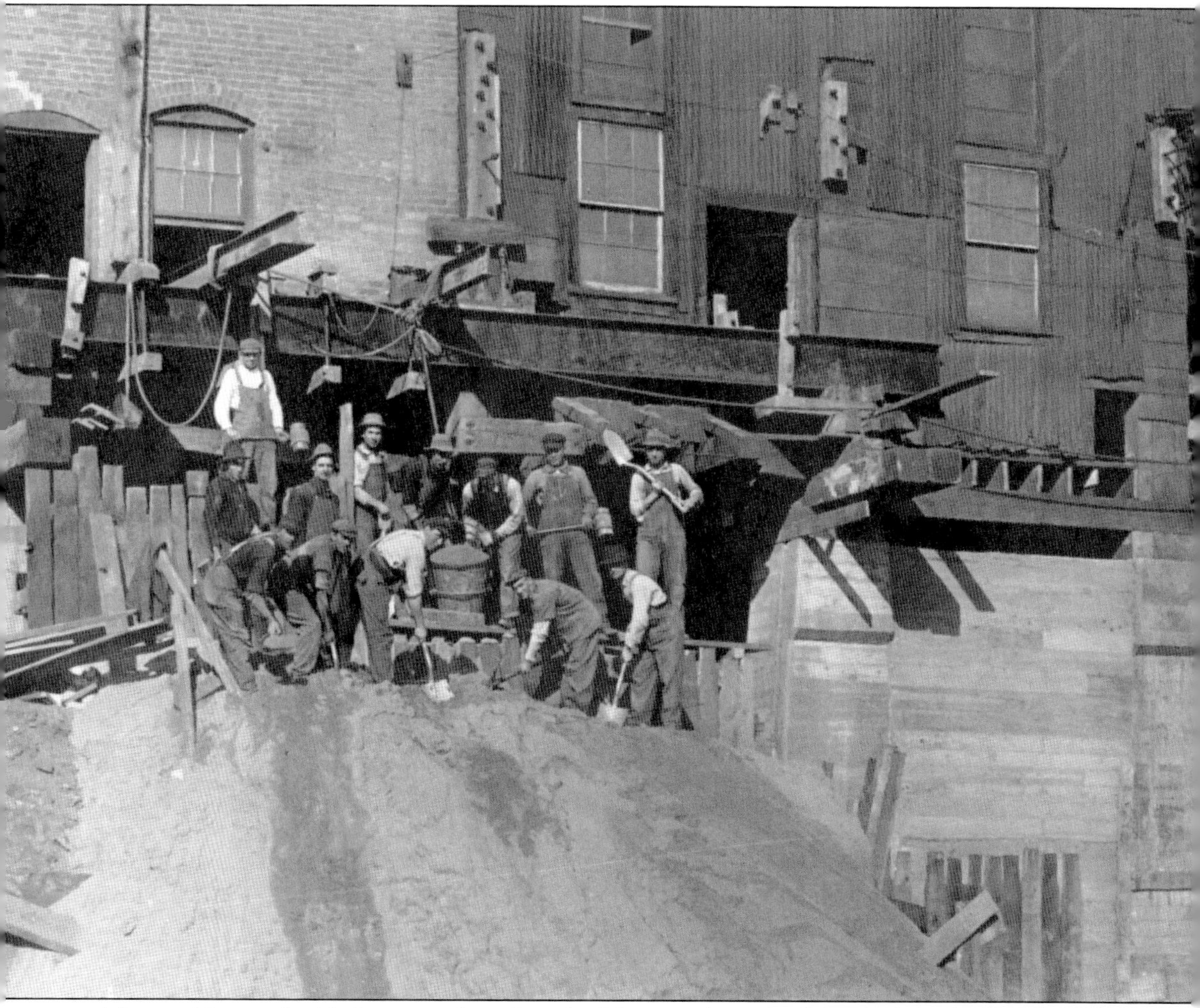

After waiting to decide how to adapt their building to the new depressed track, the Sheffield Elevator Company, located at 2843–2847 Garfield Avenue, found itself without the ability to ship or receive grain and with nearly full elevator tanks. As the result of their delay, Sheffield urgently needed to adapt their building but had to bear the complete cost of three blocks of retaining wall, expanding the span of two bridges, and underpinning two factory buildings and the elevator tanks. Workers had to use care while underpinning the tanks; a 200-horse-power engine ran continuously during construction, which necessitated a temporary steel framework that rested on top of new piers. The new foundation walls ran 36 feet below the engine house and more than 50 feet below street level. The company continued to expand the plant after the adaptation project was completed. (Minnesota Historical Society.)

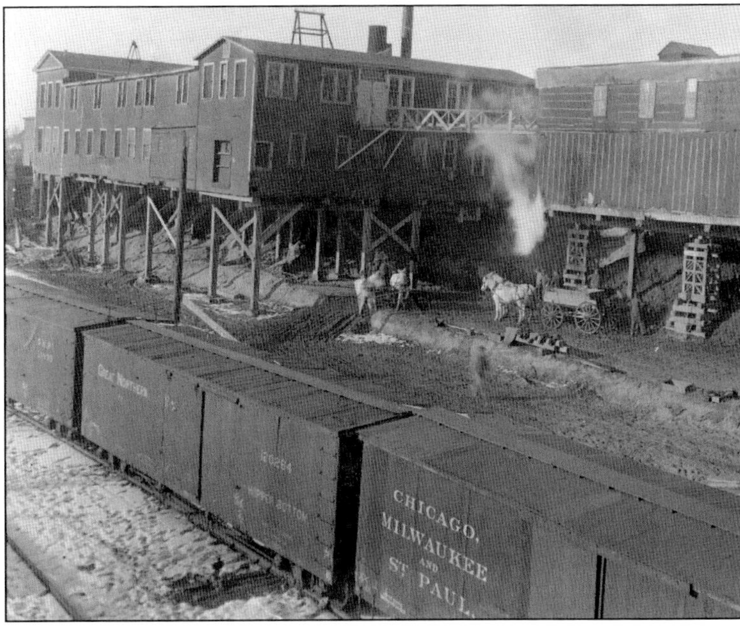

Bruer Brothers Lumber Company adapted its existing buildings by constructing a planing mill under the buildings at track level, by moving some of buildings back 60 feet, and by constructing a new office building. The company did this while allowing the plant to remain in operation. The photograph shows the underpinning that took place in 1914 to build the new mill under the existing building. (Minnesota Historical Society.)

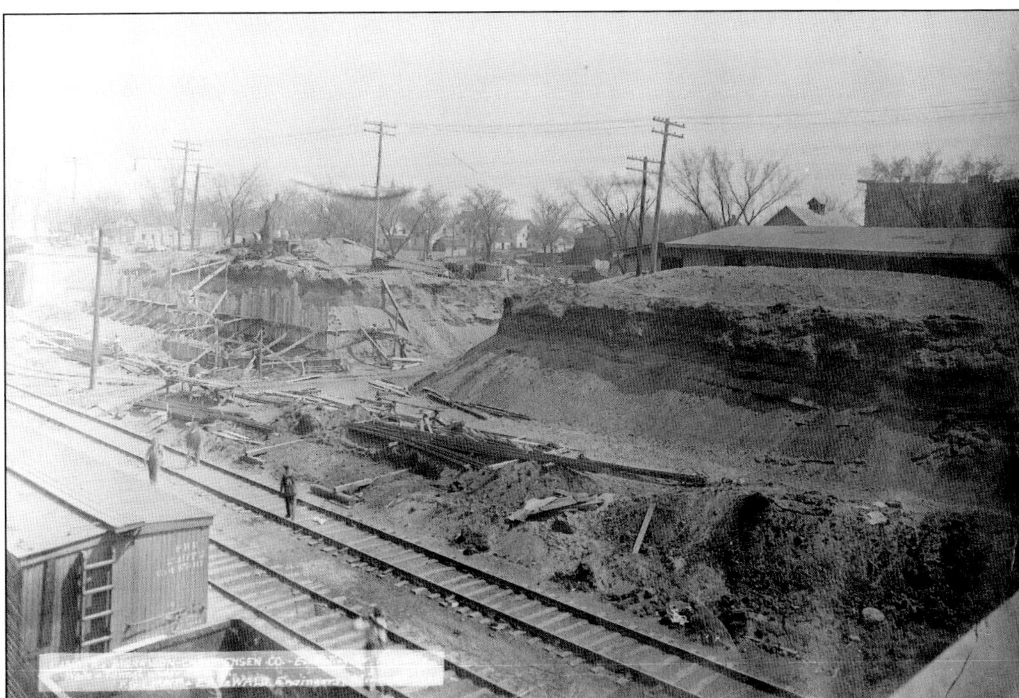

Landers, Morrison, Christensen Company, located at 2901 Dupont Avenue, planned to relocate to St. Louis Park instead of retrofitting its plant because of the costs of an adaptation plan. The engineers of the track depression project contacted Mr. Landers and suggested a plan that would use his existing buildings, increase storage space, and improve their loading operations for a cost of half of the original plan. (Minnesota Historical Society.)

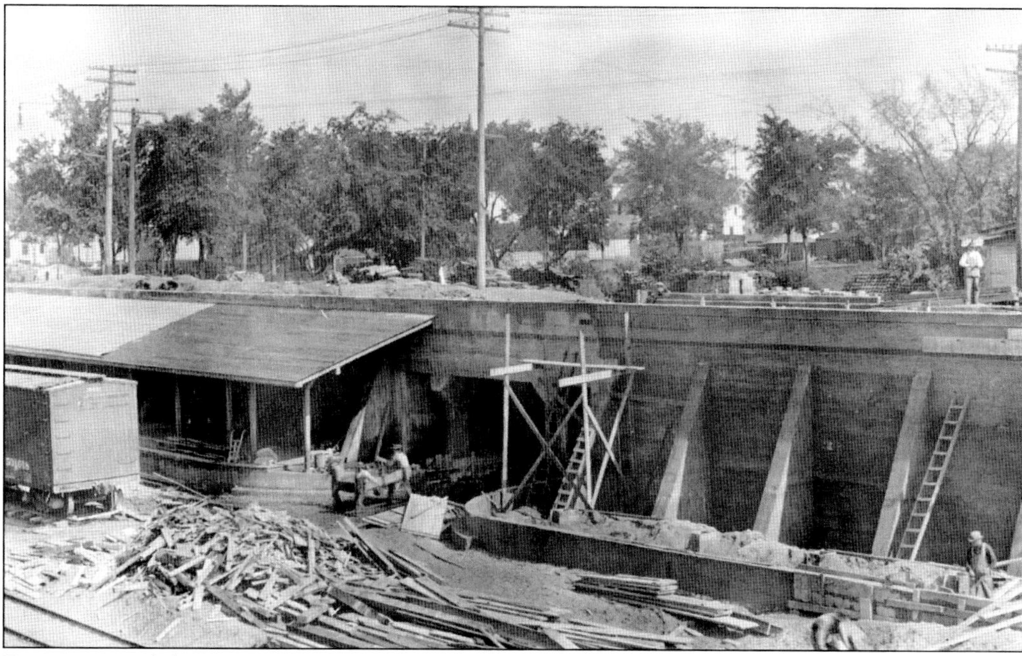

Excavation of the existing Landers site allowed for the building to be moved to track level. Twenty-ninth Street was made into a viaduct with a tunnel connecting the plant and tracks. The tunnel allowed for wagons to load from the plant to the tracks and continue up a new ramp to Twenty-ninth Street. The tunnel had space on either side to allow future conveyor belts. (Minnesota Historical Society.)

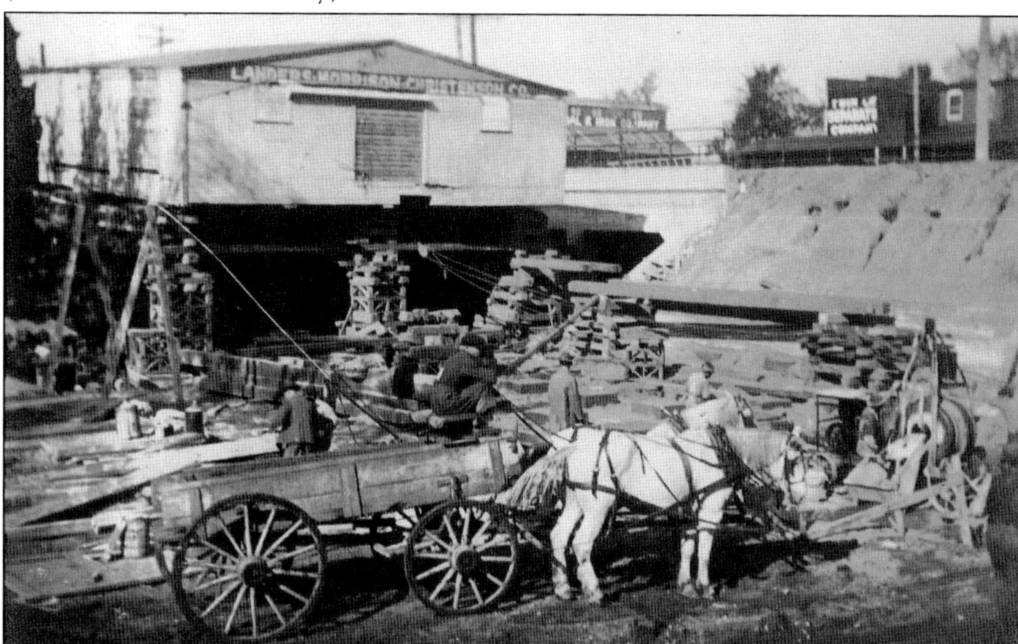

Landers, Morrison, Christensen Company was a building material supplier that provided firebrick, common brick, pressed brick, lime, and cement. The adaptation of its plant was unique, as it involved a tunnel under a road to connect the track area and the business. (Hennepin County Library.)

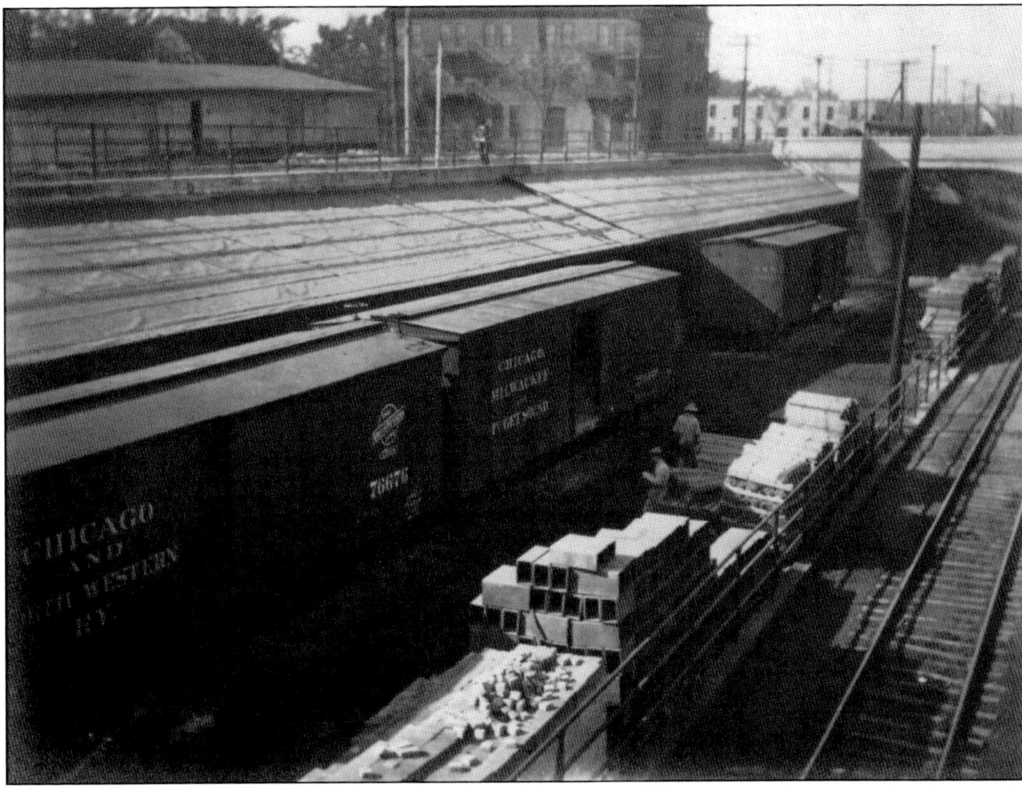

Upon completion of the adaptation, Landers, Morrison, Christensen Company had use of a siding and storage space on the trackside, utilizing the buttress retaining walls as compartments. Its effort to find a direct track connection, while unique, was similar to other businesses needing to find a new way to do business in the post-track Depression era. This photograph was taken between 1914 and 1916. (Hennepin County Library.)

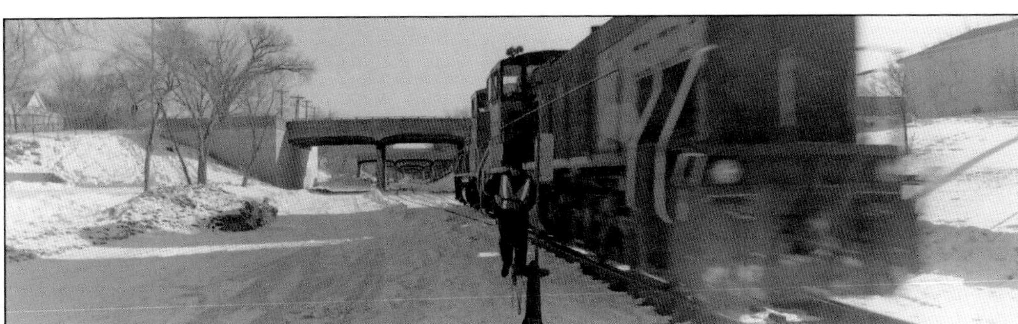

By 1993, most train traffic on the Twenty-ninth Street train tracks through Lyn-Lake had ceased. However, it was not until 1998 and after the ceremonial ground-breaking for the Midtown Greenway that all rail traffic through Lyn-Lake came to an end. This train on the tracks was one of the last to travel the corridor, which signaled the end of Lyn-Lake's once-thriving industrial era. (City of Minneapolis.)

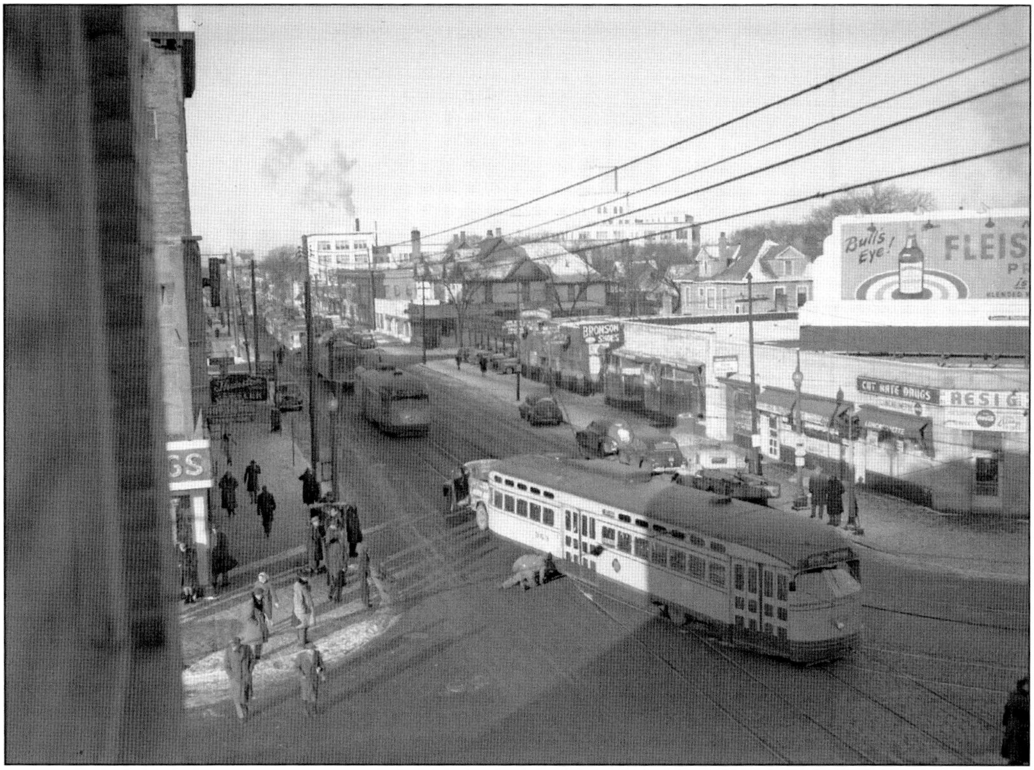

Streetcars plied the streets of the Lyn-Lake area, quickly and easily connecting residents with downtown and the commercial districts to the east and west. This 1948 photograph shows a derailed Bryant-Johnson streetcar at the intersection of Lake Street and Lyndale Avenue, which has left a long line of streetcars idling in the background. (Minnesota Historical Society; photograph by Minneapolis Star Tribune.)

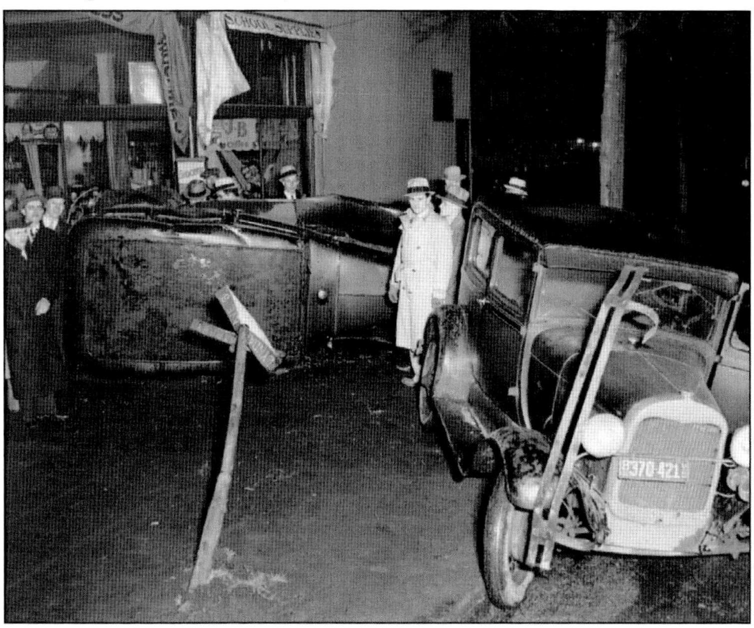

This two-car accident took place at the intersection of Lyndale Avenue and Thirty-third Street, outside Roy Austin's market. Lyndale Avenue was a heavily traveled street, and concern over balancing the needs of traffic and cars with concerns about safety, speed, and quality of life for those in the neighborhood has been a part of local conversations for more than a century. (Hennepin History Museum.)

In 1960, the City of Minneapolis Planning Commission envisioned a Whittier that was more inwardly facing, with a school and playground at its center and with its homes distinctly segregated from non-residential use. Note the proposed Twenty-eighth Street Crosstown Expressway; this was envisioned as both a way to buffer residents from industrial uses along the railroad tracks, as well as to remove traffic from city streets. (Hennepin County Library.)

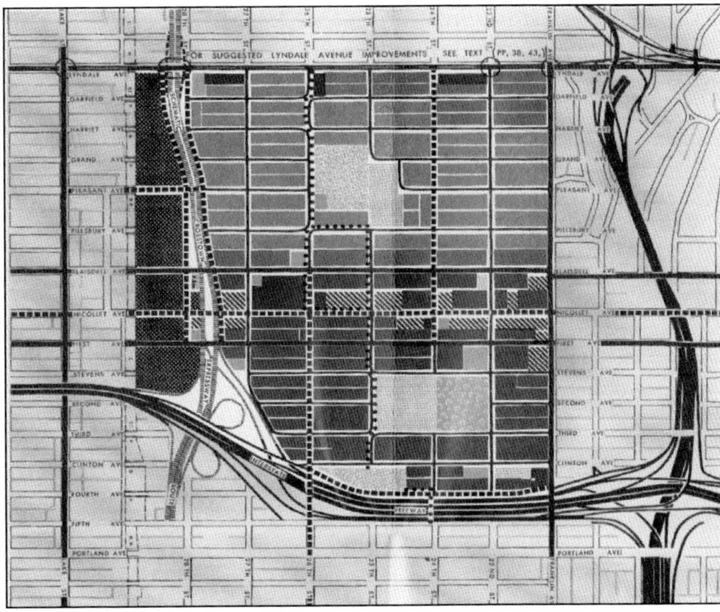

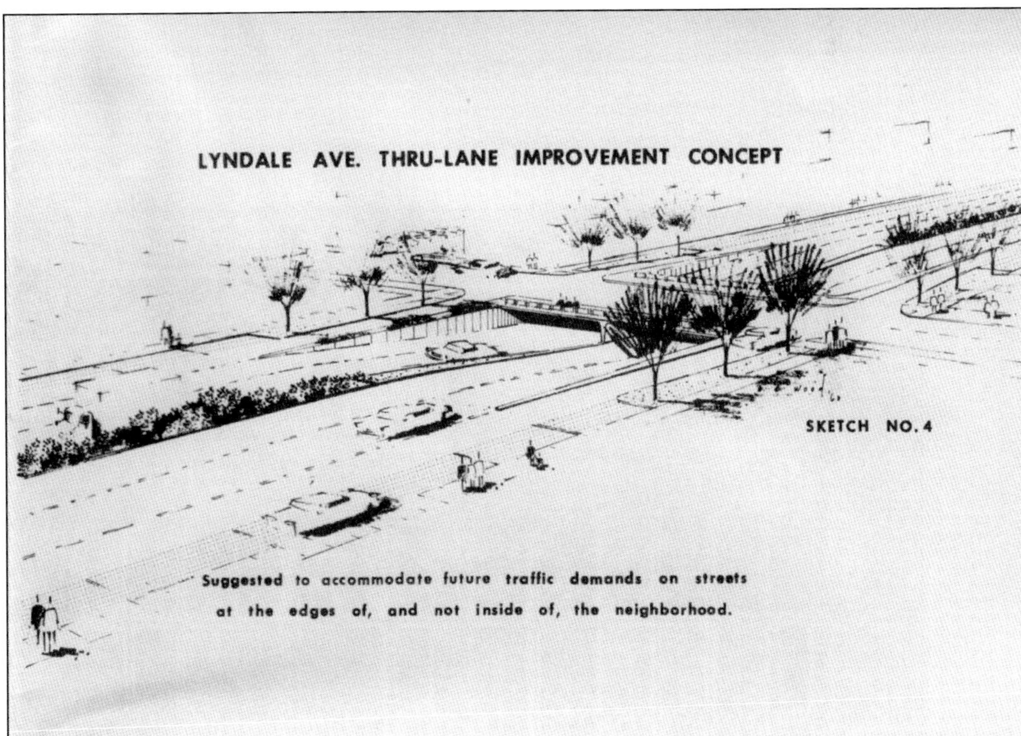

The suggested traffic separations at the intersections of Lyndale Avenue and Lake Street aimed to reduce traffic on side streets and to speed up traffic and increase capacity on the major streets. At the time, it was seen as good public planning and even as favorable to pedestrians, because it would have contributed to the segregation of residential and commercial or industrial space and decreased traffic within the neighborhood's interior. (Hennepin County Library.)

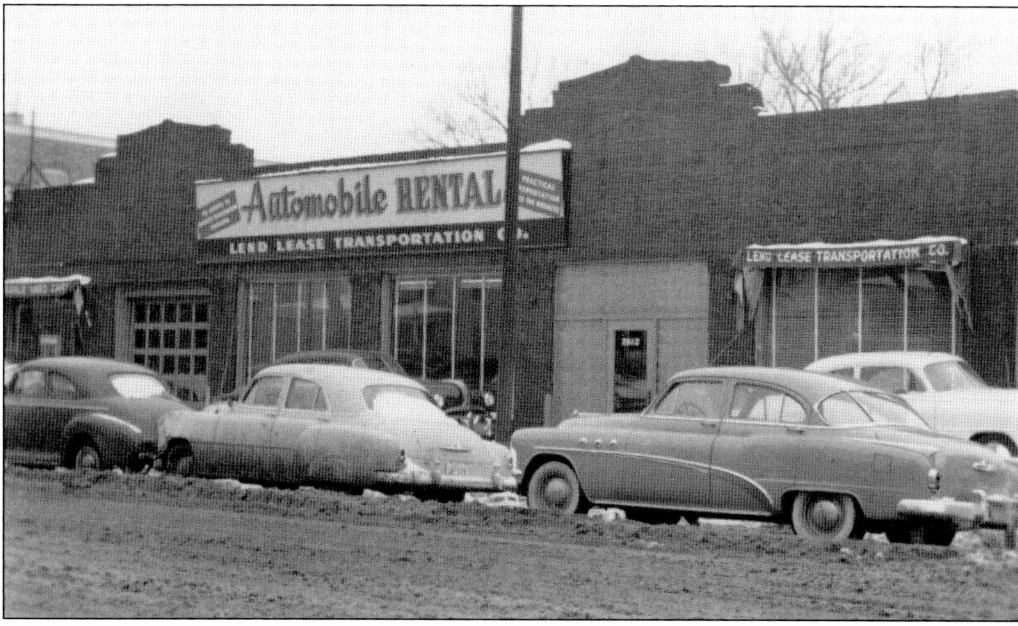

Although the Lyn-Lake area remained one of the best neighborhoods in the city for public transportation coverage, by 1955, the year of this photograph, automobiles had become the dominant form of transportation for many residents. Those in the neighborhood who did not already own a car could rent one at the Lend Lease Transportation Company, located at 2612 Lyndale Avenue. (Hennepin History Museum.)

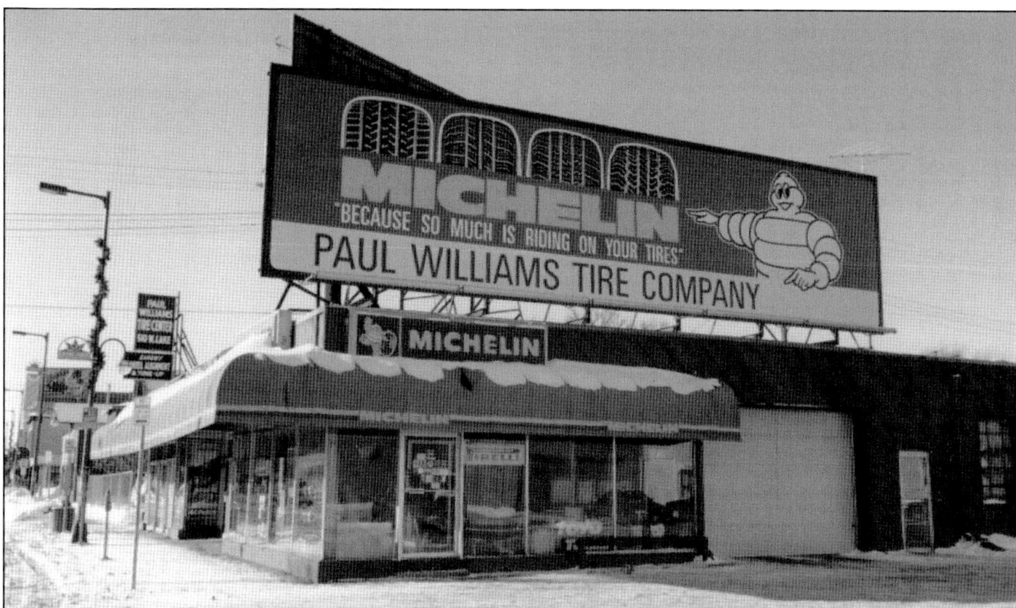

Paul Williams worked at a relative's Standard Oil station after getting out of the Navy. A company representative offered him an opportunity to run a service station at Holmes Avenue and Lake Street in 1954, followed by the station on Lake Street and East Lake Calhoun Parkway and then Thirty-Sixth Street and Lyndale Avenue. He opened Paul Williams Tire Company, at 510 West Lake Street, in 1971. This photograph dates to 1997. (LNA.)

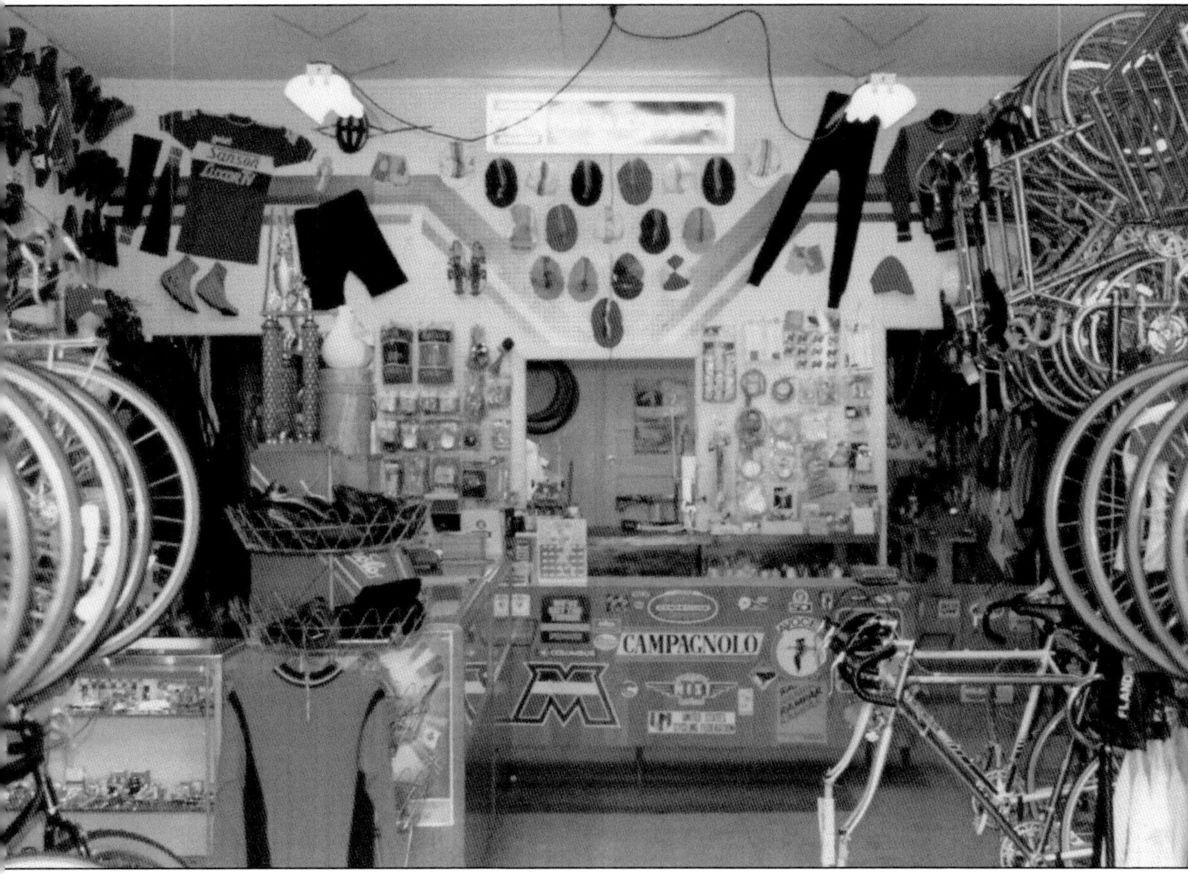

After seizing an opportunity to secure a relationship with the Italian bicycle brand Gitane, James Karusis, with his grandsons Jim and Scott Flanders, opened Flanders Brothers Cycle at 2707 Lyndale Avenue in 1973. Karusis and the Flanders brothers had learned the bicycle business while working for Wheel Goods Corporation on Hennepin Avenue at Twenty-seventh Street for several years. Jim and Scott were avid bicycle racers and were traveling to races outside of the United States in the mid- to late 1970s. In 1978, their grandfather passed away, and they decided to have Scott watch over the store while Jim traveled to train competitively at the Olympic Training Center. After the frustrating experience of having nearly made a big break but falling just short, Jim decided to return to the store full-time and compete regionally. Since then, Flanders Brothers Cycle has been outfitting riders, whether racers, commuters, or recreational bikers. (Flanders Brothers Cycle.)

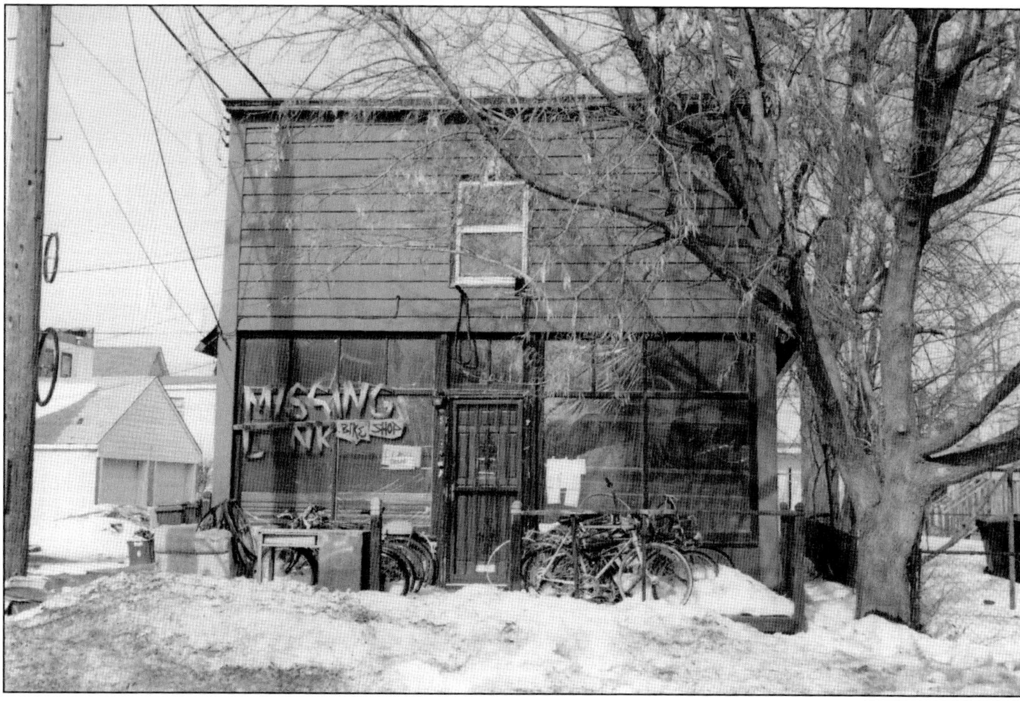

The Missing Link Bike Shop was located behind 310 West Lake Street until 1996, when the Lyndale Neighborhood Development Corporation purchased the building and ultimately had it demolished. Owner Chris Darsow was active in the neighborhood; among other things, the local Missing Link Bike Club was based out of the shop. (LNA.)

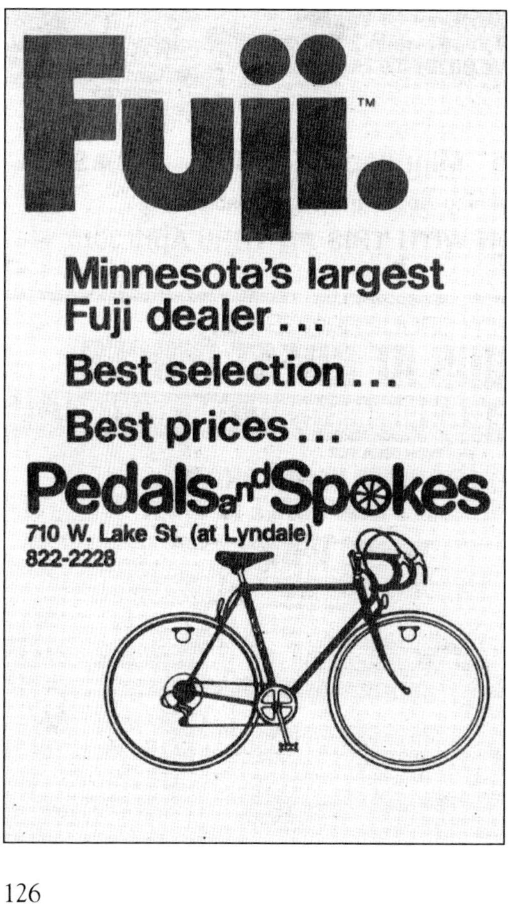

Pedals and Spokes moved to the Lyn-Lake area following the 1984 opening of Calhoun Square and the accompanying rise in rents in the adjacent area. That year, it published this advertisement with a new location, 710 West Lake Street, in the *Whittier Globe*. The store sold bikes and accessories. It operated a seasonal store, and it traditionally did not open until March 1. Penn Cycle purchased Pedals and Spokes in 1987. (Hennepin County Library.)

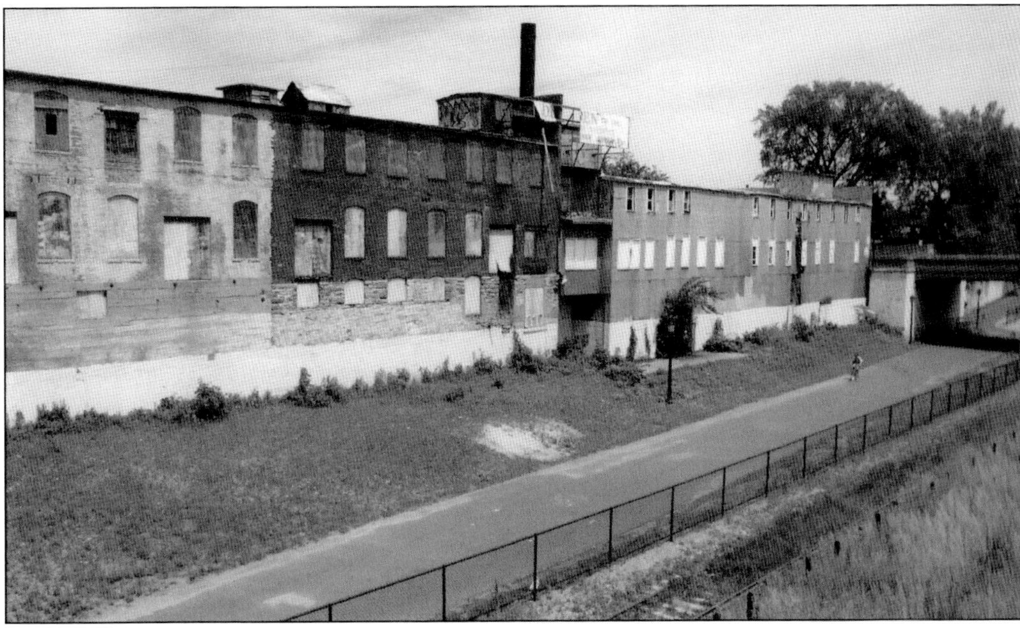

The Midtown Greenway was an ambitious plan to turn the former Milwaukee Road railroad track trench into a 5.7-mile-long bike corridor. Ground-breaking for the greenway took place in July 1998 on Bryant Avenue in Lyn-Lake; Minneapolis mayor Sharon Sayles Belton was in attendance, as were assorted officials from both city and county government and agencies. The Midtown Greenway celebrated its grand opening two years later. (LNA.)

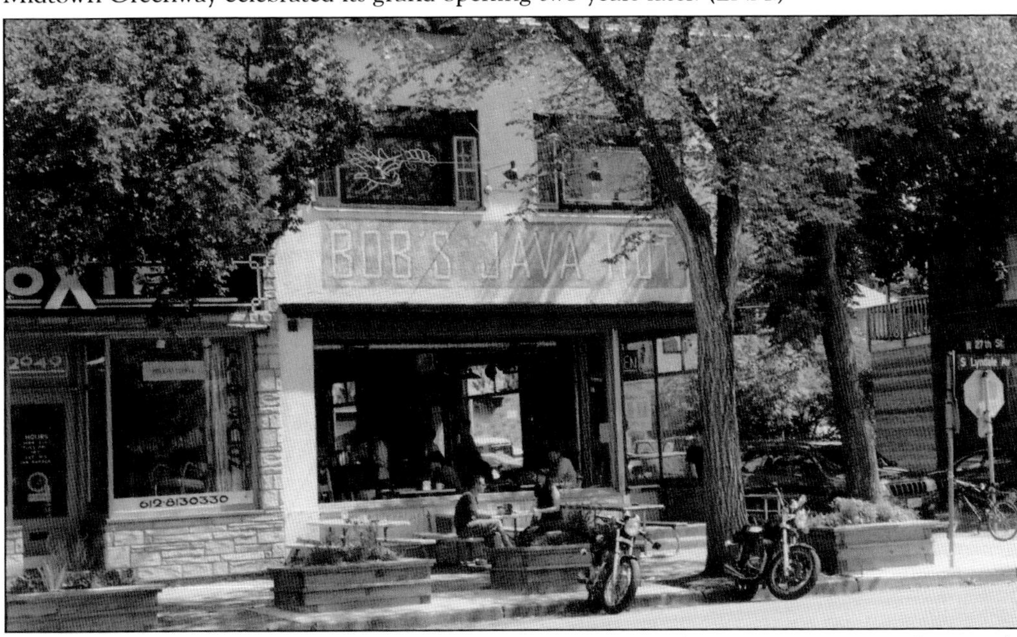

Bob's Java Hut opened in 1994 as a motorcycle-oriented coffee shop. In 1996, it moved across the street and into this corner location at Twenty-seventh Street and Lyndale Avenue. Motorcycles have been, and continue to be, a familiar part of Lyn-Lake life. Despite bikers' prominence in the neighborhood, Bob's was the first in the area to position itself as a bike-friendly coffee house. This photograph was taken in 2000. (LHENA.)